chapters 28-66

THE COLLEGE PRESS NIV COMMENTARY

ISAIAH
VOLUME 2

THE COLLEGE PRESS NIV COMMENTARY

ISAIAH
VOLUME 2

TERRY BRILEY

Old Testament Series Co-Editors:

Terry Briley, Ph.D.
Lipscomb University

Paul Kissling, Ph.D.
Great Lakes Christian College

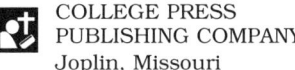
COLLEGE PRESS PUBLISHING COMPANY
Joplin, Missouri

Copyright © 2004 College Press Publishing Co.
All Rights Reserved
Printed and Bound in the United States of America

All Scripture quotations, unless indicated, are taken from
THE HOLY BIBLE: NEW INTERNATIONAL VERSION®.
Copyright © 1973, 1978, 1984 by International Bible Society.
Used by permission of Zondervan Publishing House.
All rights reserved.

Library of Congress Cataloging-in-Publication Data

Briley, Terry R., 1956–
   Isaiah/Terry R. Briley
     p. cm. – (The College Press NIV commentary. Old
  Testament series)
   Includes bibliographical references.
   ISBN 0-89900-891-7
   1. Bible. O.T. Isaiah—Commentaries. I. Title. II. Series.
BS1515.3.B75 2000
224'.1077—dc21

                                                                               99-059033

A WORD FROM THE PUBLISHER

Years ago a movement was begun with the dream of uniting all Christians on the basis of a common purpose (world evangelism) under a common authority (the Word of God). The College Press NIV Commentary Series is a serious effort to join the scholarship of two branches of this unity movement so as to speak with one voice concerning the Word of God. Our desire is to provide a resource for your study of the Old Testament that will benefit you whether you are preparing a Bible School lesson, a sermon, a college course, or your own personal devotions. Today as we survey the wreckage of a broken world, we must turn again to the Lord and his Word, unite under his banner and communicate the life-giving message to those who are in desperate need. This is our purpose.

Simplified Guide to Hebrew Writing

Heb. letter	Translit.	Pronunciation guide
א	ʾ	Has no sound of its own; like smooth breathing mark in Greek
ב	b	Pronounced like English B *or* V
ג	g	Pronounced like English G
ד	d	Pronounced like English D
ה	h	Pronounced like English H, silent at the end of words in the combination āh
ו	w	As a consonant, pronounced like English V or German W
וּ	û	Represents a vowel sound, pronounced like English long OO
וֹ	ô	Represents a vowel sound, pronounced like English long O
ז	z	Pronounced like English Z
ח	ḥ	Pronounced like German and Scottish CH and Greek χ (chi)
ט	ṭ	Pronounced like English T
י	y	Pronounced like English Y
כ/ך	k	Pronounced like English K
ל	l	Pronounced like English L
מ/ם	m	Pronounced like English M
נ/ן	n	Pronounced like English N
ס	s	Pronounced like English S
ע	ʿ	Stop in breath deep in throat before pronouncing the vowel
פ/ף	p/ph	Pronounced like English P *or* F
צ/ץ	ṣ	Pronounced like English TS/TZ
ק	q	Pronounced very much like כ (k)
ר	r	Pronounced like English R
שׂ	ś	Pronounced like English S, much the same as ס
שׁ	š	Pronounced like English SH
ת	t/th	Pronounced like English T *or* TH

Note that different forms of some letters appear at the end of the word (written right to left), as in כָּפַף (*kāphaph*, "bend") and מֶלֶךְ (*melek*, "king").

Vowels in Hebrew (except where the ו is used to represent a vowel sound), are represented by "vowel points" added to the consonant. For example: הַ (*ha*, "the"). The letter *yod* (י, *y*) also becomes a *part of* certain vowel sounds, as in the conjunction כִּי (*kî*, "that"). Originally, Hebrew was written as "unpointed" text, with just the consonants. For convenience, the different vowel points are shown below on the letter Aleph (א).

אָ	ā	Pronounced not like long A in English, but like the broad A or AH sound
אַ	a	The Hebrew short A sound, but more closely resembles the broad A (pronounced for a shorter period of time) than the English short A
אֶ	e	Pronounced like English short E

אָ	ē	Pronounced like English long A, or Greek η (eta)
אִ	i	Pronounced like English short I
אִ	î	The same vowel point is sometimes pronounced like אִי (see below)
אָ	o	This vowel point sometimes represents the short O sound
אֹ	ō	Pronounced like English long O
אֻ	u	The vowel point ֻ sometimes represents a shorter U sound and
אֻ	ū	is sometimes pronounced like וּ (û, see above)
אֵי	ê	Pronounced much the same as אֵ
אֶי	ê	Pronounced much the same as אֶ
אִי	î	Pronounced like long I in many languages, or English long E
אְ	ᵊ	An unstressed vowel sound, like the first E in the word "severe"
אֱ, אֲ, אֳ	ŏ, ă, ĕ	Shortened, unstressed forms of the vowels אָ, אַ, and אֶ, pronounced very similarly to אְ

PREFACE

The end of a long writing project like a commentary on Isaiah results in a mixture of relief and gratitude. The task is difficult, especially in the midst of many other demands, but ultimately highly rewarding. I harbor no illusions that this work represents a definitive or exhaustive treatment of Isaiah. I can only hope it provides the reader with a fraction of the benefit I have received from the time spent researching and reflecting upon the rich message of this great prophet.

Two writers who have significantly aided in my study of Isaiah, J. Alec Motyer and John N. Oswalt, have each published new works on Isaiah since the completion of the first volume of this commentary. For the sake of continuity, I have continued to cite their earlier works. I would commend these new commentaries, however, to any serious student of Isaiah. Motyer has contributed the volume on Isaiah to the Tyndale series published by InterVarsity Press. In keeping with the nature of that series, this work is more condensed and accessible than his earlier volume. Oswalt has written on Isaiah for the NIV Application Commentary series published by Zondervan. Oswalt provides many helpful preaching insights in his two-volume NICOT work, but the Application Commentary series is more directly aimed at making the transition from text to sermon.

I continue to be indebted to many individuals and groups for helping me to complete this volume. I would like to single out the following:

> Sandra Collins, for staying the course with me through the entire project and for providing a skilled second set of eyes to read this manuscript;
>
> Dru Ashwell, my editor at College Press, for his patience, prayers, and positive motivation;
>
> My family at the Natchez Trace Church of Christ, who encourage

me in so many ways and who have listened to many sermons and classes on Isaiah in recent years;

My friends and colleagues at Lipscomb University, especially those in the College of Bible and Ministry, who have inspired me with their use of God's gifts and honored me with the opportunity to serve them;

Teresa and Janis, for keeping the office functional and for protecting my writing time;

My "daughters" in Kappa Chi, whose many prayers and words of encouragement have meant so much.

Finally, I dedicate this volume to my wife, Teri, and to my sons, Nathan and Daniel. I love you and thank you for your understanding. You serve as constant reminders of how blessed I am.

INTRODUCTION TO ISAIAH 28–39

The chapters that comprise this section of Isaiah could actually be grouped under three separate headings according to literary type. Chapters 28–33 are typical prophetic oracles. Chapters 34–35 contain a proto-apocalyptic style similar to chapters 23–27 and bear a similar relationship to the preceding chapters. Chapters 36–39 represent the most extended portion of narrative in the book.

The distinctive nature and purpose of the various literary styles of Isaiah 28–39 will be briefly evaluated in this introduction. The commentary itself, however, will focus on the common theme of the section as a whole. The primary theme is the importance of trusting in God, as well as the nature of such trust. This theme is not new in Isaiah, but follows closely from the preceding chapters. Isaiah 1–12 highlights the dramatic failure of Ahaz to trust God when threatened by Israel and Syria. God's sovereignty over the nations dominates Isaiah 13–27, with the aim of encouraging Judah not to trust in or fear these nations.

The occasion of the exhortation to trust God in Isaiah 28–39 derives from the obvious destructive purpose of Assyria after the nation with which Ahaz covenanted defeated Israel and Syria. The Assyrians have revealed their intent to conquer Judah next rather than serve as a faithful covenant partner. Where should the people of Judah turn now? The proper response, of course, would be to turn to God, their true faithful covenant partner. An alternative that obviously appealed to many, however, was to seek help from Egypt instead (cf. 30:1-2; 31:1).

The first six chapters of this section flesh out the tragedy and folly of turning to Egypt for help. Through a series of woes (cf. 28:1; 29:1; 30:1; 31:1; 33:1) Isaiah points out the disastrous consequences of repeating the mistake of Ahaz. Exchanging Egypt for Assyria is, if anything, a greater sin because Egypt represents the bondage from which

God had delivered them. Isaiah stresses both the hardened condition such a decision evidences and the rejection of God it represents.

Just as Isaiah 24–27 looks beyond immediate historical circumstances to God's universal judgment and blessing, so Isaiah 34–35 expands the reader's vision. The prophet sees a day in which the world of the wicked becomes a place of permanent desolation and the world of the redeemed is transformed from a desert to a lush garden. The two alternatives present a clear and limited choice to those who would cast their lot with the nations doomed to judgment rather than with the One who will judge the nations.

Chapters 36–39 are significant in more ways than one. They present in narrative fashion the challenge Hezekiah faces as the forces of the Assyrian king Sennacherib overrun most of Judah and move toward the final target of Jerusalem. Hezekiah's faith stands in stark contrast to the fear and unbelief of Ahaz. God's dramatic deliverance of Jerusalem from the encircling Assyrian army confirms the power of such faith. Hezekiah also sees God's power in a life-and-death situation as God spares him from a deadly illness. The section ends on an ominous note, however, as Hezekiah receives Babylonian envoys ostensibly sent to celebrate Hezekiah's recovery. God reveals to Hezekiah, however, that these same Babylonians, who have expansionist ambitions, will take Jerusalem's treasures and his descendants into exile.

In addition to the way Isaiah 36–39 further illustrates the importance of faith, these chapters also play an important role in the structure of the whole book. Chapters 36–37 bring resolution to the danger from Assyria which serves as the backdrop for the book to this point. Chapters 38–39 introduce the future threat of Babylon, setting the stage for the rest of the book and its focus on the future of God's kingdom purpose in light of the Babylonian exile. It is also striking that God's promise to heal Hezekiah of his illness includes a reference to the deliverance of Jerusalem from the king of Assyria (38:4-6). This promise of future deliverance means that Hezekiah's healing preceded God's actions against the Assyrian army. The literary structure of the book thus takes precedence over the chronological order of the events. When considered in chronological sequence, however, Hezekiah's healing serves to strengthen his faith in God's power to deliver Jerusalem from Sennacherib's army.

The following outline reflects the emphasis on faith in these chapters.

OUTLINE OF ISAIAH 28–39

I. **THE FOLLY OF TRUSTING IN EGYPT** — 28:1–31:9
  A. **Woe to the Drunkards** — 28:1–29:24
    1. The Description of the Drunkards — 28:1-15
      a. The Drunkards of Israel — 28:1-6
      b. The Drunkards of Judah — 28:7-15
    2. God's Response to the Drunkards — 28:16–29:24
      a. Expose the Deceptive Refuge — 28:16-22
      b. Prepare for the Harvest — 28:23-29
      c. Humble the Proud — 29:1-4
      d. Overthrow the Enemies — 29:5-8
      e. Soften the Hardened Hearts — 29:9-16
      f. Restore the Proper Order — 29:17-24
  B. **Woe to the Obstinate Children** — 30:1–31:9
    1. The Description of the Obstinate Children — 30:1-11
      a. Judah's Determination to Ally with Egypt — 30:1-7
      b. Judah's Determination to Reject God's Word — 30:8-11
    2. God's Response to the Obstinate Children — 30:12–31:9
      a. A Removal of False Hopes — 30:12-17
      b. An Offer of Grace — 30:18-26
      c. An Offer of Vindication — 30:27-33
      d. An Offer of Restoration — 31:1-9
II. **THE WISDOM OF TRUSTING IN GOD** — 32:1–35:10
  A. **God Will Restore Righteous Rule** — 32:1-20
    1. The Transformed Society under Righteous Rule — 32:1-8
    2. The Prerequisite for the Restoration of Righteous Rule — 32:9-20
  B. **God Will Rise Up to Vindicate the Righteous** — 33:1-24
    1. The Exaltation of God against the Wicked Schemers — 33:1-12
    2. The Exaltation of God on Behalf of the Faithful of Zion — 33:13-24
  C. **God Will Judge the Nations** — 34:1-17

1. God Will Defeat the Nations' Armies — 34:1-4
2. God Will Slaughter Edom as a Sacrifice — 34:5-17
  D. God Will Give Joy to the Redeemed — 35:1-10
1. God Will Transform the Desert into a Garden — 35:1-7
2. God Will Provide a Way Home for the Redeemed — 35:8-10
III. THE EXAMPLE OF THE FAITH OF HEZEKIAH — 36:1–39:8
  A. The Challenge of Sennacherib's Invasion — 36:1–37:38
1. The Taunt from Sennacherib's Representatives to Hezekiah's Representatives — 36:1-10
2. The Warning from Sennacherib's Representatives to the People on the Walls of Jerusalem — 36:11-22
3. The Initial Response to Sennacherib's Message — 37:1-7
4. Sennacherib's Renewed Threat — 37:8-13
5. Hezekiah's Prayer to God — 37:14-20
6. God's Response to Hezekiah's Prayer — 37:21-35
7. God's Response to Sennacherib — 37:36-38
  B. The Challenge of Hezekiah's Illness — 38:1-22
1. God's Announcement of Hezekiah's Imminent Death — 38:1-3
2. God's Response to Hezekiah's Prayer — 38:4-8
3. Hezekiah's Song of Thanksgiving — 38:9-20
4. A Final Note on Hezekiah's Recovery — 38:21-22
  C. The Challenge of the Babylonian Envoys — 39:1-8
1. Hezekiah's Reception of the Babylonian Envoys — 39:1-2
2. God's Warning Regarding the Babylonians — 39:3-8

ISAIAH 28

I. THE FOLLY OF TRUSTING IN EGYPT (28:1–31:9)

A. WOE TO THE DRUNKARDS (28:1–29:24)

The first of Isaiah's series of woes[1] begins with an address to **Ephraim** (i.e., the Northern Kingdom of Israel) before its fall to the Assyrians. Prophets who minister to Judah frequently use the bitter experience of Israel to warn Judah of the same end, though with little apparent success.[2] Isaiah quickly turns his attention, therefore, from the **drunkards** of Ephraim to their counterparts in Judah, who are equally insensitive to the ways of God.

1. The Description of the Drunkards (28:1-15)

The Drunkards of Israel (28:1-6)

¹Woe to that wreath, the pride of Ephraim's drunkards, /to the fading flower, his glorious beauty, /set on the head of a fertile valley— /to that city, the pride of those laid low by wine! /²See, the Lord has one who is powerful and strong. /Like a hailstorm and a destructive wind, /like a driving rain and a flooding downpour, /he will throw it forcefully to the ground. /³That wreath, the pride of Ephraim's drunkards, /will be trampled underfoot. /⁴That fading flower, his glorious beauty, /set on the head of a fertile valley, /will be like a fig ripe before harvest— /as soon as someone sees it and takes it in his hand, /he swallows it.
⁵In that day the LORD Almighty /will be a glorious crown, /a beautiful wreath /for the remnant of his people. /⁶He will be a

---

[1] Cf. the Overview of Isaiah 28–39.
[2] Cf. Ezekiel 23 and the graphic parable of the two sisters.

spirit of justice / to him who sits in judgment, / a source of strength / to those who turn back the battle at the gate.

28:1 The word **Woe** (הוֹי, *hôy*) expresses God's dissatisfaction with and grief over the condition he observes. In this case he sees the city of Samaria, capital of the Northern Kingdom, whose walls on top of a hill resemble a **wreath** of flowers on the head of a reveler. While there is nothing wrong with an appropriate celebration, such occasions can degenerate into bouts of drunkenness. Unfortunately, this degeneracy characterizes the condition of Samaria's inhabitants. Proverbs frequently warns of the disastrous effects of intoxication, most notably in 23:29-35. Samaria's drunkenness explains how such a beautiful and **fertile** area could be **laid low**. The extent of these consequences and the larger context indicate that Isaiah points to drunkenness as a figurative description of Israel's relationship with God.

28:2-4 God will respond to Ephraim's condition by sending his **powerful and strong** agent (Assyria) in judgment. Isaiah describes this agent with two metaphors. The first is that of an overwhelming storm that will flatten the city. The other image is that of **a fig ripe before harvest** which will be plucked and eaten.

28:5-6 Remarkably, although the picture of judgment is devastating and no redeeming virtue in Ephraim is mentioned, verses 5 and 6 abruptly introduce an element of future hope. **In that day** those who remain will not trust in city walls, nor will they escape to drunken reveling. Instead, God himself **will be a glorious crown, a beautiful wreath**, as well as their **source of strength** when they face enemies **at the gate**. Nothing is said directly about how this transformation will occur, but it will be accompanied by a return to **justice**, a virtue which does not accompany drunkenness.[3] These promises are part of the larger future hope which anticipates the reunification of Israel and Judah (cf. Ezek 37:15ff.). The absence of any obvious basis for this hope indicates that the future of Israel and Judah will come about through the power and graciousness of God.

The Drunkards of Judah (28:7-15)

⁷**And these also stagger from wine / and reel from beer: / Priests and prophets stagger from beer / and are befuddled with wine; /**

---

[3]The significance and meaning of "justice" for Isaiah's message will be considered in more detail in chapters 40–66.

they reel from beer, / they stagger when seeing visions, / they stumble when rendering decisions. / ⁸All the tables are covered with vomit / and there is not a spot without filth.

⁹"Who is it he is trying to teach? / To whom is he explaining his message? / To children weaned from their milk, / to those just taken from the breast? / ¹⁰For it is: / Do and do, do and do, / rule on rule, rule on rule*ᵃ*; / a little here, a little there."

¹¹Very well then, with foreign lips and strange tongues / God will speak to this people, / ¹²to whom he said, / "This is the resting place, let the weary rest"; / and, "This is the place of repose"— / but they would not listen. / ¹³So then, the word of the LORD to them will become: / Do and do, do and do, / rule on rule, rule on rule; / a little here, a little there— / so that they will go and fall backward, / be injured and snared and captured.

¹⁴Therefore hear the word of the LORD, you scoffers / who rule this people in Jerusalem. / ¹⁵You boast, "We have entered into a covenant with death, / with the graveᵇ we have made an agreement. / When an overwhelming scourge sweeps by, / it cannot touch us, / for we have made a lie our refuge / and falsehoodᶜ our hiding place."

ᵃ*10* Hebrew / *sav lasav sav lasav* / *kav lakav kav lakav* (**possibly meaningless sounds; possibly a mimicking of the prophet's words); also in verse 13**
ᵇ*15* Hebrew *Sheol*; also in verse 18   ᶜ*15* Or *false gods*

28:7-8 Since Isaiah's primary concern is the situation in Judah, he describes their present condition and future hope in greater detail.⁴ As with Israel, the problem is described in terms of drunkenness, but here the emphasis is on the consequent dulling of the senses. In addition, the dangerous effects of intoxication are compounded when the drunkards are the ostensible leaders of the people. Following the deaths of Nadab and Abihu, God expressly prohibits priests from drinking wine or other strong drink when they approach the tent of meeting (Lev 10:8-11). The need for priests and prophets alike to have a clear head when carrying out their sacred

---

⁴Isaiah clearly turns to Judah in verse 14. Some (e.g., Oswalt) understand verses 7-13 as a continuation of the message to Israel. In this case, the word "also" in verse 7 singles out priests and prophets from the people as a whole in Israel. This commentary understands the message of Israel's future hope in verses 5 and 6, as well as the reference to priests and prophets in verse 7, to signal the transition to God's message to Judah.

duties should be obvious, but words such as **stagger**, **reel**, **befuddled**, and **stumble** describe a condition which inspires little confidence. The picture of **vomit** and **filth**[5] covering their meeting places in verse 8 completes a highly unflattering portrayal of Judah's spiritual leaders.

28:9 Once again, although literal drunkenness may have been a problem, Isaiah uses this condition to characterize a lack of spiritual perception. Individuals react differently to alcohol, but it inevitably hinders one's ability to reason and discern. One effect of alcohol is to make a person arrogant and overconfident. Such a person is certainly not going to be open to instruction. These "informed" leaders apparently consider Isaiah's message too basic and feel insulted by his condescending words. His words are more appropriate, in their opinion, to children who have just been weaned from their mother's milk.

28:10 The description of Isaiah's teaching by the offended priests and prophets in verse 10 (צַו לָצָו צַו לָצָו קַו לָקָו קַו לָקָו, *ṣaw lāṣāw ṣaw lāṣāw qāw lāqāw qāw lāqāw*) is difficult to translate. The NIV, like most translations, attempts to translate it by **Do and do, do and do, rule on rule, rule on rule**. If this translation is the proper rendering, it portrays his message as a simplistic list of rules. These opponents may, however, be describing Isaiah's words as gibberish (cf. the NIV text note). If the latter is their intention, the leaders' description of Isaiah's words would be comparable to our "blah, blah, blah," or "yadda yadda yadda." In other words, they have neither the time nor the inclination to listen to this fanatic. Another possibility, which is compatible with verse 9, is that Isaiah's words are comparable to the simple childhood exercises used in learning the alphabet.

28:11 Regardless of the option selected above, Judah's leaders disdain the words of Isaiah and, therefore, the words of God. This disrespect will have drastic consequences, for they are rejecting the message which would deliver them from the same danger faced by Israel. If they find Isaiah's message incomprehensible, though it is in their own language, God will speak to them by the **foreign lips and strange tongues** of the Assyrians. They can choose to reject the message of the

---

[5]The word used here (צֹאָה, *ṣō'āth*) typically refers to human excrement (cf. the marginal note in the Hebrew text of 36:12) and is used figuratively of the sins of the women of Zion in 4:4.

prophet, but they will have to follow the simple rules of their invaders when these people of foreign speech tell them what to do.

28:12-14a Verse 12 highlights the tragedy of Judah's subjection to a foreign power. God's message, as delivered by Isaiah, provides a promise of **rest** for the **weary**. God's promise of rest and Judah's rejection of it in favor of attempts at self-preservation are twin themes that recur throughout this section of Isaiah. The problem is not that Judah's leaders are *unable* to listen; they are *unwilling* to listen. Their stubbornness is reflected in Isaiah's designation of them as **scoffers** in verse 14.[6] Proverbs routinely rebukes scoffers (cf. 1:22; 9:7-8; 13:1; 14:6; 15:12; 24:9) because their contempt for instruction is the antithesis of wisdom. In keeping with Isaiah's drunkenness theme, wine is called a mocker in Proverbs 20:1. Such, however, are those **who rule this people in Jerusalem**.

28:14b-15 Scoffers deserve the sarcasm Isaiah directs toward them. He mocks their false confidence when the **overwhelming scourge sweeps by**[7] in the way he characterizes the object of their trust. They would certainly not say that their **covenant** is with **death** or that their **agreement** is with **the grave** (שְׁאוֹל, *šᵉ'ôl* [Sheol]). Nor would they claim that their **refuge** was a **lie**, or that they would find their **hiding place** in **falsehood**. Isaiah puts words in their mouths that express the reality about their alternative to trusting in God. Truth is found only in right relationship with God, and falsehood inevitably leads to death.

2. God's Response to the Drunkards (28:16–29:24)

Expose the Deceptive Refuge (28:16-22)

¹⁶**So this is what the Sovereign LORD says:**
"See, I lay a stone in Zion, / a tested stone, / a precious cornerstone for a sure foundation; / the one who trusts will never be dismayed. / ¹⁷I will make justice the measuring line / and righteousness the plumb line; / hail will sweep away your refuge, the lie, / and water will overflow your hiding place. / ¹⁸Your covenant with

---

[6] The words for "scoffing" in verse 14 and "mocking" in verse 22 both derive from the same root (לִיץ, *lyṣ*).

[7] Isaiah here combines the image of a flood of waters and a whip (scourge) to intensify the severity of the threat to Judah.

death will be annulled; /your agreement with the grave will not stand. / When the overwhelming scourge sweeps by, /you will be beaten down by it. / ¹⁹As often as it comes it will carry you away; / morning after morning, by day and by night, / it will sweep through."

The understanding of this message /will bring sheer terror. / ²⁰The bed is too short to stretch out on, /the blanket too narrow to wrap around you. / ²¹The LORD will rise up as he did at Mount Perazim, /he will rouse himself as in the Valley of Gibeon— /to do his work, his strange work, /and perform his task, his alien task. / ²²Now stop your mocking, /or your chains will become heavier; / the Lord, the LORD Almighty, has told me / of the destruction decreed against the whole land.

28:16 In contrast to the unstable alliances of the foolish leaders in Jerusalem, God presents a secure basis for hope in verse 16 in a building metaphor that points initially to the rebuilding efforts after the promised storm sweeps over **Zion**. The foundation is the most important part of any building project, and the **cornerstone** is the critical element in the foundation. This stone is, first, a **tested** stone, meaning one that has been proven trustworthy.[8] It is also **precious**, referring to its value to the people and/or God. This stone thus provides **a sure foundation**, but only for **the one who trusts**.

To what (or whom) does the precious cornerstone refer? Interpreters have answered this question in numerous ways.[9] The most likely possibilities are God's covenant faithfulness (cf. the description of him as Israel's "Rock" in 17:10) or, more specifically, to the embodiment of covenant promises in the Davidic messiah. Both of these interpretations are compatible with the New Testament application of this verse to the work of Christ in Ephesians 2:20 and 1 Peter 2:4-6. Particularly instructive is Romans 9:33, in which Paul combines Isaiah 8:14 and 28:16 to highlight the significance of the way one responds to God's foundational work. In that context Paul distinguishes between those who pursue righteousness by faith and those who do so as if it were by works. The truth in Isaiah's day is

---

[8]The phrase is literally "a stone of testing," which could imply that it is a stone which will test the people's faith as in 8:14. Cf. J. Alec Motyer, *The Prophecy of Isaiah* (Downers Grove, IL: InterVarsity, 1993), p. 187.

[9]For a more complete list of the proposals, cf. John N. Oswalt, *The Book of Isaiah: Chapters 1–39* (Grand Rapids: Eerdmans, 1986), p. 518.

the same as in Paul's: those who trust in their own righteousness or in any other means of human security will be put to shame, but those who trust in God will stand firm.

28:17-19 The building metaphor continues in the beginning of verse 17 as attention turns from the future rebuilding efforts to God's assessment of what his people have constructed on their own. When he applies **the measuring line** of **justice** and **the plumb line** of **righteousness** to their works, their deficiencies are determined to be fatal. What his people have built will not withstand the storms as they had anticipated.[10] These storms will reveal the flimsiness of what the Jerusalem leaders have trusted in (cf. verse 15) as they come in waves and beat down and carry away those whose trust is not in God. The storms will turn the former complacency to **sheer terror**.

28:20 Verse 20 uses another image to describe the futility of Jerusalem's condition. The bed is a place to which people turn for peaceful rest. In this case, however, their **bed is too short** and their **blanket too narrow** to cover them. It is impossible to find rest when one's feet are hanging off the end of the bed and there are not enough covers to keep one warm. God offers rest (v. 12), but the inhabitants of Jerusalem prefer an uncomfortable and deficient alternative of their own design.

28:21 The foolish choices of the scornful leaders of Jerusalem force God into a **strange work**, an **alien task**. When God first entered into covenant with Israel, he promised to give them peace in the land and victory over their enemies (cf. Lev 26:6-8; Deut 28:7). They would enjoy victory because God would fight for them, as illustrated when God broke out as a flood against the Philistines at **Mount Perazim** (2 Sam 5:20) and when he hurled hailstones upon the Canaanites **in the Valley of Gibeon** (Josh 10:11). God's covenant promises of victory, however, are contingent upon Israel's faithfulness to the covenant. The counterparts to these promises guarantee defeat if the people prove untrue (cf. Lev 26:17; Deut 28:25). Sadly, God must now give victory to his people's enemies. Just as God had "stormed" against these enemies in the past, now he must make the enemies an overwhelming flood against Judah.

28:22 In one sense God's acts of judgment are neither strange nor alien because they are true to his holy and righteous nature. They are distressing when they must be directed against his

---

[10]Cf. Jesus' teaching on the wise and foolish builders in Matt 7:24-27.

covenant people, however, because of the special relationship he has with them and the special purpose they have in bringing salvation to the nations. These judgments are ultimately redemptive, however, as they purify a remnant through whom he can continue his work. Perhaps this goal is behind the warning in verse 22. The more hardened the people are in their resistance to God, the more devastating God's **destruction** must be. If they persist in responding to faithful prophets like Isaiah (vv. 9-10), they will not be liberated but their **chains will become heavier**. Sin is a restrictive burden which only becomes more burdensome the more one continues in it.

Prepare for the Harvest (28:23-29)

²³Listen and hear my voice; /pay attention and hear what I say. / ²⁴When a farmer plows for planting, does he plow continually? / Does he keep on breaking up and harrowing the soil? / ²⁵When he has leveled the surface, / does he not sow caraway and scatter cummin? / Does he not plant wheat in its place,ᵃ /barley in its plot,ᵃ /and spelt in its field? / ²⁶His God instructs him /and teaches him the right way.

²⁷Caraway is not threshed with a sledge, / nor is a cartwheel rolled over cummin; /caraway is beaten out with a rod, /and cummin with a stick. / ²⁸Grain must be ground to make bread; /so one does not go on threshing it forever. / Though he drives the wheels of his threshing cart over it, /his horses do not grind it. / ²⁹All this also comes from the LORD Almighty, /wonderful in counsel and magnificent in wisdom.

ᵃ25 The meaning of the Hebrew for this word is uncertain.

28:23-28 Since the scoffers who rule in Jerusalem have been placed in the category of fools, it is appropriate that the first woe ends with a wisdom passage. The biblical concept of wisdom assumes that true wisdom originates with God and may be found only by those who possess "the fear of the LORD." Because the world was created by God's wisdom, however (cf. Prov 8:22ff.), an astute observer of creation can discern the wisdom inherent in its workings. God has not published a book on agriculture, but the wise farmer is instructed by God (v. 26) through observation and experience.

It is possible to interpret this passage as a rebuke to the "enlightened" leaders of Jerusalem as Isaiah contrasts them with the simple but wise farmer. The emphasis upon the necessarily "violent" aspects of farming, however, such as plowing, breaking up the soil, threshing, beating, and grinding, points in another direction. These verses highlight further God's positive intention in the painful ways he must deal with his foolish people.

28:29 The farmer does not keep on breaking up the soil as an end in itself, but only to prepare it for planting. This image recalls other prophetic messages which exhort the people to break up the fallow ground in their hearts so that they can receive God's word (cf. Jer 4:3-4; Hos 10:11-12). Similarly, the wise farmer threshes neither destructively nor endlessly. His goal is to reap a useful harvest from his labors. In the same way, God does not treat his people with severity apart from his wise and good purpose. He is powerful, but he is also **wonderful in counsel and magnificent in wisdom**. God's people must trust in his wisdom and benevolent purpose. This message was especially relevant for Isaiah and others of the faithful remnant if they were to maintain their faith through the hard times ahead.

ISAIAH 29

Humble the Proud (29:1-4)

¹**Woe to you, Ariel, Ariel,** / **the city where David settled!** / **Add year to year and let your cycle of festivals go on.** / ²**Yet I will besiege Ariel;** / **she will mourn and lament, she will be to me like an altar hearth.**[a] / ³**I will encamp against you all around;** / **I will encircle you with towers** / **and set up my siege works against you.** / ⁴**Brought low, you will speak from the ground;** / **your speech will mumble out of the dust.** / **Your voice will come ghostlike from the earth;** / **out of the dust your speech will whisper.**

[a] **2** The Hebrew word for *altar hearth* sounds like the Hebrew for *Ariel*.

Whereas Isaiah's first woe addressed Judah by beginning with the parallel situation of Ephraim, his second woe is directed to Jerusalem at the outset via the figurative name "Ariel." The emphasis in this woe is similar to the first: God must humble a proud, imperceptive people in order to continue his purpose through them. The reader should remember that even though this series of woes may appear redundant at times, the *book* of Isaiah is largely a collection and arrangement of the spoken *oracles* of the prophet. Like any good preacher, he would address persistent root problems by attacking them repeatedly in different ways. In this woe Isaiah presents four important actions God must take to bring his people from their sinful condition to where he wants them to be. He first must humble them.

29:1 The double reference to **Ariel** in verse 1 (and once again at the beginning of verse 2) makes a proper name of the term for an "altar hearth" (אֲרִיאֵל, *'ărî'ēl*), as it is translated at the end of verse 2. This is the place where the portion of the sacrificial offering given to God is consumed. Too often Israel, and the residents of Jerusalem (**the city where David settled**) in particular, presume that they are secure solely because of the presence of this sacred site. In language reminiscent of 1:10-14, God sarcastically exhorts them to continue their annual **cycle of festivals** which condemn rather than sustain them in light of their hypocrisy.

29:2 As in 28:21, God again speaks of devastating warfare against his people. The encircling army will consist of foreign soldiers, but the invaders' success will be God's doing. It is in light of this scenario that the reader must consider in what sense Jerusalem will become **like an altar hearth**. The unbelief and rebellion of the inhabitants of Jerusalem will make their offerings meaningless, so their false confidence will lead them to become the sacrificial victims consumed in this holy place. God is, after all, a consuming fire even to his people when they persist in rebellion against him (cf. Exod 24:17; Deut 4:24; Heb 12:29).

29:3-4 As a result of God's judgment, the people will be brought so **low** that they must speak **out of the dust**. Their words are not recorded, but being brought low is equivalent to being humbled. In 57:15 the exalted God reveals that he dwells "with him who is contrite and lowly in spirit." Since humility is a prerequisite to the saving presence of God, the state to which God brings his people makes sense of the seemingly illogical reversal of circumstances in verse 5.

Overthrow the Enemies (29:5-8)

⁵**But your many enemies will become like fine dust, / the ruthless hordes like blown chaff. / Suddenly, in an instant, / ⁶the LORD Almighty will come / with thunder and earthquake and great noise, / with windstorm and tempest and flames of a devouring fire. / ⁷Then the hordes of all the nations that fight against Ariel, / that attack her and her fortress and besiege her, / will be as it is with a dream, / with a vision in the night— / ⁸as when a hungry man dreams that he is eating, / but he awakens, and his hunger remains; / as when a thirsty man dreams that he is drinking, / but he awakens faint, with his thirst unquenched. / So will it be with the hordes of all the nations / that fight against Mount Zion.**

29:5-6 God promises to reduce **in an instant** the invading armies at Jerusalem's gates to **fine dust** and **blown chaff**. This promise fits well with what God does to Sennacherib's forces in 37:36-37. The **devouring fire** which transforms Jerusalem into an altar hearth is now directed at the arrogant, unbelieving invaders. In another mixed metaphor, the storms which earlier devastated Ephraim

(28:2) and Judah (28:15) now overwhelm the **ruthless hordes** that comprise Israel's **many enemies**.[1]

29:7-8 The sudden turn of events leaves Ariel's attackers bewildered. What once seemed so real now becomes like a **dream**. When one dreams of success and awakens to find that the success was but an illusion, the effects can be frustrating. The enemies' **hunger** and **thirst** remains unsatisfied as God delivers his people from their grasp. This reversal refers not only to the failure of Sennacherib's "certain" conquest of Jerusalem, but also to the illusory nature of any apparent success in opposing God. Only frustration and failure await those with such plans. No matter how many battles are won or how close the final victory appears, God alone will prevail in the war for the territory he has claimed (**Zion**). As with chapters 13–23, this message is directed more to Israel than to the attackers as it calls those who humbly trust in God to share in his victory.

Soften the Hardened Hearts (29:9-16)

⁹**Be stunned and amazed, / blind yourselves and be sightless; / be drunk, but not from wine, / stagger, but not from beer. /** ¹⁰**The LORD has brought over you a deep sleep: /He has sealed your eyes (the prophets); / he has covered your heads (the seers).**

¹¹**For you this whole vision is nothing but words sealed in a scroll. And if you give the scroll to someone who can read, and say to him, "Read this, please," he will answer, "I can't; it is sealed."** ¹²**Or if you give the scroll to someone who cannot read, and say, "Read this, please," he will answer, "I don't know how to read."**

¹³**The Lord says:**

"These people come near to me with their mouth /and honor me with their lips, / but their hearts are far from me. / Their worship of me / is made up only of rules taught by men.ᵃ **/** ¹⁴**Therefore once more I will astound these people /with wonder upon wonder; /the wisdom of the wise will perish, / the intelligence of the intelligent will vanish." /** ¹⁵**Woe to those who go to great depths /to hide their plans from the LORD, / who do their work in darkness and think, / "Who sees us? Who will know?" /** ¹⁶**You turn things upside down, /as if the potter were thought to be like the clay! / Shall what**

---

[1]Ironically, the Assyrian armies that made up the overwhelming flood against Israel and Judah (8:6-8) are the ones that now will be swept away.

is formed say to him who formed it, / "He did not make me"? / Can the pot say of the potter, / "He knows nothing"?

^a*13 Hebrew; Septuagint* They worship me in vain; / their teachings are but rules taught by men.

Unfortunately, invaders such as the Assyrians are not the only ones whose perception is faulty. As we have seen, God uses these deluded would-be conquerors to bring his people back to the humility they need for a relationship with him. These verses, however, return to the time before that change of heart has occurred. Judah's hardness of heart is a more serious and complex problem than the political and military arrogance of the Assyrians. God knows, however, how to win this war as well.

29:9-10 Who is responsible for the spiritual stupor in Jerusalem? On the one hand, verse 9 alleges that the people are **sightless** and **stagger** as drunkards (though not from literal alcohol) by their own choice. On the other hand, as verse 10 compares their lack of perception to a person in a **deep sleep**,[2] God is designated as the agent of their condition. God has put them to sleep by sealing their **eyes** and covering their **heads**. As with the drunkenness, the sleepiness in Judah is figurative. Those who are "asleep on the job" are the **prophets** and **seers**. God has sent faithful prophets like Isaiah to warn the people, but he also permits the false prophets to proclaim their message. These prophets who preach what the people want to hear have lulled them into a false security. In the final analysis, therefore, those who are blind and asleep and drunk are so because they have chosen to be in that condition.

29:11 Due to Jerusalem's unhealthy spiritual condition, the message God reveals through Isaiah is like **words sealed in a scroll**.[3] The message is not literally sealed, but it might as well be in light of the unreceptive spirit of the people. Illiterates could not read the scroll even if it were opened, whereas the more educated would know not to open a sealed scroll. The result is a no-win situation for Judah. The truth is actually hidden in plain sight. In keeping with God's warning to Isaiah at the time of his call, the more he proclaims the truth the less capable the people are of receiving it. God has not sealed the scroll; their hardened hearts have.

---

[2]The same word used here (תַּרְדֵּמָה, *tardēmāh*) appears in Genesis 2:21 when God puts Adam to sleep to remove the rib from which he forms Eve.

[3]The words "nothing but" in the NIV of verse 11 obscure the Hebrew, which says that the vision is "*like* words sealed in a scroll."

29:12 What is the solution, then, to this tangled web of responsibility? Since the people have sinned against God's clear revelation, he imposes upon them a further hardening (cf. Rom 1:18 ff) which ultimately brings them to a point where they can perceive clearly again (see below). They are thus responsible for their hardened condition, but God acts through both true and false prophets to expose the full extent of their hardness. He is also, however, the one who will act to break their downward spiral (cf. v. 14).

29:13-16 In contrast to his imperceptive people, God sees their futile, scheming ways only too clearly. In verses 13-16 he exposes their delusional thinking and explains how he will overturn it. The root issue here, as is commonly the case with those whose relationship with God is in disarray, is a deficient view of the nature of God. They are convinced that they can **hide their plans** from God and keep him in the dark because they deny the distinction between the creator and the creation. Perhaps God aims to inject a note of sarcasm in describing this foolishness, since those who seek to equate the **potter** and the **clay** conclude that the potter **knows nothing**. They are thus striving to be like one who, by their own admission, is ignorant. When humans seek to mold God into their likeness, the result is not liberating but enslaving.

Foolish thinking by religious people inevitably manifests itself in their worship. When God's people act as if Yahweh can be manipulated by hypocritical acts of worship, they insult him by equating him with the petty gods of paganism. In a physical sense people cannot distance **their lips** from **their hearts**, but in worship such a separation is quite common. By "the heart," of course, God refers to the true commitment of the inner person. To utter pious words in worship with no intention of responding accordingly with one's life exposes a worship motivated either by superstitious fear or a desire to manipulate. The fearful in Jerusalem also manifest a lack of logic, for why would they bother to seek the favor of one so much like themselves?

The words of verse 13 are familiar to the Christian since Jesus applies them to the Pharisees when they undermine God's commandments by their traditions (Matt 15:1-9; Mark 7:1-13). These words are indeed relevant to Jesus' conflict with the Pharisees, but that context must not obscure the slightly different one in Isaiah's day. There are more ways to transform the **worship**[4] of God into

---

[4] Literally, "fear" (יִרְאָה, *yir'āh*).

something consisting **only of rules taught by men** than by following certain traditions, Pharisaic or otherwise.

Isaiah's contemporaries prefer "a commandment of men" (מִצְוַת אֲנָשִׁים, *miṣwath 'ănāšîm*), i.e., "a human commandment," to fearing God. While fearing God can be a synonym for worship, in a broader sense the expression refers to the entire heart-response to God (Eccl 12:13). The opposite of fearing God is to act according to human wisdom. This distinction explains why godly wisdom is so closely tied to "the fear of the LORD" (cf. Job 28:28; Ps 111:10; Prov 1:7). Those in Jerusalem, and especially the leaders, foolishly choose to plot and scheme rather than trust. They are more confident in their abilities to work out a solution than they are in the provision of God. They cannot, therefore, be filled with the sense of awe at the glory of God which both leads to and flows from heartfelt worship.

How can God restore the people's confidence in his ability to deliver them? He will **astound** them **with wonder upon wonder**. The words **once more** highlight the graciousness of God's actions. He has multiplied wonders before his people time and again, but they repeatedly forget. As a result of their forgetfulness, they are in no position to return to him until he again reveals himself powerfully. The **wisdom** and **intelligence** which will disappear as a result refer to the false human wisdom described above. Human wisdom must be leveled before the foundation of godly wisdom may be laid.

Restore the Proper Order (29:17-24)

[17]In a very short time, will not Lebanon be turned into a fertile field / and the fertile field seem like a forest? / [18]In that day the deaf will hear the words of the scroll, / and out of gloom and darkness / the eyes of the blind will see. / [19]Once more the humble will rejoice in the LORD; / the needy will rejoice in the Holy One of Israel. / [20]The ruthless will vanish, / the mockers will disappear, / and all who have an eye for evil will be cut down— / [21]those who with a word make a man out to be guilty, / who ensnare the defender in court / and with false testimony deprive the innocent of justice.

[22]Therefore this is what the LORD, who redeemed Abraham, says to the house of Jacob:

"No longer will Jacob be ashamed; / no longer will their faces grow pale. / [23]When they see among them their children, / the work of my hands, / they will keep my name holy; / they will acknowledge the holiness of the Holy One of Jacob, /and will stand in awe of the God of Israel. / ²⁴Those who are wayward in spirit will gain understanding; / those who complain will accept instruction."

The last major section of this woe elaborates upon the deliverance promised briefly in verses 5-8 and 14. Pride has led the people to false theology and false wisdom, producing a society characterized by deafness, blindness, and injustice. God promises that the humility he engenders will reverse those traits and yield a society that truly acknowledges him.

29:17 The chronological reference, **In a very short time**, in verse 17 is parallel to the more frequent, vague "in that day" in verse 18. The former stresses the certainty and swiftness of God's intervention when the threat against his people reaches the critical point (cf. 10:25; 17:14). Such imminence language frequently (as here) entails not only the overthrow of enemies, but the transformation of God's people as well. This fact should focus the reader's attention on God's ability to bring about a total change in the present order rather than on calculations and date predictions.

The image in verse 17 clearly pictures a radical reversal like the one God will bring about among his people. The precise nuance of the imagery is less obvious. Similar language appears in 32:15 to describe the transforming effect of the Spirit's outpouring. In 32:15 the desert rather than Lebanon becomes a fertile field. In the positive context of that verse, the fact that the fertile field seems like a forest must be a good thing. In 29:17, therefore, the point may be that the outwardly mighty must be brought low before being exalted again.

29:18-19 The emphasis in the verses that follow is upon the restoration of the senses that have become dulled and the resulting change in the governance of society. Once God's most recent wonders free his people from the shackles of attempted self-preservation, they will be able to **hear the words of the scroll** and **the eyes of the blind will see** the wisdom of trusting in him. As with Jesus' beatitudes, joy will come to **the humble** and **the needy**. These are the ones who survive and enjoy God's blessings anew because they are the ones whose hearts have been turned back to God.

29:20-21 On the other hand, individuals such as **the ruthless** and **the mockers** (cf. 28:14,22) will perish. They are the leaders who govern by their own wisdom rather than by God's. Because they have no reverence for God, they make a mockery of justice (v. 21). Even when they witness God's powerful acts, they remain unchanged and are thus swept away in judgment. The removal of the irreparably hardened is a prerequisite to God's renewal of a remnant. In a sense, then, God's wonders enable the blind to see, but there are those devoid of the capacity to see with the eyes of faith for whom even these wonders cannot accomplish their work.

29:22 The summarizing element (**Therefore**, v. 22) of this woe begins by describing God as the one **who redeemed Abraham**. This reference reminds God's people again of his long-standing covenant faithfulness. Abraham longed for a child through whom the covenant promises could be fulfilled, and God overcame the odds to give him that child. The prospect for descendants may have seemed equally remote for Isaiah's fellow Israelites, but God will once again overcome their fears (**no longer will their faces grow pale**).

29:23a Verse 23 begins with the word "for" (omitted by the NIV), indicating that when the people **see among them their children**, this sight will vividly remind them of God's freshly-revealed faithfulness. God can describe these children as **the work of my hands**, not only as the creator of all, but also as the cultivator of a covenant people. Only in this light can they truly appreciate and properly respond to the holiness of God. People will either deny or flee in fear from God's holiness unless they see him as a committed, loving father.

29:23b-24 A proper appreciation of **the Holy One of Jacob** also results in changed lives. Even the **wayward** and **those who complain** have hope if they **will accept instruction**. This prospect exposes again the complex relationship between divine sovereignty and human responsibility. Among the inhabitants of Jerusalem are the ruthless and the mockers, those so hardened by sin that they refuse to see and respond to God and thus perish. Yet other sinners humbly accept God's instruction and experience the joy of God's forgiveness and a restoration of the covenant blessings. The proper response to God is essential, but impossible apart from God's gracious, persistent revelation of himself. This woe highlights, therefore, the holiness and graciousness of God, while at the same time it stresses the need for a sincere and trusting commitment by his people to the truth about God.

ISAIAH 30

B. WOE TO THE OBSTINATE CHILDREN (30:1–31:9)

The next two woes (30:1-33; 31:1-9) reflect more clearly the historical background to the entire section. Judah is eager to seek support from Egypt in order to obtain relief from the Assyrian threat (cf. Isaiah 18–20). The stubborn and faithless pursuit of this path will yield only disappointment and divine judgment. Yet even under these circumstances God is at work to redeem and to restore.

1. The Description of the Obstinate Children (30:1-11)

Judah's Determination to Ally with Egypt (30:1-7)

¹"Woe to the obstinate children," / declares the LORD, / "to those who carry out plans that are not mine, / forming an alliance, but not by my Spirit, / heaping sin upon sin; / ²who go down to Egypt / without consulting me; / who look for help to Pharaoh's protection, / to Egypt's shade for refuge. / ³But Pharaoh's protection will be to your shame, / Egypt's shade will bring you disgrace. / ⁴Though they have officials in Zoan / and their envoys have arrived in Hanes, / ⁵everyone will be put to shame / because of a people useless to them, / who bring neither help nor advantage, / but only shame and disgrace."
⁶An oracle concerning the animals of the Negev:
Through a land of hardship and distress, / of lions and lionesses, / of adders and darting snakes, / the envoys carry their riches on donkeys' backs, / their treasures on the humps of camels, / to that unprofitable nation, / ⁷to Egypt, whose help is utterly useless. / Therefore I call her / Rahab the Do-nothing.

30:1 The book of Isaiah opens with God's charge that his children are rebellious (1:2), a charge that recurs in this woe. The language used in 30:1 (בָּנִים סוֹרְרִים, *bānîm sôrᵊrîm*) is the same as that used of the rebellious son in Deuteronomy 21:18-21.[1] The fact that such a child is to be put to death casts an ominous shadow over this text. Like all rebellious children, the people of Judah possess an unhealthy desire for independence that leads them to act without consulting or even considering the will of their father. Those who are suffering for their sins and respond by **carrying out plans** without seeking the will of God inevitably compound their problems, a result described here as **heaping sin upon sin**.

30:2-6 By seeking **protection** (מָעוֹז, *mā'ôz*) and **shade** (צֵל, *ṣēl*) from Egypt, Judah not only violates the injunction against turning back to Egypt for help (Deut 17:16), but also rejects God's willingness to provide those same benefits.[2] The determination to seek Egyptian aid has proceeded to the point that representatives of Judah are already in the Egyptian cities of **Zoan** and **Hanes**. This move, however, will result only in **shame** and **disgrace**, because Egypt is **useless** (לֹא־יוֹעִילוּ, *lō'-yô'îlû*)[3] as an ally. From the standpoint of a political/military strategy, turning to Egypt is a foolish decision because the Egyptians have already proven ineffective against Assyria. From the standpoint of Judah's relationship with God, turning to Egypt is an even more foolish decision because of God's history of faithfulness and power to save.

30:7 In order to illustrate the folly of trusting in Egypt, Isaiah delivers a sarcastic **oracle** depicting the dangerous and fruitless journey of a Judean delegation in their vain search for deliverance. Travel through the barren **Negev** south of Judah would be difficult because of both the climate and the dangerous animals they might encounter. The **envoys carry their riches** to profit a nation which can offer them nothing in return. By labeling Egypt as **Rahab**, Isaiah recalls the ancient Near Eastern myth of the powerful sea monster whom the gods were barely able to subdue. Biblical writers use this myth to affirm that it is Yahweh who prevails over all hostile forces (cf. 51:9; Job 26:12). In this case, however, Egypt as Rahab does not

---

[1] Barry G. Webb, *The Message of Isaiah* (Downers Grove, IL: InterVarsity, 1996), p. 127.

[2] Isaiah 25:4 uses the same words to refer to God's blessings (cf. 4:5-6).

[3] This word (also translated "advantage" in the next line) refers to the vanity of trusting in idolatry in 44:9-10. It is used of vain confidences in general in a number of passages (cf. Isa 57:12; Jer 2:8; 7:8; Prov 10:2; 11:4).

represent a fearsome power, but is rather **the Do-Nothing**.[4] As Oswalt colorfully summarizes the situation, "A caravan loaded with treasures struggles through wild terrain infested with lions and snakes, all to buy the help of an old dragon who is in fact helpless."[5]

Judah's Determination to Reject God's Word (30:8-11)

⁸**Go now, write it on a tablet for them, / inscribe it on a scroll, / that for the days to come / it may be an everlasting witness. / ⁹These are rebellious people, deceitful children, / children unwilling to listen to the LORD's instruction. / ¹⁰They say to the seers, / "See no more visions!" / and to the prophets, / "Give us no more visions of what is right! / Tell us pleasant things, / prophesy illusions. ¹¹Leave this way, / get off this path, / and stop confronting us / with the Holy One of Israel!"**

30:8-9 Isaiah returns to his role as a faithful **witness** (cf. 8:1-2,16) to a generation of **children unwilling to listen to the LORD's instruction** (תּוֹרָה, *tôrāh*). His formal record of both Judah's stubbornness and God's faithfulness will provide an opportunity for those in **days to come** to know the truth about how to enjoy a meaningful relationship with God. The word for **deceitful** (כְּחָשׁ, *keḥāš*) carries the connotation of failure or disappointment.[6] These children have not responded to their father as they should, but God will deal with this failure in such a way that future generations will.

30:10-11 As in 28:15, Isaiah in verses 10-11 sarcastically puts words in the mouths of the rebellious children which, while not verbatim quotes, reflect their true attitude. Their response to true prophets who call them to return to the covenant is **"Give us no more visions of what is right!"** In other words, "Stop giving us a clear picture of the way things really are!" What they prefer are the **pleasant things** and the **illusions**[7] that the false prophets (those who seek to please man rather than God) willingly offer (cf. Jer 6:13-14; Micah 3:5).

---

[4]Literally, "one who sits" (הֵם שָׁבֶת, *hēm šābeth*).

[5]Oswalt, *Isaiah* 1, p. 547.

[6]As Oswalt puts it (*Isaiah* 1, p. 551), "it is not so much that the sons tell lies as that they *are* lies."

[7]The same root of this word (תלל, *tll*) is used in 44:20 to refer to the "deluded" heart of one who cannot even see that the idol he holds in his right hand is a lie.

It is not surprising that children who have no interest in their father's instruction want prophets like Isaiah to diverge from their normal **way** because the covenant of their father calls the children to walk in all his ways. The true prophet cannot compromise, however, because there are only two ways: one leads to "life and prosperity," and the other leads to "death and destruction" (Deut 30:15ff.).

Isaiah's particular "offense" is his continual reminder that the God he serves is **the Holy One of Israel**. A holy God is bothersome because his holiness requires that he be approached with reverent awe and that his worshipers pursue holiness in their own lives. Isaiah has been transformed by his vision of the one honored as "holy, holy, holy," but those to whom he preaches have no interest in duplicating his experience. The situation is somewhat like the occasion when God revealed himself to Israel at Sinai. Moses was transformed by going into the presence of God, but the people as a whole preferred to maintain their distance, both physically and spiritually. In both cases, failing to acknowledge the holiness of God marks a dangerous state of denial.

2. God's Response to the Obstinate Children (30:12–31:9)

A Removal of False Hopes (30:12-17)

¹²**Therefore, this is what the Holy One of Israel says:**
"Because you have rejected this message, / relied on oppression / and depended on deceit, / ¹³this sin will become for you / like a high wall, cracked and bulging, / that collapses suddenly, in an instant. / ¹⁴It will break in pieces like pottery, / shattered so mercilessly / that among its pieces not a fragment will be found / for taking coals from a hearth / or scooping water out of a cistern."

¹⁵**This is what the Sovereign LORD, the Holy One of Israel, says:**
"In repentance and rest is your salvation, / in quietness and trust is your strength, / but you would have none of it. / ¹⁶You said, 'No, we will flee on horses.' / Therefore you will flee! / You said, 'We will ride off on swift horses.' / Therefore your pursuers will be swift! / ¹⁷A thousand will flee / at the threat of one; / at the threat of five / you will all flee away, / till you are left / like a flagstaff on a mountaintop, / like a banner on a hill."

30:12 Isaiah obviously has no intention of bowing to popular opinion and changing his ways because he responds to the people's wishes with another message from **the Holy One of Israel**. God will not allow his people to continue living in denial. By exposing the frailty of their illusory objects of trust, God seeks not to be vindictive but redemptive. God's kindness does not allow people to remain oblivious to their folly when they desperately need him.

The popular path of Isaiah's day is not simply a vain hope for those who pursue it; it is also a **sin**. Denying the truth about God is sinful in itself, but such a denial inevitably leads to further evil. The people hope to be supported[8] by **oppression** and **deceit**. The latter term (נָלוֹז, *nālôz*) is translated "perverse" by the NIV in Proverbs 3:32 and "devious" in Proverbs 14:2. Brutality and scheming characterize systems of government that operate without a clear sense of the nature of God and their accountability before him. Judah should show the world a radically different system but has not, as Isaiah has already revealed (cf. chapter 3).

30:13-14 God uses two analogies for Judah's false hope and its inevitable end in verses 13-14. He first compares it to a **high wall** that is obviously weak and fragile. The higher one builds a wall, the more likely it is to collapse and injure those it is intended to protect. The second comparison is to **pottery**, composed of inherently weak material. Clay implements can serve a variety of important functions, especially in securing and storing water. Even broken fragments of pottery can be useful, but in this case the vessel will be so shattered that **not a fragment will be found** that is salvageable. Walls and pottery are valuable human inventions, but in this case they represent the futility of human provisions in the face of life's ultimate challenges.

30:15 Before dismantling one more false hope, God[9] reminds his people of the alternative to their feverish but hopeless attempts at self-preservation. He contrasts their scheming and building fortifications with the **rest** and **quietness** he offers. This contrast anticipates the questions in chapter 55 about why the people spend all of their money and labor on what is not food while God offers a free

---

[8]The word translated "depended" (שָׁעַן, *šʿn*) literally means "lean upon."
[9]In verse 15 Isaiah adds "Sovereign Lord" (אֲדֹנָי יהוה, *ʾădōnāy YHWH*) to his designation of God. This multiplication of divine titles adds greater seriousness to Judah's decision to reject him.

feast. The "catch" in this case is the call for **repentance** and **trust**. God's grace is only available to those who turn from their ways to his and recognize him as the only true basis of confidence. These responses are not meritorious acts of self-justification, but they represent such a radical departure from humanity's customary sinful ways that many people will refuse God's gracious offer. Such was true of Isaiah's contemporaries, who **would have none of it**.[10]

30:16-17 In this case the people prefer "flying off on horses to resting in God's care."[11] The twice-repeated **therefore** in verse 16 implies that the people will need to **flee on horses** and they will need **swift horses** because their **pursuers will be swift!** In other words, those who put their trust in something other than God will find themselves in need of that object of trust, but they will also find it to be inadequate. On the other hand, those who trust in God will not need other objects of trust. This lesson in reality is, once again, the work of God to discipline and instruct his people. The numbers in verse 17 reflect a reversal of the covenant promise in Leviticus 26:8, further demonstrating that God is directly at work in this process. The picture of the remnant of Judah as a **flagstaff on a mountaintop** recalls the equally lonely picture of the devastated "Daughter of Zion" in 1:8.

An Offer of Grace (30:18-26)

¹⁸**Yet the LORD longs to be gracious to you; / he rises to show you compassion. / For the LORD is a God of justice. / Blessed are all who wait for him!**

¹⁹**O people of Zion, who live in Jerusalem, you will weep no more. How gracious he will be when you cry for help! As soon as he hears, he will answer you.** ²⁰**Although the Lord gives you the bread of adversity and the water of affliction, your teachers will be hidden no more; with your own eyes you will see them.** ²¹**Whether you turn to the right or to the left, your ears will hear a voice behind you, saying, "This is the way; walk in it."** ²²**Then you will defile your idols overlaid with silver and your images covered with gold; you will throw them away like a menstrual cloth and say to them, "Away with you!"**

---

[10]Literally, "you were not willing," as in verse 9.
[11]Oswalt, *Isaiah* 1, p. 554.

²³He will also send you rain for the seed you sow in the ground, and the food that comes from the land will be rich and plentiful. In that day your cattle will graze in broad meadows. ²⁴The oxen and donkeys that work the soil will eat fodder and mash, spread out with fork and shovel. ²⁵In the day of great slaughter, when the towers fall, streams of water will flow on every high mountain and every lofty hill. ²⁶The moon will shine like the sun, and the sunlight will be seven times brighter, like the light of seven full days, when the LORD binds up the bruises of his people and heals the wounds he inflicted.

30:18 On a much more positive note, these verses contain one of Scripture's most beautiful expressions of the graciousness of God. God will not expose the false hopes of his people without standing by ready to offer himself again as their true refuge. The word translated **longs** (חכה, *ḥkh*) in verse 18 is the same word rendered **wait** at the end of the verse. What an amazing picture of God as the one who "waits" for his people to return to him! The only reason for the delay of God's actions is the stubborn insistence of his people on running after other options. The NIV's **yet** (לָכֵן, *lākēn*) at the beginning of verse 18 would be more accurately rendered "therefore." *Because* Judah pursues foolish alternatives, God must wait before he can be gracious to them.

The second line of verse 18,[12] in which God **rises** to extend **compassion** to his people, is parallel to the first. This line clarifies the active nature of God's waiting. If God were to sit on the sidelines and wait idly, Judah's situation would go from bad to worse. As he manifests his patience, he is also at work to *turn* his people back to him. God is thus exalted[13] when he exposes the futility of rival objects of trust (cf. vv. 12-17) because such a work is essential before his people will see their folly and turn to him for compassion.

God's corrective work is also highlighted by the explanation (cf. the opening **For**) that he is a **God of justice**. Isaiah 5:15-16 claims that God is "exalted by his justice" when he humbles the proud. Justice (מִשְׁפָּט, *mišpāṭ*), broadly speaking, has to do with making

---

[12]"Therefore" precedes this line in the Hebrew as well, but is omitted by the NIV.

[13]One of the senses of the verb (רום, *rwm*), translated here as "rises" (cf. Ps 21:14; 46:10; 57:5,11; 108:5).

things right.[14] God will bring about the circumstances in which his people will acknowledge their foolish ways and turn to him. Nothing could be more right or, consequently, more exalting to God. In a context dominated by woes, blessedness[15] comes to **all who wait for** the one who actively and graciously waits for them.

30:19-21 Verses 19-22 anticipate the changes those who wait for God will experience in their relationship with him. Though they may weep when they **cry for help**, God will move swiftly to remove weeping from their experience. One of the major emphases of these verses is the renewed intimacy and immediacy of access they will enjoy with God. The spare diet of **adversity** and **affliction** with which God has fed them will last only as long as it takes to open their eyes to legitimate **teachers** such as Isaiah. These teachers are not presently **hidden** in a literal sense, but the people do not possess eyes to see them. God will also open their ears so that they will **hear a voice** telling them which way to go. Moses had told Israel in Deuteronomy 30:11-14 that one need not "ascend into heaven" or "cross the sea" to gain access to God's guidance. Instead, "the word is very near you; it is in your mouth and in your heart so you may obey it." Isaiah does not promise each person a personal, private revelation from God, but a renewed ability to hear what God has clearly been saying all along. Instead of telling the prophets to "leave this way" (v. 11), they will welcome the words, **this is the way**.

30:22 When Paul describes his changed perspective after his conversion, he says that the things he lost for the sake of Christ appear to him as "rubbish" (Phil 3:8). Isaiah tells his audience that when God renews their sight the idols they now so much value (**overlaid with silver** and **with gold**) and trust will be seen as defiling objects **like a menstrual cloth** (cf. Ezek 7:19-20) to be summarily dismissed.

30:23-24 Woes are associated with the covenant curses, so Isaiah concludes God's offer of grace with the inevitable blessings that will

---

[14]Cf. the close connection between "justice" and "righteousness" in Isaiah 1:27; 5:7,16; 16:5; 28:17; 32:1,16; 59:9,14.

[15]The word translated "blessed" (אַשְׁרֵי, *'ašrê*) is used in passages such as Psalms 1:1; 32:1; 112:1 and is parallel to μακάριος (*makarios*) in the Beatitudes. In distinction to בָּרַךְ (*bārak*), which refers to praise given to God or blessings bestowed by God, the word used here conveys a commendation or congratulation to the individual so characterized. Frequently, as in Isaiah 30:18, the person is commended for making a wise choice in relation to God.

ensue (vv. 23-26). The indications of a healthy covenant relationship between God and Israel (cf. Lev 26:3-13; Deut 28:1-14) include **rain** in its seasons and the **food that comes from the land** as a result (as opposed to the idols that could not bless, but only hinder God's blessing). "Abundant food contrasts with the afflictive bread of the matching verse 20."[16] The food will be so abundant, in fact, that even the animals will enjoy a rich feast.

30:25-26 Although the apparently literal aspects of covenant blessing in verses 23-24 are consonant with God's promises to Israel, verses 25-26 are more figurative in nature and point to the broader scope of God's purpose. The **day of great slaughter, when the towers fall** alludes to earlier passages that speak of God's humbling the arrogant forces arrayed against his people (cf. 2:12-17).[17] These forces, used by God to discipline his people, ultimately become a barrier to be removed before he can bless them. No direct connection exists between the defeat of these enemies and literal **streams of water**, but these waters represent the blessings that flow from God (cf. 32:2; 41:18). Similarly, a literal fulfillment of the promises concerning the **moon** and the **sun** would be destructive rather than beneficial. The fact that they will shine brightly stands in contrast to the scenes of judgment in which they are darkened (cf. 13:10; 24:23).

In Isaiah 1:5-6 the prophet describes the nation as a person beaten and bruised from head to toe, whose wounds were untreated. As Isaiah's message has unfolded, it has become clear that God is the ultimate source of these wounds. They remain untreated because Judah stubbornly refuses to turn to the one who can heal them. The blessings promised in verses 23-26 look forward to the day when that tragic situation changes and God **heals the wounds he inflicted**. God's primary intent is to heal, but sometimes he must wound until the need for and source of healing become clear.

An Offer of Vindication (30:27-33)

[27]See, the Name of the LORD comes from afar, / with burning anger and dense clouds of smoke; / his lips are full of wrath, / and his tongue is a consuming fire. / [28]His breath is like a rushing torrent, rising up to the neck. / He shakes the nations in the sieve of destruction; / he places in the jaws of the peoples / a bit that leads

---

[16]Motyer, *Prophecy*, p. 251.
[17]This reference also anticipates verses 27-33.

them astray. /²⁹And you will sing /as on the night you celebrate a holy festival; /your hearts will rejoice /as when people go up with flutes /to the mountain of the LORD, /to the Rock of Israel. /³⁰The LORD will cause men to hear his majestic voice /and will make them see his arm coming down /with raging anger and consuming fire, /with cloudburst, thunderstorm and hail. /³¹The voice of the LORD will shatter Assyria; /with his scepter he will strike them down. / ³²Every stroke the LORD lays on them /with his punishing rod /will be to the music of tambourines and harps, /as he fights them in battle with the blows of his arm. /³³Topheth has long been prepared; /it has been made ready for the king. /Its fire pit has been made deep and wide, /with an abundance of fire and wood; /the breath of the LORD, /like a stream of burning sulfur, sets it ablaze.

When present circumstances run counter to the will of God, the proper response of God's people is to long for and to cry out for God's intervention. Isaiah will cry out in this fashion in later chapters, but perhaps nowhere more forcefully than in 64:1: "Oh, that you would rend the heavens and come down . . . ." The lament psalms contain many such cries. The goal of these cries is that God will not only deliver and thus vindicate his people before the nations, but that he will vindicate himself. These verses contain a promise that God will accomplish that goal.

30:27 When God reestablished his relationship with Israel through Moses, great emphasis was placed on the revelation of his **Name** (cf. Exod 3:13-15; 6:2-3). His name is not just an arbitrary label, but the revelation of who he is. On the occasion celebrated here, he will reveal that nature again. In light of the strong language he uses to convey God's judgment, Isaiah emphasizes that such actions reveal a fundamental aspect of who he is. As in the time of Egyptian bondage, God cannot redeem his people without defeating their oppressors.

The picture of God coming **from afar** has two possible applications (not mutually exclusive). It can relate to the nature of a lament, in which God seems distant.[18] As such, this language serves as a word of encouragement to Isaiah's original audience in light of their present difficulties and the delay of God's action. The notion of God's distance also ties in to the imagery of God's judgment as an

---

[18]Cf. "Why are you so far . . .?" in Psalm 22:1.

approaching storm. This storm is very personal, however, in its association with God's name and the anthropomorphic references to his **lips**, his **tongue**, and his "breath."

30:28 The reference to flood waters **rising up to the neck** of God's adversaries recalls the same image in 8:8 as the Assyrians invade Judah. In that case, God proves to be "Immanuel" to his people and rescues them. In the present context, the **rushing torrent** parallels the opposite image of "burning anger" and "consuming fire" to convey destruction. As Isaiah typically multiplies mixed metaphors, he also describes God's use of a **sieve**[19] in which he sifts **the nations** and a **bit** that he places **in the jaws of the peoples** to turn them from their hostile intentions. The latter image also appears in God's reassurance to Hezekiah during Sennacherib's assault of Jerusalem (37:29) and is a strong assertion of God's sovereignty.

30:29-32 Some might be disturbed not so much by the description of the scene when God **will shatter Assyria** as by Judah's celebration over the destruction.[20] Is it appropriate for God's people to **sing** and **celebrate** and **rejoice** to the accompaniment of **flutes** and **tambourines** and **harps** as God's blows rain down on these enemies? A similar celebration follows the fall of Babylon in Revelation 19:1ff. In some of the more extreme lament psalms, imprecations (curses) are called down upon enemies and the fulfillment of these curses is sometimes seen as cause for rejoicing (cf. Psalms 58; 137). The point of these psalms, however, is not to promote anger, hatred, or personal vengeance. The concern is for the vindication of God (cf. Psalms 58:11; 59:13; 79:9-10; 94:1-7). The same is true of the celebration in Isaiah 30:29ff. and Revelation 19. The joy is not rooted in sadistic pleasure over the sufferings of others, but over the defeat of evil and the resulting opportunity for God's purpose to move forward.

30:33 Topheth was located in the Valley of Hinnom, south of Jerusalem, and became a place where some Israelites offered their sons and daughters in the fire to Molech (Jer 7:31). Josiah desecrated the site during his reforms (2 Kgs 23:10) to eliminate such actions in the future. Jeremiah prophesied that God would change the name of the "Valley of Hinnom" to the "Valley of Slaughter" through a

---

[19]It is a "sieve of destruction." The word for destruction (שָׁוְא, *šāw'*) generally refers to that which is empty or vain, so the sorting out in this case is designed to "expose the false and the worthless" (Motyer, *Prophecy*, p. 252).

[20]Cf. Webb, *Message*, p. 131.

judgment so great that the bodies could not be buried and would be picked over by vultures (7:31-32; 19:5ff.).[21] God knows the blasphemous pride of Sennacherib (cf. 37:9-13), so this unclean place **has long been prepared** as the Assyrian king's ultimate destination.[22]

---

[21]During the intertestamental period the Valley of Hinnom (גֵּי הִנֹּם, *gê hinnōm*), or Gehenna, came to be viewed as the realm of the evil dead (cf. Matt 5:22).

[22]Cf. the "unexpected" arrival of the king of Babylon in Sheol (14:9-11).

ISAIAH 31

An Offer of Restoration (31:1-9)

¹Woe to those who go down to Egypt for help, / who rely on horses, / who trust in the multitude of their chariots / and in the great strength of their horsemen, / but do not look to the Holy One of Israel, / or seek help from the Lord. / ²Yet he too is wise and can bring disaster; / he does not take back his words. / He will rise up against the house of the wicked, / against those who help evildoers. / ³But the Egyptians are men and not God; / their horses are flesh and not spirit. / When the Lord stretches out his hand, / he who helps will stumble, / he who is helped will fall; / both will perish together.

⁴This is what the Lord says to me:

"As a lion growls, / a great lion over his prey— / and though a whole band of shepherds / is called together against him, / he is not frightened by their shouts / or disturbed by their clamor— / so the Lord Almighty will come down / to do battle on Mount Zion and on its heights. / ⁵Like birds hovering overhead, / the Lord Almighty will shield Jerusalem; / he will shield it and deliver it, / he will 'pass over' it and will rescue it."

⁶Return to him you have so greatly revolted against, O Israelites. ⁷For in that day every one of you will reject the idols of silver and gold your sinful hands have made.

⁸"Assyria will fall by a sword that is not of man; / a sword, not of mortals, will devour them. / They will flee before the sword / and their young men will be put to forced labor. / ⁹Their stronghold will fall because of terror; / at sight of the battle standard their commanders will panic," / declares the Lord, / whose fire is in Zion, / whose furnace is in Jerusalem.

31:1 Although this chapter begins by recalling the **Woe to those who go down to Egypt for help** as in 30:1-2, the focus shifts quickly to a reminder of God's willingness and capacity to save. Even though his people have been looking everywhere but **to the Holy One of Israel**, he is prepared to defend and prove his trustworthiness to them.

31:2 In a classic example of understatement, Isaiah asserts that even though the Egyptians are noted for their wisdom, God **too is wise**. In fact, in 19:11-15 Isaiah has already prophesied of the day when God will expose the vaunted wisdom of the Egyptians as foolishness in comparison to his wisdom. Furthermore, unlike the Egyptians who do not possess the military might to stop the Assyrians, God has the power to **bring disaster** against his people's enemies. The Egyptians are not only foolish and weak but also unreliable covenant partners, unlike God who **does not take back his words**.

31:3 Even though God is **spirit** (רוּחַ, *rûaḥ*), he is actually more substantial than the **men** who make up the Egyptian army and the **flesh** of their **horses**. From the time of the golden calf when the Israelites were encamped at Sinai, this people has fallen prey to the common human temptation to trust in what eyes can see and hands can touch even when God has proven himself to be eminently reliable. Israel should have learned by now, on the other hand, that when man turns to man for deliverance instead of to God, the only result can be that both **he who** [allegedly] **helps** and **he who** [allegedly] **is helped** will **stumble** and **fall** to their destruction **together**.[1]

31:4-5 In verse 4 God begins his positive offer of restoration to Judah. God portrays his power to save by introducing himself as a **lion** that cannot be deterred from finishing off his **prey** (the Assyrians) as he fights on behalf of **Mount Zion** even if **a whole band of shepherds is called together against him**. The imagery for God then changes from that of a warrior lion to that of the protective wings of **birds**, recalling the way God "carried [Israel] on eagles' wings" in the exodus (Exod 19:4; cf. Deut 32:11; Isa 40:31). The exodus allusion continues in verse 5 in God's promise to **"pass over"** (פסח, *psḥ*) Jerusalem as he rescues it. The anticipated destruction within Sennacherib's army encamped around Jerusalem (cf. vv. 8-9) while the inhabitants of the city remain safe recalls the distinction God made between Israel and Egypt in the plagues.

31:6-7 For those who have **so greatly revolted against**[2] God, the only proper response to his gracious offer of restoration is to **return**

---

[1] Cf. Matthew 15:14 in which the blind lead the blind and both fall into the ditch.

[2] Literally, the Israelites have "made deep" (הֶעְמִיקוּ, *heʿmîqû*; the same word used in 30:33 for making the fire pit "deep") their turning away from God.

to their former relationship with him. They have turned away from God to their harm; he has provided the means and the motivation for them to turn back to him. As in 30:22, the renewal of their relationship with God will enable them to see their **idols of silver and gold** for what they are and **reject** them. The relationship of events here illustrates again the complex problem of human sinfulness and the need for God to initiate any positive change. Idolatry, in whatever form, blinds individuals to the truth about God so that they cannot recognize the truth about either their idols or God unless he helps them to see.

31:8-9a Isaiah 37:36ff. records the divine intervention that ends the Assyrian assault against Jerusalem **by a sword that is not of man**. Isaiah 31:8-9 also looks beyond that event, however, to the swift and complete collapse of the Assyrian empire that follows. As is normally the case, God accomplishes his victory in such a way that his people cannot claim credit. A false sense of self-reliance leads to forgetting God and is as dangerous as any other form of idolatry (cf. Deuteronomy 8).

31:9b Isaiah states the promise of God's victory as a prophetic oracle (**declares the LORD** = נְאֻם־יְהוָה, *nəʾum-YHWH*) to give it additional weight and to assure its reliability. He further affirms God's commitment to **Zion** by reminding the people of God's fiery protective presence there. The similar image of Jerusalem as an "altar hearth" in 29:1ff. is intended to teach the inhabitants of that city that the presence of a holy God is dangerous for those who disregard his holiness (cf. the fear in 33:14). Ezekiel will even warn later citizens of Jerusalem that the presence of God can be withdrawn if their uncleanness becomes too severe (Ezekiel 8–10). In this passage, however, the nature of God as a consuming fire stands as a warning to any who would threaten God's covenant promises regarding Zion.

ISAIAH 32

II. THE WISDOM OF TRUSTING IN GOD (32:1–35:10)

A. GOD WILL RESTORE RIGHTEOUS RULE (32:1-20)

The "woe" (הוֹי, *hôy*) with which each of the previous four chapters begins undergoes an abrupt reversal in 32:1 (**See**, הֵן, *hēn*). Although one woe remains (33:1), it addresses Judah's traitorous oppressor Assyria. Judah's sinful condition continues to be in view in chapters 32–35, but the emphasis shifts from the woes that have resulted from Judah's covenant unfaithfulness to the blessings that will flow from God's covenant faithfulness toward his people, and through them to all peoples.

1. The Transformed Society under Righteous Rule (32:1-8)

¹See, a king will reign in righteousness / and rulers will rule with justice. / ²Each man will be like a shelter from the wind / and a refuge from the storm, / like streams of water in the desert / and the shadow of a great rock in a thirsty land.
³Then the eyes of those who see will no longer be closed, / and the ears of those who hear will listen. / ⁴The mind of the rash will know and understand, / and the stammering tongue will be fluent and clear. / ⁵No longer will the fool be called noble / nor the scoundrel be highly respected. / ⁶For the fool speaks folly, / his mind is busy with evil: / He practices ungodliness / and spreads error concerning the LORD; / the hungry he leaves empty / and from the thirsty he withholds water. / ⁷The scoundrel's methods are wicked, / he makes up evil schemes / to destroy the poor with lies, / even when the plea of the needy is just. / ⁸But the noble man makes noble plans, / and by noble deeds he stands.

From the outset of his message, Isaiah has attacked the corrupt leadership in Judah that constitutes at least part of the cause as well as the result of his people's sinful condition (cf. chapters 3-5). In Isaiah 5:16 the prophet contrasts the humbling of arrogant men with the exaltation of God, the one who manifests justice and righteousness. God further reveals to Isaiah that a descendant of David will mediate God's rule over his people by the just and righteous nature of his government (cf. 9:7; 11:4).[1]

32:1-2 As Isaiah 32 opens, God returns to the notion of a **king** as pivotal to the happier and more productive future he foresees for the covenant people. This connection links the future envisioned in this text with the messianic expectation earlier in Isaiah.[2] Up to this point, the Davidic line has failed to sustain righteous and just rule. Even virtuous rulers like Hezekiah and Josiah could not usher in lasting change. As in the days of the judges, the people became even worse after these deliverers passed from the scene (cf. Judg 2:18-19). The figurative blessings described in verse 2 derive from God himself (cf. 25:4; 30:25). In contrast to God's role as **shelter** and **refuge**, Micah 7:4 compares Judah's typical leaders to briars and thorns, images normally reserved for Israel's adversaries (Num 33:55; Josh 23:13; Judg 2:3) or for the land when under God's curse (Isa 5:6; 7:23-25).

32:3-8 If the Davidic line cannot maintain God's standards within itself, how can it bring about the reversal of the people's spiritual condition envisioned in verses 3-8? Israel's dulled senses will be restored (vv. 3-4) and their upside-down values will be righted (vv. 5-8). Once again, these are works beyond the scope of any ordinary human ruler. When the **fool . . . spreads error concerning the LORD** (cf. 3:12; 9:16) yet is called **noble**, when the **scoundrel** plots to **destroy the poor with lies** yet is **highly respected**, radical measures are necessary to restore a society to the proper perspective. When

---

[1]Ezekiel 34 draws the same contrast in greater detail. In that passage God condemns Israel's leaders as shepherds who feed off the flock rather than protect it. The result of this self-serving rule is a "survival of the fittest" mentality within the flock. God promises to shepherd the people himself (vv. 11-16), but he also vows to place David over them as shepherd (vv. 23-24).

[2]The "rulers" in the second line of verse 1 are simply part of the picture of an organized government such as the people of that day would have known. God typically uses familiar concepts to prefigure the greater future he has for his people.

one of God's primary barometer's of his people's spiritual condition is their treatment of the weak, the neglect of the **hungry** and the **thirsty** and the corruption of justice for the **needy** cries out for God's intervention. Just as Psalm 1 contains God's promise to establish the righteous and leave no place for the wicked to "stand," here God promises a future in which a person **stands** by **noble plans** and **noble deeds**. Who but the Messiah is adequate to bring about this transformation?

2. The Prerequisite for the Restoration of Righteous Rule (32:9-20)

⁹You women who are so complacent, /rise up and listen to me; /you daughters who feel secure, /hear what I have to say! / ¹⁰In little more than a year /you who feel secure will tremble; /the grape harvest will fail, /and the harvest of fruit will not come. / ¹¹Tremble, you complacent women; /shudder, you daughters who feel secure! /Strip off your clothes, /put sackcloth around your waists. / ¹²Beat your breasts for the pleasant fields, /for the fruitful vines /¹³and for the land of my people, /a land overgrown with thorns and briers— /yes, mourn for all houses of merriment /and for this city of revelry. / ¹⁴The fortress will be abandoned, /the noisy city deserted; /citadel and watchtower will become a wasteland forever, /the delight of donkeys, a pasture for flocks, /¹⁵till the Spirit is poured upon us from on high, /and the desert becomes a fertile field, /and the fertile field seems like a forest. / ¹⁶Justice will dwell in the desert /and righteousness live in the fertile field. / ¹⁷The fruit of righteousness will be peace; /the effect of righteousness will be quietness and confidence forever. / ¹⁸My people will live in peaceful dwelling places, /in secure homes, /in undisturbed places of rest. / ¹⁹Though hail flattens the forest /and the city is leveled completely, /²⁰how blessed you will be, /sowing your seed by every stream, /and letting your cattle and donkeys range free.

In 3:16–4:1, Isaiah speaks of the reversal of circumstances of the pampered women of Zion whose luxury has come at the neglect of, if not at the expense of, the oppressed poor in Judah. Perhaps Isaiah singles them out to indicate their complicity in their husbands' corruption, or perhaps the disregard for the poor even by the women highlights how hardened the people as a whole have become. In

32:9-20, these women appear again as they are called to make the necessary response to God's actions if the transformation described in the preceding verses is to occur.

32:9-13 The biggest problem of the women in this passage is not their wealth per se (even though the way in which it has been acquired is highly suspect), but the fact that they feel **complacent** and **secure** as a result of their standing. That their security is misplaced will be obvious in a **little more than a year** when God withholds the produce from the **harvest**. In light of the bleak days ahead, the proper responses are humility and penitence (**Tremble . . . shudder . . . Strip off your clothes . . . put sackcloth around your waists . . . Beat your breasts . . . mourn**).

The mere announcement of disaster will not, however, bring about the humility and penitence God seeks from his complacent people. What will be required is the disaster itself. In describing Jerusalem as a **city of revelry**, Isaiah uses a root (עלז, *'lz*) he applies to Tyre (23:7,12), but also to Israel (5:14; 22:2), in each case in a context of judgment (cf. also 24:8). The revelry refers to a triumphant celebration. In Judah's case the celebration is unwarranted, and it must be overturned before God can move forward with his people. God must forge at least a remnant that will be receptive to him.

32:14-15 When Isaiah receives the painful news in chapter 6 about the hardened hearts with which his message will be met, he asks the question, "For how long, O Lord?" (v. 11). God responds that the condition will persist until the land is devastated and deserted, although a stump, consisting of the "holy seed" will remain. The holy seed is the remnant that will emerge from the devastation. In 32:15, God elaborates on what must happen to bring God's judgment to an end. The devastation will continue **till the Spirit is poured** out on the people by God. The painful process of defeat and exile will expose Israel's false security and make the remnant open to God, which in turn will prepare the way for the outpouring of his Spirit.[3] The role of God's Spirit strengthens the messianic context of this chapter (cf. 11:2).

32:16-18 God first describes the transforming work of the Spirit

---

[3]A similar connection exists in Joel, where the locust invasion results in a call for the people to rend their hearts and return to God (2:12ff.), leading to the promise of the outpouring of the Spirit in 2:28ff.

in terms of the restoration of the devastated land (cf. 29:17; 35:1-2). As verses 16-18 make clear, however, God is not as interested in agriculture as he is in the return of **justice** and **righteousness** and their "fruits" to the land. These traits appear at the beginning of the chapter in the description of the future king's rule; here we see that they ultimately derive from the work of God's Spirit. The resulting **peace** and security are far more stable than the false confidence of the women. The word for **undisturbed** (שַׁאֲנַנּוֹת, ša'ănannôth) in verse 18 is the same as the word for the "complacent" women in verse 9. The word for **secure** (מִבְטָחִים, mibṭaḥîm) in verse 18 is from the root of the same word in verses 9 and 10. "The prophet would disrupt their empty complacency in order to replace it with true security."[4]

32:19-20 Verses 19 and 20 summarize the message of this chapter. The destruction that lies in Judah's immediate future, here compared to a devastating **hail** storm, will not end the hopes for a **blessed** future but will actually help to make it possible.[5] As in 28:17, the hail is God's way of sweeping away the deceptive alternative refuges so that his people find **quietness and confidence forever** in him.[6]

---

[4]Motyer, *Prophecy,* p. 261.
[5]The word "though" with which the NIV begins verse 19 is an interpretation of the simple Hebrew conjunction and might imply that verses 19 and 20 describe contrasting circumstances taking place with two groups at the same time. This view does not seem to fit the context.
[6]The words for "quietness and confidence" (הַשְׁקֵט וָבֶטַח, hašqēṭ wabeṭaḥ) in verse 17 are the same as those used for the "quietness and trust" of 30:15 that the people rejected in favor of fast horses.

ISAIAH 33

B. GOD WILL RISE UP TO VINDICATE THE RIGHTEOUS (33:1-24)

God uses hostile powers like Assyria to discipline his people and awaken them to their need for him. For his ultimate goal to be realized, however, he must both overthrow the hostile powers that are interested in their own conquest rather than accomplishing God's purposes, and also restore his newly penitent people. The two major sections of this chapter deal, respectively, with those two matters.

1. The Exaltation of God against the Wicked Schemers (33:1-12)

¹Woe to you, O destroyer, / you who have not been destroyed! / Woe to you, O traitor, / you who have not been betrayed! / When you stop destroying, / you will be destroyed; / when you stop betraying, / you will be betrayed.
²O LORD, be gracious to us; / we long for you. / Be our strength every morning, / our salvation in time of distress. / ³At the thunder of your voice, the peoples flee; / when you rise up, the nations scatter. / ⁴Your plunder, O nations, is harvested as by young locusts; / like a swarm of locusts men pounce on it. / ⁵The LORD is exalted, for he dwells on high; / he will fill Zion with justice and righteousness. / ⁶He will be the sure foundation for your times, / a rich store of salvation and wisdom and knowledge; / the fear of the LORD is the key to this treasure.ᵃ
⁷Look, their brave men cry aloud in the streets; / the envoys of peace weep bitterly. / ⁸The highways are deserted, / no travelers are on the roads. / The treaty is broken, / its witnessesᵇ are despised, / no one is respected. / ⁹The land mournsᶜ and wastes away, / Lebanon is ashamed and withers; / Sharon is like the Arabah, / and Bashan and Carmel drop their leaves.

¹⁰"Now will I arise," says the LORD. / "Now will I be exalted; / now will I be lifted up. / ¹¹You conceive chaff, / you give birth to straw; / your breath is a fire that consumes you. / ¹²The peoples will be burned as if to lime; / like cut thornbushes they will be set ablaze."

ᵃ6 Or *is a treasure from him*   ᵇ8 Dead Sea Scrolls; Masoretic Text / *the cities*   ᶜ9 Or *dries up*

33:1 These verses begin with the final "woe" of the series (v. 1),[1] followed by a confident prayer to God (vv. 2-6) and an anticipation of the overthrow of Judah's enemies (vv. 7-12). The **woe** presents a scene of poetic justice to one portrayed as a **destroyer** and a **traitor**. These terms presumably refer to the Assyrians. Ahaz had entered into a covenant with them (2 Kgs 16:7ff.), but the Assyrians did not stop their advance after conquering Aram and Israel. The primary point of reference here, however, is Sennacherib's invasion of Judah even after Hezekiah had paid him tribute (2 Kgs 18:13ff.). Sennacherib's defeat at Jerusalem and death at the hands of his sons (Isa 37:36-38) satisfy the terms of the woe.

33:2-4 Isaiah's prayer appeals both to God's **gracious** nature toward his people and to his **strength** by which he sustains and protects them. The expressions **at the thunder of your voice** and **when you rise up** point to the tension of a believer who accepts God's power but at the time in question does not see it in evidence. When God does choose to act, however, the **plunder** that the **nations** have gathered will disappear like vegetation before an invasion of **locusts**.

33:5 Isaiah's confidence in God's intervention ultimately derives from his understanding of God's nature. Since God **is exalted**, he will not allow the arrogant powers that oppose him or disregard him to prevail.[2] The traits of **justice and righteousness** that are so precious to God cannot **fill**[3] **Zion** until Zion's enemies fall.

33:6 God's character and ability ensure that he will prevail. But who will share in the spoils[4] of his victory? It will be those who value not only the **salvation** God has to offer, but also his **wisdom and**

---

[1] The second "woe" in verse 1 is added by the NIV.

[2] The same word for "exalted" (נִשְׂגָּב, *niśgab*) is used in 2:11,17 to refer to the day when the proud are humbled and God alone is "lifted high."

[3] The verb used here is another example of the prophetic perfect, referring to a future event as if it were an accomplished act.

[4] Both "rich store" (חֹסֶן, *ḥōsen*) and "treasure" (אוֹצָר, *'ôṣār*) refer to an abundance of wealth.

knowledge. The latter have not been in abundant supply at a time when human wisdom has been valued above God's wisdom. Much of God's work in Isaiah's time and in the ensuing generations seeks to overthrow human wisdom (cf. 29:14,24). By stripping away all bases of human pride, God either uncovers or creates a faithful remnant of individuals like Isaiah, those whose clearer vision of God leads them to faith and humility.

The NIV's translation of the last line of verse 6 (**the fear of the LORD is the key to this treasure**) is rather interpretive. Oswalt's rendering, "The fear of the Lord, it is his treasure,"[5] is more literal. The possessive pronoun in "his treasure" apparently refers to God. Rather than serving as a "key" to a treasure *from* God, this trait constitutes the treasure itself because it is the foundation of a meaningful relationship *with* God.[6] God's goal from the time of the first sin has been to restore such a relationship with creatures who typically fail to see the need for it or the value of it. After God responds to the prayer to defeat the traitorous destroyers (who embody the world's harmful alternatives to him), in the latter part of the chapter he invites his people to return to this relationship.

33:7-9 It must have been extremely difficult to envision a secure existence in light of the present distress. Verses 7-9 describe the aftermath of Assyria's treachery in violating its **treaty** (בְּרִית, *bᵊrîth*) with Judah. Judah's officials can only **weep bitterly**. The mourning will have no more effect than treaty negotiations because, from the Assyrian perspective, **no one is respected**. Those intent on conquest and power have no regard for the feelings and needs of the individuals who stand in their way.[7] Not only do the people mourn, but the land also suffers from the Assyrian invasion. Isaiah thus personifies the land's reaction to these circumstances as the most beautiful and fertile areas experience devastation.

33:10 God's assurance that he will **arise** against the enemies of his people vindicates Isaiah's confidence that the God who is **exalted** by the very nature of his "dwelling place" (v. 5) will not allow his

---

[5]Oswalt, *Isaiah* 1, p. 590. Cf. the NIV footnote.

[6]The Messiah in 11:3 is said to "delight in the fear of the LORD." See the commentary on that verse for the positive use of "the fear of the LORD" in the Old Testament.

[7]The word אֱנוֹשׁ, (*ᵊnôš*) in the last line of verse 8 frequently refers to humanity in the context of weakness and mortality (cf. 51:12; Ps 8:4 [5 in Hebrew]; 9:20 [21 in Hebrew]; 90:3; 103:15.

name to be disrespected. When it appears that all hope is lost, God intervenes to restore order. God takes a covenant relationship very seriously, and even though Judah should not have been in league with Assyria, God will neither violate his covenant with his people nor overlook Assyria's covenant unfaithfulness.

33:11-12 Isaiah combines vivid and familiar images in verse 11 to describe the end of those who operate as the Assyrians do. Their time of aggression is like a pregnancy, but when they **give birth**, the result will not turn out like they had anticipated (cf. 26:18; 59:4). The volatile combination of **straw** and **fire** points to the self-destructive nature of their actions (cf. 1:31). From God's perspective there was no future for them from the beginning. To say that they **conceive chaff** indicates that their plans have been founded upon the useless and insubstantial (cf. Ps 1:4). In one sense, then, Assyria's plans will fall short through inherent weakness. The timing and completeness (**burned as if to lime**) of their fall, however, result from the work of God. They will burn like dry, brittle **thornbushes**, but **they will be set ablaze** by God.

2. The Exaltation of God on Behalf of the Faithful in Zion (33:13-24)

¹³**You who are far away, hear what I have done;** / **you who are near, acknowledge my power!** / ¹⁴**The sinners in Zion are terrified;** / **trembling grips the godless:** / **"Who of us can dwell with the consuming fire?** / **Who of us can dwell with everlasting burning?"** / ¹⁵**He who walks righteously** / **and speaks what is right,** / **who rejects gain from extortion** / **and keeps his hand from accepting bribes,** / **who stops his ears against plots of murder** / **and shuts his eyes against contemplating evil—** / ¹⁶**this is the man who will dwell on the heights,** / **whose refuge will be the mountain fortress.** / **His bread will be supplied,** / **and water will not fail him.**

¹⁷**Your eyes will see the king in his beauty** / **and view a land that stretches afar.** / ¹⁸**In your thoughts you will ponder the former terror:** / **"Where is that chief officer?** / **Where is the one who took the revenue?** / **Where is the officer in charge of the towers?"** / ¹⁹**You will see those arrogant people no more,** / **those people of an obscure speech,** / **with their strange, incomprehensible tongue.**

²⁰**Look upon Zion, the city of our festivals;** / **your eyes will see**

Jerusalem, /a peaceful abode, a tent that will not be moved; /its stakes will never be pulled up, /nor any of its ropes broken. / ²¹There the LORD will be our Mighty One. /It will be like a place of broad rivers and streams. /No galley with oars will ride them, /no mighty ship will sail them. /²²For the LORD is our judge, /the LORD is our lawgiver, /the LORD is our king; /it is he who will save us.

²³Your rigging hangs loose: /The mast is not held secure, /the sail is not spread. /Then an abundance of spoils will be divided /and even the lame will carry off plunder. /²⁴No one living in Zion will say, "I am ill"; /and the sins of those who dwell there will be forgiven.

33:13-14a Isaiah returns to the fearful condition of those in Judah, but now their fear derives from the manifestation of God's holiness rather than from Assyrian betrayal. When God appears to have abandoned his people, they fear their enemies; when God rises up and powerfully reveals his glorious presence, they fear him (in the unhealthy sense). When God makes his **power** known to those both **far** and **near**, he does so to reaffirm his commitment to Zion. Yet it is the **sinners in Zion** who are **terrified**, the **godless**[8] who tremble with fear. The scene is reminiscent of Israel's reaction to God's dramatic self-revelation at Sinai (cf. Exod 19:16).

3314b-16 The questions raised in verse 14b, as well as God's response in verses 15-16, call to mind Psalms 15 and 24. Entering the presence of a holy God should never be taken lightly. The entire book of Leviticus stresses both the challenges and the opportunities of a sinful people living with a holy God in their midst. Isaiah's own intimate encounter with the "holy, holy, holy" God affirms the same realities. Yet whereas Leviticus and Isaiah 6 highlight the *possibility* of dwelling in God's presence, the questions posed by the frightened sinners in Zion assume the *impossibility* of doing so. Surely a God perceived as a **consuming fire** or as **everlasting burning** would obliterate any mere mortal who drew too close.

This passage, along with Psalms 15 and 24, assumes that the gracious provisions of God for purification are essential for enjoying fellowship with him. In addition, God requires that those among whom he dwells separate themselves from idolatry and walk in his

---

[8]Isaiah applies the same root (חנף, *ḥnp*), which refers to those who are profane, or irreligious, to the "godless nation" (Israel) against whom God sends Assyria in 10:6.

ways with sincerity and purity of heart. He does not require an impossible standard of perfection, or the sacrifices and other means of ritual cleansing would be irrelevant. In 2 Corinthians 3 Paul calls his readers to follow the example of Moses, who enjoyed intimacy with God, rather than the example of the Israelites, who withdrew in fear. Isaiah pursues a similar goal here. Unrepentant sinners should tremble in fear before God. If, however, the citizens of Zion will turn their hearts to God and seek his ways, God will provide them **refuge** and satisfy their needs.

33:17a In the closing verses of this chapter, Isaiah shifts his vision from a fearful Zion to a restored Zion. As in the opening of chapter 32, the ideal ruler stands at the center of the picture. The earlier glimpse emphasized his righteous rule; here Isaiah envisions **the king in his beauty**. A king's royal attire calls attention to the significance of his position and encourages the celebration of his rule. Fancy clothing, however, does not offset a king's lack of character or effectiveness as a leader. As in the comments on 32:1ff., the description of the righteous king's rule cries out for a messianic fulfillment.[9] By the end of this chapter, the bar will be raised even higher.

33:17b-19 The exiles who will return first from Babylon will occupy a small territory around Jerusalem. They will remain under Persian rule and will experience external opposition and internal struggle and discouragement. In the time Isaiah envisions, however, the people will **view a land that stretches afar**.[10] The **former terror**[11] occasioned by the oversight and taxation of foreign overlords will be a faint memory. In 28:9ff., the rejection of Isaiah's message as empty babbling leads to the conquest of the land by those who speak an unfamiliar language (28:11). The future removal of **arrogant people** with their **obscure speech** and **strange, incomprehensible tongue** assumes a time when God's people have come to hear his words again.

33:20 In the Old Testament, foreign rule threatened the freedom to worship God. When Moses first went to Pharaoh, God tested the Egyptian ruler's willingness to allow Israel to go into the

---

[9]Motyer (*Prophecy,* p 267) observes that the same word used in 33:17 for the king's beauty (יֳפִי, *yōphî*) also describes the ideal king in Psalm 45:2 (v. 3 in Hebrew).

[10]Cf. God's promise to Abraham in Genesis 13:14-17.

[11]The word "former" is not present in the Hebrew, but the NIV addition conveys the intent of the passage.

wilderness to worship him (Exod 4:21-23).[12] The peaceful conditions in **Zion** will allow it to be **the city of our festivals**, that is, the place where God's people can freely assemble to worship him. The description of Zion as a **tent** recalls Israel's nomadic existence in the wilderness, but here the image stresses permanence because this is a tent whose **stakes will never be pulled up**.

33:21 This verse begins the close association between God and a bright future. Isaiah describes him as Israel's **Mighty One** (cf. 10:34). The word for "mighty" (אַדִּיר, *'addîr*) implies majesty more than brute force. The same word is used for the **mighty ship** at the end of the verse. The image of **broad rivers and streams** would be particularly meaningful to a people with limited sources of water (cf. 41:18). The rivers that flow through Nineveh and Babylon also make them vulnerable to attack by their enemies,[13] but God will not allow such an attack in Zion.[14]

33:22 God's role in the future security of his people emerges more explicitly in verse 22. The future will be brighter because (**For**) God will resume his rightful place as the **judge**, **lawgiver**, and **king** of his people. In the absolute sense, God has always held these positions. His people, however, have frequently refused to acknowledge his authority. When the Israelites demanded a king from Samuel, God told the aging leader that they were rejecting God as their king (1 Sam 8:7). God granted their request for a king, but the people quickly learned that human kings possess many flaws. The failures of these rulers fueled the anticipation for the Messiah, the anointed king who would succeed where his predecessors had failed. At numerous points Isaiah has presented this ideal ruler as one whose titles and accomplishments require divine empowerment. In 33:22 he presents God, not as the one who *empowers* the king, but as the

---

[12]For the implications of exile for worship, cf. Deut 4:27-28; 28:36,64; Jer 16:13; Ps 137:4.

[13]Webb, *Message*, p 141.

[14]The image of "broad rivers and streams" through or near Zion points to the figurative nature of Isaiah's depiction of the future. Ezekiel 47 presents a similar picture in the life-giving river that flows from the temple. Ezekiel's vision is rooted in the river in Eden (Gen 2:10), and finds its fulfillment in the "river of the water of life" in the new Jerusalem (Rev 22:1). Isaiah's rivers that nourish yet do not allow access to enemies are also comparable to John's vision of gates in the heavenly city that never close yet do not allow anything evil or unclean to enter (Rev 21:25-27).

one who *resumes the role of* king in the eyes of his people. Those who insisted that Samuel appoint a human king over them wanted someone to fight their battles as the kings of the other nations did (1 Sam 8:19-20). Isaiah promises that God will **save**[15] them, a promise that sets the covenant people apart from all the other nations.

33:23-24 In verse 23 Isaiah returns to the imagery of a ship. God's people must neither fear attacks from enemy ships, nor take pride in their own prowess. God will be recognized as the one who saves only when those who are saved realize their inadequacy. A ship with loose **rigging**, a wobbly **mast**, and a limp **sail** is helpless in the water. In spite of this situation, God's victory will be so dramatic and complete that **even the lame will carry off plunder**. Finally, the removal of sickness and the forgiveness of sins are also works that depend upon the power of God. Only the King of kings can win these battles and share his victory with the inhabitants of **Zion**, his covenant people.

---

[15]The word "he" in "it is he who will save us" is emphatic in the Hebrew.

ISAIAH 34

Isaiah 34-35 functions similarly to chapters 24-27. Both passages culminate sections that focus on specific historical circumstances for Israel, in particular the Assyrian threat and the temptation to turn to Egypt for aid. Both apply the implications of these circumstances to a larger context as they universalize God's purpose in both his acts of judgment and his work of redemption. These two aspects of God's activity are clearly delineated between chapter 34 and chapter 35.

C. GOD WILL JUDGE THE NATIONS (34:1-17)

1. God Will Defeat the Nations' Armies (34:1-4)

¹Come near, you nations, and listen; / pay attention, you peoples! / Let the earth hear, and all that is in it, / the world, and all that comes out of it! / ²The LORD is angry with all nations; / his wrath is upon all their armies. / He will totally destroy[a] them, / he will give them over to slaughter. / ³Their slain will be thrown out, / their dead bodies will send up a stench; / the mountains will be soaked with their blood. / ⁴All the stars of the heavens will be dissolved / and the sky rolled up like a scroll; / all the starry host will fall / like withered leaves from the vine, / like shriveled figs from the fig tree.

[a]2 The Hebrew term refers to the irrevocable giving over of things or persons to the LORD, often by totally destroying them; also in verse 5.

34:1 The opening verses of this chapter reveal in unmistakable terms that a day will come when God will hold all nations accountable for their sins and will inflict a frightening penalty for their rebellion. God calls them to **attention** in light of their future. At some point God's devastation of the sinful nations will be irrevocable; until that time there is still hope. This universal judgment will not fall upon the redeemed, of course, a group which will include many from the nations who turn to God.[1] The purpose of this passage is not primarily to exhort the nations to repent but to reassure the covenant people that God will deal with those who would jeopardize the security the previous chapter describes.

34:2-3 Does this passage indicate a specific reason God is **angry with all nations**? Why will he **totally destroy** (הֶחֱרִים, *heḥĕrîm*) these peoples? God uses the same language in commanding the destruction of the Canaanites (cf. Deut 7:1-2). In that context the sins of those nations had reached their full measure (Gen 15:16), and their survival jeopardized the faithfulness of Israel to God (Deut 7:3-4). Verse 2a provides a hint, one that later verses will corroborate, that a slightly different issue evokes God's judgment here. God's **wrath is upon all** [the] **armies** of the nations. The shameful exposure of **their dead bodies** compares to the treatment of the hostile forces of Gog (Ezekiel 39) and those conquered by the rider on the white horse (Rev 19:17-21). While the nations doubtless deserve God's judgment in general, and the ungodly always pose a threat to the faithful, God's greatest anger is reserved for those who actively oppose his purpose and his people.[2]

34:4 The effects of God's judgment extend even to the removal of the **stars of the heavens**. A similar idea appears in the prophecy of Babylon's defeat (13:10),[3] as well as the description of the world's

---

[1] Isaiah's seemingly all-inclusive language is similar to John's designation of the "inhabitants of the earth" in Revelation (3:10; 6:10; 8:13; 11:10; 13:8,14; 17:8). The context (especially 13:8; 17:8) indicates that this group, who will experience God's judgment, consists of all the "worldly," those who refuse to acknowledge God.

[2] This interpretation does not deny the notion of universal judgment. In this context, however, the key concern is to reassure the covenant people that God will not allow their enemies to deny them the peace and stability he intends for them (33:18-22). These enemies ultimately oppose God himself, ensuring their destruction. For this reason the language of this chapter is extreme.

[3] The fall of the king of Babylon in 14:12 is compared to the "morning star" crashing to earth. The description of Babylon's judgment illustrates how language that apparently refers to final judgment can actually apply to a specific situation. Such language is apocalyptic in nature, however, allowing the possibility of a broader application at a later time.

judgment in 24:23. Jesus combines Isaiah 13:10 and 34:4 as part of his discourse on the destruction of Jerusalem and "the end of the age" (Matt 24:29). When the time comes for God to judge the wicked, whether in an individual case or in the final judgment, his actions may be compared to the dissolution of the physical creation. After all, creation shares in the burden of sin (Rom 8:20-22).

2. God Will Slaughter Edom as a Sacrifice (34:5-17)

⁵My sword has drunk its fill in the heavens; /see, it descends in judgment on Edom, / the people I have totally destroyed. / ⁶The sword of the LORD is bathed in blood, /it is covered with fat—/the blood of lambs and goats, /fat from the kidneys of rams. / For the LORD has a sacrifice in Bozrah /and a great slaughter in Edom. / ⁷And the wild oxen will fall with them, / the bull calves and the great bulls. / Their land will be drenched with blood, /and the dust will be soaked with fat.
⁸For the LORD has a day of vengeance, /a year of retribution, to uphold Zion's cause. / ⁹Edom's streams will be turned into pitch, /her dust into burning sulfur; /her land will become blazing pitch! / ¹⁰It will not be quenched night and day; /its smoke will rise forever. / From generation to generation it will lie desolate; /no one will ever pass through it again. / ¹¹The desert owl[a] and screech owl[a] will possess it; /the great owl[a] and the raven will nest there. / God will stretch out over Edom / the measuring line of chaos /and the plumb line of desolation.
¹²Her nobles will have nothing there to be called a kingdom, / all her princes will vanish away. / ¹³Thorns will overrun her citadels, /nettles and brambles her strongholds. / She will become a haunt for jackals, /a home for owls. / ¹⁴Desert creatures will meet with hyenas, /and wild goats will bleat to each other; / there the night creatures will also repose /and find for themselves places of rest. / ¹⁵The owl will nest there and lay eggs, /she will hatch them, and care for her young under the shadow of her wings; /there also the falcons will gather, /each with its mate.
¹⁶Look in the scroll of the LORD and read:
None of these will be missing, /not one will lack her mate. / For it is his mouth that has given the order, /and his Spirit will gather them together. / ¹⁷He allots their portions; / his hand distributes

them by measure. / They will possess it forever / and dwell there from generation to generation.

^a*11 The precise identification of these birds is uncertain.*

34:5 At first glance verse 5 appears to signal a dramatic shift from the universal to the particular as God singles out the **judgment on Edom**. In reality, the message has not changed from the first five verses. Edom stands as a prototypical example of a nation that is hostile to Israel.[4] Since the Edomites are the descendants of Esau, in a sense this conflict extends back to the time when Jacob and Esau struggled in Rebekah's womb (Gen 25:21-23). It climaxes in Edom's rejoicing over Judah's defeat and exile at the hands of the Babylonians (Ps 137:7; Obad 10-14). Edom's adversarial role in Israel's history strengthens the argument that the Edoms of the earth are the primary focus of God's judgment in this passage.

34:6-7 God's destruction of the Edomites[5] by his **sword** takes on a distinctive nuance in verses 6-7 as Isaiah portrays them as sacrificial animals. The **blood** and **fat** of sacrifices were to be strictly reserved for God.[6] This principle leads some interpreters to see in the sacrificial imagery that "in judgment the Lord seeks what is peculiarly his, that to which he alone has a right."[7] While that understanding may be valid, one should also remember that sacrificial creatures by definition suffer death. Sinners either receive the gracious atonement provided by God or they experience God's judgment themselves. For those who rebel like the Edomites in opposing God's redemptive purpose, there no longer remains a sacrifice for their sins (cf. 1 Sam 3:14). Instead, they will *become* a sacrifice (see below). They reflect the negative side of God's promise to Abraham and his descendants in Genesis 12:3 — "I will bless those who bless you, and whoever curses you I will curse."

34:8 This verse also points to God's judgment upon those who directly oppose his people. God's **vengeance** (נָקָם, *nāqām*) is paralleled with his **retribution** (שִׁלּוּמִים, *šillûmîm*). The same two root

---

[4]For a helpful summary of the troubled relationship between Israel and Edom, cf. Motyer, *Prophecy*, pp. 268-269.

[5]"Bozrah" (v. 6) was the capital of Edom.

[6]Cf. Leviticus 3:17; 7:22-27; 17:10-12. Contrast the dangerous abuse of power by Eli's wicked sons Hophni and Phinehas when they seized their preferred portions of the sacrifices without honoring God in this way (1 Sam 2:16-17).

[7]Motyer, *Prophecy*, p. 271.

words appear in Deuteronomy 32:35, where God promises, "It is mine to avenge; I will repay" (cf. Rom 12:19; Heb 10:30). In light of the discussion about the solidarity between God and his people and about Edom as a sacrifice, the parallelism a few verses later (Deut 32:43) is interesting. God's claim that "he will avenge the blood of his servants" is equated with "he will take vengeance on his enemies" (i.e., those who shed the blood of his servants are his enemies). The last line of the verse then adds, "and make atonement for his land and people." From the beginning God has committed himself to avenge his people's enemies himself. Only he can determine when individuals' (or nations') sins are so great that only their destruction will atone. The word behind God's promise to **uphold** the **cause** (רִיב, *rîb*) of Zion at the end of verse 8 often reflects a legal context (cf. 3:13; 50:8), which is appropriate here as God is the ultimate judge. In the end, God cannot vindicate and establish his people (and thus himself) without condemning and destroying their enemies.

34:9-10 Verses 9-17 present a figurative picture of "Edom" after God's judgment. The picture reinforces the thoroughness of God's judgment by means of an image of a land so totally and permanently devastated that human beings will never occupy it again. The references to **burning sulfur** and **blazing pitch** recall God's judgment on Sodom and Gomorrah (Gen 19:24-25) that left those cities a wasteland. In this scene, however, the **smoke will rise forever** from the fiery destruction. Isaiah's account of the destruction of Babylon (13:19-22) includes an explicit reference to Sodom and Gomorrah, as well as the description of the land as permanently uninhabitable by anyone but "desert creatures." John picks up the theme, consigning those who worship the beast and receive his mark to be tormented with burning sulfur forever (Rev 14:9-11). The smoke from the burning of the great prostitute, avenging the blood of God's servants, also "goes up for ever and ever" (Rev 19:1-3).

34:11-15 The end of verse 11 portrays Edom's end as a reversal of God's work of creation. The words for **chaos** (תֹהוּ, *tōhû*) and **desolation** (בֹהוּ, *bōhû*) refer to the disordered state in Genesis 1:2 before God completed his work of creation.[8] The builder's tools of a **measuring line** and a **plumb line** symbolize God's means of evaluating people (cf. 2 Kgs 21:13; Amos 7:7-8). Sin inevitably injects

---

[8] The words are translated "formless" and "empty" in the NIV of Genesis 1:2.

chaos into the order God created. One result of the first sin was the struggle with "thorns and thistles" (Gen 3:18) in the land. **Thorns and nettles and brambles** likewise **will overrun** Edom. Whereas the original appearance of these nuisances simply made the production of food more of a toilsome process, this judgment reverts so far to the original chaos that what is left does not deserve **to be called a kingdom**. Every kingdom that asserts itself against God will meet the same end.

34:16-17 These verses conclude this picture by presenting a covenant relationship between God and the creatures who inherit Edom's former territory. God promises each of them its **mate**. Just as he did for Israel in the promised land, God **allots their portions** (cf. Num 26:52-56). Since God's **mouth** has committed to these promises and his **Spirit** brings them to fulfillment, they are certain. This certainty, based on God's reliability and power, is the point of using covenant language. The creatures will **dwell there from generation to generation** because Edom "will lie desolate" for the same length of time (v. 10).

Interpreters differ as to how **the scroll of the LORD** relates to this covenant with the wild creatures.[9] No prophecy prior to Isaiah clearly refers to it. Perhaps it is best to view this scroll as a reference to Isaiah's own record. A significant part of Isaiah's ministry, in light of the hardened condition of most of his generation, consists of leaving behind faithful testimony for future generations. In 8:16 the exhortation rings out to "bind up the testimony and seal up the law among my disciples." In 29:11-12 Isaiah's message might as well be a sealed scroll for all the hearing it is receiving in his day. Finally, 30:8 calls for Isaiah to "inscribe [God's revelation] on a scroll, that for the days to come it may be an everlasting witness." In the same fashion, 34:16 encourages future recipients of Isaiah's record to **look in the scroll** to see that God brings his enemies to an end.

---

[9]Oswalt lists four alternatives, none without difficulties, and concludes "that the invitation is only a literary device" (pp. 617-618).

ISAIAH 35

D. GOD WILL GIVE JOY TO THE REDEEMED (35:1-10)

God's certain and complete judgment of his enemies finds its counterpart in this chapter. Judgment is an essential element of God's purpose, but the only direct good news in chapter 34 addresses the animals that inherit devastated Edom. Chapter 35, however, promises the total transformation of the circumstances of the covenant people from their crippling spiritual condition and their own experience of God's judgment. The primary imagery of the chapter, a transformed desert, provides a fitting contrast to Edom's degeneration to a home for desert creatures.

1. God Will Transform the Desert into a Garden (35:1-7)

¹The desert and the parched land will be glad; / the wilderness will rejoice and blossom. / Like the crocus, ²it will burst into bloom; / it will rejoice greatly and shout for joy. / The glory of Lebanon will be given to it, / the splendor of Carmel and Sharon; / they will see the glory of the LORD, / the splendor of our God.
³Strengthen the feeble hands, / steady the knees that give way; / ⁴say to those with fearful hearts, / "Be strong, do not fear; / your God will come, / he will come with vengeance; / with divine retribution / he will come to save you."
⁵Then will the eyes of the blind be opened / and the ears of the deaf unstopped. / ⁶Then will the lame leap like a deer, / and the mute tongue shout for joy. / Water will gush forth in the wilderness / and streams in the desert. / ⁷The burning sand will become a pool, / the thirsty ground bubbling springs. / In the haunts where jackals once lay, / grass and reeds and papyrus will grow.

35:1-2 The outer frame of this section (vv. 1-2 and 6b-7) paints the picture of the transformed desert. This formerly barren land that **will burst into bloom** is personified as it rejoices over its new look. Barrenness, of course, stems from a lack of water. The word for **parched land** (צִיָּה, *ṣiyyāh*) refers to dryness or drought. The word rendered **wilderness** (עֲרָבָה, *'ărābāh*) is transliterated as the Arabah at times in reference to the desolate area south of the Dead Sea (cf. Deut 2:8).[1] What is needed to change such land is water, so it is not surprising that verses 6b-7 emphasize "streams" gushing forth, "springs" bubbling up to form pools, and water-loving plants like "reeds" and "papyrus" growing.

In 33:9 Isaiah also personifies the land when its most fertile regions mourn and shed their beauty in light of Assyria's treacherous breach of covenant. In 35:2 the whole land will enjoy the fertility of **Lebanon** and **Carmel** and **Sharon**. This promise contains a strong hint that the real problem is more significant than an arid climate and that the solution requires more than streams of literal water. The **glory** and **splendor** that have been lost will return because **they will see the glory of the LORD, the splendor of our God**. The land, in other words, will reflect the nature of God. The outward condition of the land of promise might serve as a measure of the health of the covenant relationship, but God's fundamental concern is for the relationship itself. The core of this section in verses 3-6a draws the focus to the place where God longs most deeply to see new life blossom — in the hearts of his people.

35:3-4 Isaiah has seen the glory of the Lord in chapter six and has become a changed person as a result. Unfortunately, the majority of Isaiah's contemporaries are not open to sharing his vision. Until they do, they are doomed to experience **feeble hands** and **knees that give way** and **fearful hearts**. These traits describe the condition of Judah in the days of Ahaz and the emerging Assyrian threat when "the hearts of Ahaz and his people were shaken, as the trees of the forest are shaken by the wind" (7:2). God counseled Isaiah at that time not to fear like those with no faith (8:12). The Israelite approach to warfare illustrates the antithesis between fear and faith. Soldiers were not to be afraid because "the LORD your God is the one who goes with you to fight for you against your enemies to give you victory" (Deut 20:3-4).

---

[1] The designation "Arab" also derives from this root.

Fear is an aspect of the vicious cycle of sin. One must trust God in order to be blessed by him, but fear results in turning to other sources of help, just as Ahaz turned to Assyria when he was afraid of Israel and Aram. That tragic first move away from God further erodes one's capacity for trusting him. Ironically, however, "hitting rock bottom" in this regard can lead to a restoration of relationship with God. Near the end of the covenant curses in Deuteronomy 28 (vv. 65-66), Moses describes the depths of fear. "Among those nations you will find no repose, no resting place for the sole of your foot. There the LORD will give you an anxious mind, eyes weary with longing, and a despairing heart. You will live in constant suspense, filled with dread both night and day, never sure of your life." The fact that God "gives" (נתן, *ntn*) this condition reveals that even though living in dread is a consequence of sin, it is designed to encourage openness to salvation from the only true source.

35:5-7 In 35:4, the encouragement of the fearful is based on the promise of God appearing to avenge and to "save."[2] Only at this point (**then**) can healing come, not to a barren land but to a people who are **blind** and **deaf** and **lame** and **mute**. This parallel image to the transformed desert could simply serve to add variety to Isaiah's portrait. It certainly anticipates the healing miracles of Jesus. But just as Jesus' healings demonstrate his capacity to address a deeper problem, Isaiah typically uses physical ailments to convey more significant spiritual ills (cf. 6:10; 29:18; 30:20-21; 32:3-4). God's actions on behalf of his people will restore their health and vigor as certainly as water causes life to break forth in a parched land.

2. God Will Provide a Way Home for the Redeemed (35:8-10)

⁸And a highway will be there; / it will be called the Way of Holiness. / The unclean will not journey on it; / it will be for those who walk in that Way; / wicked fools will not go about on it.ᵃ / ⁹No lion will be there, / nor will any ferocious beast get up on it; / they will not be found there. / But only the redeemed will walk there, / ¹⁰and the ransomed of the LORD will return. / They will enter Zion

---

[2] As in the previous chapter, the expression of God's anger against the wicked is integrally related to his work of salvation.

with singing; / everlasting joy will crown their heads. / Gladness and joy will overtake them, / and sorrow and sighing will flee away.

ᵃ8 Or / the simple will not stray from it

35:8a The final image of the glorious future, a **highway** (מְסִלּוּל, *maslûl*), anticipates the highway of 40:3 (מְסִלָּה, *mᵉsillāh*). Although the exiles return to Judah on a literal road, Isaiah's message that begins in chapter 40 stresses the work of God that makes it possible for the exiles to return and looks ahead to an even greater work of God. Similarly, the designation of this road as a **Way of Holiness** indicates an interest in something more than a means of physical transportation. God's nature as "the Holy One of Israel" demands that his people walk in holiness. Just as God is the one who saves (v. 4b), he is also the one who provides the way. His people do not construct this highway; it **will be there** for them.

35:8b-9 Travel in the ancient world presented many dangers. The presence of a **lion** or other **ferocious beast** along the way could bring death to a traveler. Those seeking to follow the **Way of Holiness** face greater threats from the **unclean** and **wicked fools**.³ The path God constructs, however, is open only to the **redeemed**.⁴ God will protect those who walk in his ways from these defiling and destructive influences. In the midst of a great expression of confidence in God, the psalmist cries out, "Teach me your way, O LORD; lead me in a straight path because of my oppressors" (Ps 27:11).

35:10 The chapter closes with the highest hope of the Judean exiles: that they **will return** to **Zion**. Verse 10, which is repeated in 51:11, bursts with the language of unbridled celebration. Zion's association with their covenant with God makes joyful **singing** flow

---

³It is possible to interpret the last line of v. 8 in the sense that the way will be so clear that even the fool can stay on it. The NIV footnote, for example, suggests the alternate translation, "the simple will not stray from it." This rendering us unlikely, however, for this particular designation for the fool (אֱוִיל, *'ĕwîl*) "means not merely a simpleton but that morally perverse person who knowingly chooses the opposite to God's truth" (Oswalt, *Isaiah* 1, p. 625).

⁴The root for "redeemed" (גָּאַל, *g'l*) occurs frequently in chapters 40–66. It is the same root for the "kinsman-redeemer" (*gô'ēl*), the one who acts on behalf of a next-of-kin who experiences debt (Lev 25:25) or murder (Num 35:12). God is the ultimate Redeemer. The closely related root for "ransomed" (פָּדָה, *pdh*) refers to the payment of the price for that which rightfully belongs to God, such as a firstborn son (cf. Leviticus 27).

at the occasion of this renewed pilgrimage (cf. the "songs of ascents" in Psalm 120–134). The covenant blessings (**gladness and joy**) are like one wave that **will overtake them** and continually break over them, whereas the remnants of their painful past (**sorrow and sighing**) are like another wave that is past them and **will flee away** from them forever. What a hopeful picture of the future this brief song paints before Isaiah returns to the painful realities of his day.

ISAIAH 36

III. THE EXAMPLE OF THE FAITH OF HEZEKIAH (36:1–39:8)

This commentary groups Isaiah 36–39 with chapters 28–35. Such a connection is legitimate because these chapters, though they vary in style, all stress the folly of foreign alliance and the wisdom of trusting in God.[1] Isaiah 36–39 should also be considered in isolation, however, because these chapters serve a literary function in the structure of Isaiah.[2] They have been described as a "hinge" or "bridge" linking chapters 1–35 with chapters 40–66.[3]

Several factors validate this view. First, Isaiah 1–35 and 40–66 are written almost exclusively in poetry, whereas Isaiah 36–39 provides the only extended narrative segment of the book. Second, the content of these chapters relates to the two larger poetic blocks surrounding it. The first thirty-five chapters of Isaiah describe a crisis of faith occasioned by the threat of Assyrian invasion. Ahaz refuses to trust God and enters a covenant with Assyria that actually brings the Assyrians into the land. God responds by announcing that he will use the Assyrians as the "rod of his anger" against his people, but he also promises to deliver them from Assyria. Isaiah 36–37 records the devastation of Judah by the Assyrians, as well as God's miraculous deliverance of Jerusalem when all hope appears to be lost. In so doing God responds to the faith of Hezekiah, which stands in stark contrast to Ahaz's earlier rejection of God. Isaiah 40–66 presupposes a future

---

[1] Cf. the brief comments in the introduction to chapters 28–39.

[2] The material in Isaiah 36–39 recurs almost verbatim in 2 Kings 18:13–20:19. The only major variation is the exclusion of Hezekiah's prayer of thanksgiving in 38:9-20 from Kings.

[3] Cf. Herbert M. Wolf, *Interpreting Isaiah: The Suffering and Glory of the Messiah* (Grand Rapids: Zondervan, 1985), pp. 39-41; Oswalt, *Isaiah* 1, pp. 629-631.

Babylonian exile and a return by the power of God. Not only is this return a glorious event in itself, but it also provides a basis of confidence that God will fulfill the promises he made to bless all nations through Abraham's seed. This future work of God will cause his deliverance of Judah from Assyria to pale by comparison, but the earlier deliverance demonstrates what can happen when people trust God. Chapters 38-39 set the stage for Babylon's role in God's future plans as Hezekiah extends an overly warm welcome to Babylonian envoys sent to rejoice with him in his recovery from a serious illness.

The final factor is the deliberate reversal of the chronological order of chapters 36-37 and chapters 38-39 to suit the purpose described above. When God promises to spare Hezekiah and extend his life (38:5), he also promises to defend Jerusalem from the king of Assyria as well (38:6). The most plausible reason for placing Hezekiah's illness and encounter with the Babylonians after the account of the deliverance promised in 38:6 is to connect the events of chapters 38-39 with the Babylonian context of chapters 40-66.[4] An awareness of the proper sequence of events, however, reveals that once again God prepares for great tests of faith. The Hezekiah who trusts God when surrounded by the Assyrian army is the same one who has experienced God's power over life and death.

A. THE CHALLENGE OF SENNACHERIB'S INVASION (36:1-37:38)

1. The Taunt from Sennacherib's Representatives to Hezekiah's Representatives (36:1-10)

The test of faith that Hezekiah faces in Isaiah 36-37 results directly from the failure by Ahaz to trust God in Isaiah 7. It also represents a much greater test. The immediate cause of Ahaz's fear was the alliance of Israel and Aram; Hezekiah faces a direct assault from the Assyrian army that was a more distant threat in the days of Ahaz. From the outset of his reign, however, Hezekiah is characterized as

---

[4]This explanation also supports the view that the author of Kings used the account in Isaiah 36-39 rather than the other way around. The same argument for the reversal of order does not apply in Kings.

a man of faith. According to 2 Kings 18:5, "Hezekiah trusted in the LORD, the God of Israel. There was no one like him among all the kings of Judah, either before him or after him." This trust leads the king not only to reform Judah's idolatrous religion (2 Kgs 18:4), but also to refuse to give allegiance to Assyria (2 Kgs 18:7). After the Assyrian king Shalmaneser's defeat of Israel (2 Kgs 18:9-11), Shalmaneser's son Sennacherib eventually responds to this rebellion and attacks Judah.

¹**In the fourteenth year of King Hezekiah's reign, Sennacherib king of Assyria attacked all the fortified cities of Judah and captured them. ²Then the king of Assyria sent his field commander with a large army from Lachish to King Hezekiah at Jerusalem. When the commander stopped at the aqueduct of the Upper Pool, on the road to the Washerman's Field, ³Eliakim son of Hilkiah the palace administrator, Shebna the secretary, and Joah son of Asaph the recorder went out to him.**

⁴**The field commander said to them, "Tell Hezekiah,**

"'This is what the great king, the king of Assyria, says: On what are you basing this confidence of yours? ⁵You say you have strategy and military strength—but you speak only empty words. On whom are you depending, that you rebel against me? ⁶Look now, you are depending on Egypt, that splintered reed of a staff, which pierces a man's hand and wounds him if he leans on it! Such is Pharaoh king of Egypt to all who depend on him. ⁷And if you say to me, "We are depending on the LORD our God"—isn't he the one whose high places and altars Hezekiah removed, saying to Judah and Jerusalem, "You must worship before this altar"?

⁸**"'Come now, make a bargain with my master, the king of Assyria: I will give you two thousand horses—if you can put riders on them! ⁹How then can you repulse one officer of the least of my master's officials, even though you are depending on Egypt for chariots and horsemen? ¹⁰Furthermore, have I come to attack and destroy this land without the LORD? The LORD himself told me to march against this country and destroy it.'"**

36:1-3 Sennacherib's invasion of Judah in 701 B.C. is swift and successful.[5] Egypt is unable to stop their advance, disappointing

---

[5]For a discussion of the difficulties of reconciling Sennacherib's 701 B.C. invasion with Hezekiah's fourteenth year, cf. Oswalt, *Isaiah* 1, p. 631.

anyone in Judah who was hoping for assistance from that front. Hezekiah's faith apparently falters at this point, because he gives the king of Assyria all the silver and gold he can gather from the temple and his palace (2 Kgs 18:13-16). The Assyrians, however, continue their assault, perhaps prompting the lament over treachery in Isaiah 33:7ff. The last of the **fortified cities of Judah** still standing other than Jerusalem is **Lachish**, a royal fortress approximately 27 miles southwest of Jerusalem. Sennacherib's strategy is obviously to delay until last the siege of Jerusalem, the most difficult fortified city in Judah, in hopes that a protracted siege can be avoided. He thus sends his representatives with a **large army** to intimidate and persuade the people of Jerusalem to surrender.

The location of the meeting between the Assyrian delegation and Hezekiah's representatives[6] is not an incidental detail. The **aqueduct of the Upper Pool, on the road to the Washerman's Field** is the very site where Isaiah reassured Ahaz that he need not fear the "two smoldering stubs of firewood" that were threatening him (Isa 7:3ff.). This geographical note draws attention to the significant contrast between Ahaz the father and Hezekiah the son. God sent Isaiah to Ahaz and had him address the king as "house of David" to remind him of the security of his covenant relationship with God; Hezekiah's first instinct is to send word to Isaiah of his trust in God (Isa 37:1-4).

36:4-6 The strategy of Sennacherib's **field commander** is to undermine any basis of **confidence** to which the people of Jerusalem might cling in resisting **the great king, the king of Assyria**.[7] Most of his arguments contain a considerable amount of truth and even resemble in some cases the arguments Isaiah uses to oppose ungodly alliances. He first attacks **Egypt, that splintered reed of a staff, which pierces a man's hand and wounds him if he leans on it!** In other words, Egypt's broken strength means that anyone who trusts in that nation as an ally will suffer harm rather than find support.

36:7 The fatal flaw in the Assyrian program of discouragement is its attacks against Judah's God. The attacks will become more blasphemous later, but the first charge in verse 7 betrays a pagan mis-

---

[6]Note in verse 3 that the reversal of roles between Shebna and Eliakim predicted in 22:15ff. has apparently already taken place.

[7]The Assyrian spokesman uses no formal title for the Judean king, referring to him simply as "Hezekiah."

understanding of the nature of the true God. In any other ancient Near Eastern context, Hezekiah's actions in removing all **high places** and **altars** other than the ones in Jerusalem would have offended the gods and assured defeat in battle. What the Assyrians do not realize is that Hezekiah is one of the few Israelite kings who pleases God by honoring the command for centralized worship in Deuteronomy 12.[8] This provision of the law was designed to protect Israel from idolatrous and polytheistic practices that other nations would consider virtuous.

36:8-9 In verse 8 the field commander taunts the Judean representatives with an offer to provide them with **two thousand horses**, presumably to yield a fairer fight — except for the fact that the Jerusalem forces could not **put riders on them**. Perhaps Judah's military shortcomings could be overcome by reinforcements of **chariots and horsemen** from **Egypt**. God has already warned that turning to Egypt is both sinful and futile (cf. 30:1ff.). The Assyrians reinforce God's warning by reiterating the painful current evidence of the folly of **depending**[9] on Egypt.

36:10 The final claim in the first round of verbal warfare asserts that Israel's God is actually on Assyria's side. Sennacherib's claim that **The LORD himself told me to march against this country** may be an exaggeration, but the Assyrians would interpret their military success as an indication of divine favor. To an extent the claim is truer than he realizes because God has revealed to Isaiah that Assyria will serve his purpose as a razor to shame his people by shaving them (7:20), an overflowing river to flood them (8:7-8), and the rod of his anger to discipline them (10:5-6). What the Assyrian king does not comprehend, however, is that God's favor will turn to anger if Assyria becomes proud and oversteps its bounds (10:7ff.). God has ordained that the Assyrians will assault Judah, but he has not commanded them to **destroy it**.

---

[8]Hezekiah's reforms are briefly described in 2 Kings 18:4.

[9]The word (בְּטֹחַ, *bṭḥ*) could also be translated "trusting." The use of this word repeatedly in the Assyrian proclamation should painfully remind the hearers of Judah's recent history of trusting in almost every resource except God (cf. 22:8-11).

2. The Warning from Sennacherib's Representatives to the People on the Walls of Jerusalem (36:11-22)

¹¹Then Eliakim, Shebna and Joah said to the field commander, "Please speak to your servants in Aramaic, since we understand it. Don't speak to us in Hebrew in the hearing of the people on the wall."

¹²But the commander replied, "Was it only to your master and you that my master sent me to say these things, and not to the men sitting on the wall—who, like you, will have to eat their own filth and drink their own urine?"

¹³Then the commander stood and called out in Hebrew, "Hear the words of the great king, the king of Assyria! ¹⁴This is what the king says: Do not let Hezekiah deceive you. He cannot deliver you! ¹⁵Do not let Hezekiah persuade you to trust in the LORD when he says, 'The LORD will surely deliver us; this city will not be given into the hand of the king of Assyria.'

¹⁶"Do not listen to Hezekiah. This is what the king of Assyria says: Make peace with me and come out to me. Then every one of you will eat from his own vine and fig tree and drink water from his own cistern, ¹⁷until I come and take you to a land like your own—a land of grain and new wine, a land of bread and vineyards.

¹⁸"Do not let Hezekiah mislead you when he says, 'The LORD will deliver us.' Has the god of any nation ever delivered his land from the hand of the king of Assyria? ¹⁹Where are the gods of Hamath and Arpad? Where are the gods of Sepharvaim? Have they rescued Samaria from my hand? ²⁰Who of all the gods of these countries has been able to save his land from me? How then can the LORD deliver Jerusalem from my hand?"

²¹But the people remained silent and said nothing in reply, because the king had commanded, "Do not answer him."

²²Then Eliakim son of Hilkiah the palace administrator, Shebna the secretary, and Joah son of Asaph the recorder went to Hezekiah, with their clothes torn, and told him what the field commander had said.

36:11-12 The request by Hezekiah's representatives for the Assyrians to speak in the standard diplomatic language of **Aramaic** reveals a clever strategy by the foreign emissaries. They no doubt could speak in Aramaic, but their surprising ability to use **Hebrew** and the decision to do so reflects their intent to demoralize any

Israelites within listening distance. The Assyrian spokesman now removes all pretense and heightens his psychological warfare against **the people on the wall**. He reminds anyone who will listen of the unthinkable conditions facing those who expose themselves to a protracted siege. When attackers surround a city and cut off its supplies of food and water, hunger and thirst can eventually drive those trapped inside to consume their own bodily wastes.[10]

36:13-14 The first argument addressed to the people, that Hezekiah **cannot deliver** them, would seem undeniable. He has not been able to slow the Assyrian advance so far, so why should anyone believe that the situation will change now? Has Hezekiah even *attempted* to "**deceive**" his citizens by proclaiming his ability to save them? Perhaps this message from the Assyrian king serves God's purpose as an ironic reminder of the folly of Israel's original request for a king to "go out before us and fight our battles" (1 Sam 8:20).

36:15 In the second claim, however, the commander again treads on dangerous ground as he calls into question *God's* ability to deliver. He takes a position the external facts would seem to support, but he is not aware of all the circumstances or the unique relationship between Yahweh and Israel. Although Hezekiah's attempt to avert the Assyrian advance by payment of tribute exposes the limitations of his faith, this context indicates that he is indeed calling upon his citizens **to trust in the LORD** for deliverance. Assyria's arrogance and presumption are actually Jerusalem's greatest hope for deliverance. Jerusalem is not invulnerable, as those who falsely trust in "the temple of the Lord, the temple of the Lord, the temple of the Lord" (Jer 7:4) will discover. For those who humble themselves before God and lay claim to his honor and his promises, however, hope remains.

36:16-17 Before returning to his attempt to undermine Jerusalem's confidence in God, the commander makes a promise to those he is encouraging to surrender. Rather than endure a long, painful, futile siege, the people within Jerusalem can enjoy a peaceful existence in their own land until the king of Assyria moves them to an equally good land where they can settle.[11] This promise squares

---

[10]Leviticus 26:29 and Deuteronomy 28:53ff. even speak of cannibalism as a result of siege warfare.

[11]The image of "the vine and the fig tree" represents the blessings God promises his people under the covenant (cf. Deut 8:8; 1 Kgs 4:25; Micah 4:4; Zech 3:10).

with the Assyrian policy of relocating captive peoples in order to control them more easily. Making the relocation process sound like a pleasure trip, however, does not conform to the record of Assyrian brutality in applying this policy.

36:18-20 In verse 7 Sennacherib claims that God will not help Jerusalem because Hezekiah's religious reforms have angered God. In verse 10 he claims that God is on his side. Finally, verses 18-20 elaborate what verse 15 implies: any call by Hezekiah to trust God is vain because he is no more able to deliver Jerusalem from Assyria than are the gods of the nations that have already fallen. By clearly revealing that Assyria views Yahweh like all the other gods — and by implication inferior to the gods of Assyria — a point of decision has arrived. God must either defend his name or allow it to suffer reproach in the fall of Jerusalem. The latter alternative is not out of the question. God allowed the ark of the covenant to be captured by the Philistines (1 Samuel 4–6), and Jerusalem will fall to the Babylonians. In every such case, however, God ultimately vindicates himself.

36:21-22 The people on the wall truly have a vital stake in the response to the Assyrians, so their silence at Hezekiah's command indicates a significant level of respect for their king.[12] They are willing at this point to wait for Hezekiah's response to the Assyrian challenge. The fact that the Judean delegation reports to the king **with their clothes torn** reveals the extent of the challenge. As Webb summarizes the situation, "the ball is firmly back in Hezekiah's court. . . . The people will follow where he leads; in a sense, the lives of them all are in his hands. What will he do, and what resources can he call on at this fateful moment?"[13]

---

[12]According to 2 Chronicles 32:6-8, Hezekiah had prepared the people of Jerusalem for the Assyrian assault by reminding them that "there is a greater power with us than with him." As a result of this speech, "the people gained confidence" (literally, they "supported themselves" on Hezekiah's words).

[13]Webb, *Message*, p. 149.

ISAIAH 37

3. The Initial Response to Sennacherib's Message (37:1-7)

Chapter 37 provides the resolution to the dilemma raised by Sennacherib's successful invasion of Judah. Can the seemingly airtight case the Assyrians have made for the surrender of Jerusalem be overcome? Will the sinfulness of Judah result in a devastating defeat like the one the Assyrians recently inflicted upon Israel? As the note at the end of the previous chapter indicates, the answers to these questions depend largely upon Hezekiah's next move. Will he turn to God or will fear drive him to another rash and foolish action?

¹When King Hezekiah heard this, he tore his clothes and put on sackcloth and went into the temple of the LORD. ²He sent Eliakim the palace administrator, Shebna the secretary, and the leading priests, all wearing sackcloth, to the prophet Isaiah son of Amoz. ³They told him, "This is what Hezekiah says: This day is a day of distress and rebuke and disgrace, as when children come to the point of birth and there is no strength to deliver them. ⁴It may be that the LORD your God will hear the words of the field commander, whom his master, the king of Assyria, has sent to ridicule the living God, and that he will rebuke him for the words the LORD your God has heard. Therefore pray for the remnant that still survives."
⁵When King Hezekiah's officials came to Isaiah, ⁶Isaiah said to them, "Tell your master, 'This is what the LORD says: Do not be afraid of what you have heard—those words with which the underlings of the king of Assyria have blasphemed me. ⁷Listen! I am going to put a spirit in him so that when he hears a certain report, he will return to his own country, and there I will have him cut down with the sword.'"

37:1 Hezekiah's first step is encouraging. Like his representatives, he takes on the signs of mourning. In addition to tearing his clothes, he also puts on **sackcloth** before entering God's presence. These symbols indicate either a response to highly undesirable circumstances or penitence for sin. This situation perhaps involves both. The Assyrian assault qualifies as a cause for grief regardless of the cause, but Hezekiah may also be mindful of his earlier lack of faith when he attempted to purchase his relief from the invasion rather than trust God. When the Syrians were besieging Samaria, the Israelite king Jehoram (Joram) encountered two women who were quarreling over their pact to cannibalize their children. The Israelite king tore his clothes, revealing sackcloth underneath (2 Kgs 6:30). This secret mourning, along with his threat against God's prophet Elisha (2 Kgs 6:31), reveals a different spirit from the one Hezekiah manifests in his actions to follow.

37:2-4 God sent Isaiah to strengthen Ahaz, but that ruler had no interest in hearing a word from God that might point him away from his sinful intentions. Hezekiah, on the other hand, sends his representatives to seek the prophet's intercession for divine aid. Hezekiah characterizes the current crisis as **a day of distress and rebuke and disgrace**. He also uses the familiar Isaianic image of frustrated childbirth to describe the present problem. This particular use of the image emphasizes the lack of strength to complete the task, the awareness of which should cause one to see the need for God's assistance. Jonathan manifested humble faith when going up against a Philistine garrison accompanied only by his armor-bearer ("It may be that the Lord will work for us, for nothing can hinder the Lord from saving by many or by few" – 1 Sam 14:6). Daniel's companions did the same when threatened with the fiery furnace ("Our God is able to deliver . . . but if not . . ." – Dan 3:16-18). In the same way, Hezekiah refuses to presume upon God's deliverance ("It may be that the Lord your God will hear the words of the field commander . . ." – Isa 37:4) as he puts his trust in God. The king realizes that his surest hope lies in God's rebuking Sennacherib for sending his servants to **ridicule the living God**.[1] Isaiah has addressed the idea of a remnant before, and now Hezekiah seeks prayers for the survival of a **remnant** after so much of Judah has already fallen.

37:5-7 Isaiah's exhortation to Hezekiah deliberately hearkens

---

[1]The designation "living God" typically occurs, as here, in contexts involving God's sovereignty over the nations or their idols (cf. 1 Sam 17:26,36; Jer 10:10; Dan 6:26).

back to his message to Ahaz in chapter 7. In the same way that the prophet had dismissed the kings of Aram and Israel as "smoldering stumps of firewood," he now encourages Hezekiah to recognize the relative insignificance of **the underlings of the king of Assyria**. The basis for Hezekiah's courage is not to be Assyria's weakness in human terms but, as the king had hoped, Sennacherib's foolish blasphemy against God. As a result of this capital offense, God will have him **cut down with the sword**. Rather than slaying him in battle, however, God has a purpose in bringing about his downfall in **his own country**. Three aspects of God's plan for Sennacherib display his sovereignty: bringing about events that will send a troubling **report** to the king; putting a **spirit in him** that will lead him to **return to his own country** in response to the report; and causing him to fall in his own country.

The nature of the spirit God will give to Sennacherib is unclear. God hardened Pharaoh's heart in Exodus. In warning Israel of the consequences of covenant unfaithfulness, he spoke of giving them "an anxious mind, eyes weary with longing, and a despairing heart" (Deut 28:65) and of making "their hearts so fearful in the lands of their enemies that the sound of a windblown leaf will put them to flight" (Lev 26:36). When God rejected the disobedient king Saul and removed his Spirit from him, he inflicted him with "an evil spirit"[2] instead. In each of these cases, God afflicts those who are already hardened in rebellion with a deeper measure of the consequences of their rebellion. The same principle would apply to the blatantly arrogant king of Assyria. God has not made Sennacherib an insolent person, but he will make use of the insecurity that typically accompanies such pride to expose the king's folly.

4. Sennacherib's Renewed Threat (37:8-13)

⁸When the field commander heard that the king of Assyria had left Lachish, he withdrew and found the king fighting against Libnah.

⁹Now Sennacherib received a report that Tirhakah, the Cushite[a] king ⌊of Egypt⌋, was marching out to fight against him. When he

---

[2]This "evil spirit" (1 Sam 16:14) is not the same as the demonic possession of the New Testament, but a punishing or afflicting force from God (cf. "injurious" in the NIV margin).

heard it, he sent messengers to Hezekiah with this word: ¹⁰"Say to Hezekiah king of Judah: Do not let the god you depend on deceive you when he says, 'Jerusalem will not be handed over to the king of Assyria.' ¹¹Surely you have heard what the kings of Assyria have done to all the countries, destroying them completely. And will you be delivered? ¹²Did the gods of the nations that were destroyed by my forefathers deliver them—the gods of Gozan, Haran, Rezeph and the people of Eden who were in Tel Assar? ¹³Where is the king of Hamath, the king of Arpad, the king of the city of Sepharvaim, or of Hena or Ivvah?"

ᵃ9 That is, from the upper Nile region

37:8 Although the chronological relationship between verses 7 and 8 is not stated, the text indicates that the fulfillment of God's promise to Hezekiah begins almost immediately. Sennacherib's move from **Lachish** to **Libnah**³ is apparently a defensive move in response to the news of Tirhakah's attempt to stop the Assyrian advance toward Egypt.⁴ Perhaps this news accounts for the withdrawal of Sennacherib's spokesman in Jerusalem as well.

37:9-13 The prospect of Egyptian resistance on one front and a long siege against Jerusalem on the other leads the Assyrian king to raise the level of his threats against Jerusalem. His first representatives have obviously failed to turn the people against Hezekiah and against God. His next message goes to Hezekiah himself. Whereas in 36:18 he charged Hezekiah with deceiving the people into believing that God could deliver them, now he warns Hezekiah that God is deceiving the king into trusting him. The summary of the way the gods of the other nations have failed to deliver in verses 11-13 essentially repeats the charge of 36:18b-20. While these words are serious in questioning God's power, the allegation that Yahweh cannot be trusted by his people strikes even closer to the heart of the covenant relationship.

---

³The location of Libnah is uncertain.

⁴For details about the historical issues surrounding the Cushite Tirhakah and his reign in Egypt, cf. Oswalt, *Isaiah* 1, pp. 649-650, and Motyer, *Prophecy,* p. 280, n. 1.

5. Hezekiah's Prayer to God (37:14-20)

¹⁴Hezekiah received the letter from the messengers and read it. Then he went up to the temple of the LORD and spread it out before the LORD. ¹⁵And Hezekiah prayed to the LORD: ¹⁶"O LORD Almighty, God of Israel, enthroned between the cherubim, you alone are God over all the kingdoms of the earth. You have made heaven and earth. ¹⁷Give ear, O LORD, and hear; open your eyes, O LORD, and see; listen to all the words Sennacherib has sent to insult the living God.

¹⁸"It is true, O LORD, that the Assyrian kings have laid waste all these peoples and their lands. ¹⁹They have thrown their gods into the fire and destroyed them, for they were not gods but only wood and stone, fashioned by human hands. ²⁰Now, O LORD our God, deliver us from his hand, so that all kingdoms on earth may know that you alone, O LORD, are God.[a]"

[a]20 Dead Sea Scrolls (see also 2 Kings 19:19); Masoretic Text *alone are the* LORD

37:14 Both Hezekiah's *response* in prayer and the *content* of his prayer reveal his accurate understanding of the situation he faces. God is his only hope for deliverance, and the Assyrian offense against God is his only basis for an appeal for deliverance. The symbolic act of spreading out the hard evidence in the **letter** before God in the **temple** establishes these points as well.

37:15-20 Hezekiah's prayer highlights the distinction the Assyrian boasts have failed to appreciate. The religious dimension of the prior Assyrian victories actually means nothing since the gods of the conquered peoples **were not gods but only wood and stone, fashioned by human hands**. Yahweh of Hosts (**LORD Almighty**), on the other hand, who is the **God of Israel**, is the only God and the one who rules **over all the kingdoms of the earth**. His status as universal ruler, however, remains somewhat veiled. He is **enthroned between the cherubim**,[5] hidden from human sight in the Holy of Holies. Judah's sinfulness further obscures God's dominion by hindering the working of his powerful presence among them.

Sennacherib's ultimatum thus challenges the truth of Hezekiah's bold faith statement. For this reason Judah's king prays that God will

---

[5]Isaiah also understands that God is enthroned in heaven (40:22; 66:1), but the point here is that God's dominion and Jerusalem's status overlap.

hear and see this insult that ties God's reputation and the fate of his people so closely together. How ironic that a blind and deaf people depend so greatly on the sensitivity of God's "eyes" and "ears." If God truly rules all the kingdoms of the earth, his defense of his throne at Jerusalem is vital, **so that all kingdoms on earth may know that** he **alone** is **God**.

6. God's Response to Hezekiah's Prayer (37:21-35)

²¹Then Isaiah son of Amoz sent a message to Hezekiah: "This is what the LORD, the God of Israel, says: Because you have prayed to me concerning Sennacherib king of Assyria, ²²this is the word the LORD has spoken against him:
"The Virgin Daughter of Zion /despises and mocks you. / The Daughter of Jerusalem /tosses her head as you flee. / ²³Who is it you have insulted and blasphemed? / Against whom have you raised your voice /and lifted your eyes in pride? /Against the Holy One of Israel! / ²⁴By your messengers /you have heaped insults on the Lord. /And you have said, / 'With my many chariots / I have ascended the heights of the mountains, / the utmost heights of Lebanon. / I have cut down its tallest cedars, / the choicest of its pines. / I have reached its remotest heights, / the finest of its forests. / ²⁵I have dug wells in foreign lands[a] /and drunk the water there. / With the soles of my feet / I have dried up all the streams of Egypt.'
²⁶"Have you not heard? /Long ago I ordained it. /In days of old I planned it; /now I have brought it to pass, /that you have turned fortified cities /into piles of stone. / ²⁷Their people, drained of power, /are dismayed and put to shame. / They are like plants in the field, /like tender green shoots, /like grass sprouting on the roof, /scorched[b] before it grows up.
²⁸"But I know where you stay /and when you come and go /and how you rage against me. / ²⁹Because you rage against me / and because your insolence has reached my ears, / I will put my hook in your nose / and my bit in your mouth, /and I will make you return /by the way you came.
³⁰"This will be the sign for you, O Hezekiah:
"This year you will eat what grows by itself, /and the second year what springs from that. / But in the third year sow and reap, /plant

vineyards and eat their fruit. / ³¹Once more a remnant of the house of Judah / will take root below and bear fruit above. / ³²For out of Jerusalem will come a remnant, / and out of Mount Zion a band of survivors. / The zeal of the LORD Almighty will accomplish this.

³³"Therefore this is what the LORD says concerning the king of Assyria:

"He will not enter this city / or shoot an arrow here. / He will not come before it with shield / or build a siege ramp against it. / ³⁴By the way that he came he will return; / he will not enter this city," / declares the LORD. / ³⁵"I will defend this city and save it, / for my sake and for the sake of David my servant!"

ª*25* Dead Sea Scrolls (see also 2 Kings 19:24); Masoretic Text does not have *in foreign lands.*   ᵇ*27* Some manuscripts of the Masoretic Text, Dead Sea Scrolls and some Septuagint manuscripts (see also 2 Kings 19:26); most manuscripts of the Masoretic Text *roof / and terraced fields*

37:21 God obviously receives Hezekiah's prayer with favor. In ways that transcend human comprehension, prayer changes the course of earthly events. The fact that Hezekiah's brief but God-centered prayer reflects faith, in contrast to the self-reliant (or Assyria-reliant) approach of Ahaz, leads God to respond to Sennacherib's boasting with a boast of his own. Before God addresses the Assyrians directly, however, he describes the confidence Jerusalem will feel as a result of trusting him.

37:22 Isaiah has referred to Jerusalem as **Daughter of Zion** before (cf. 1:8; 10:32; 16:1). Here he adds the designation **Virgin** (בְּתוּלָה, *bᵉthûlāh*) to the name. The effect is twofold. First, Jerusalem will maintain her virginity in that the Assyrians will not violate her. In addition, this imagery ridicules the mighty and boastful Assyrians by presenting Jerusalem as a girl who **despises and mocks** them.

37:23-25 The real issue that has sealed Sennacherib's fate is the identity of the one he has **insulted and blasphemed: the Holy One of Israel**. This title emphasizes both God's exalted nature (in contrast to the empty gods of the pagan nations) and his special relationship with his covenant people. He is also **the Lord** (אֲדֹנָי, *'ădōnāy*),[6] a label that acknowledges God's sovereignty over all, including Assyria. Sennacherib's boastful claims, poetically expressed in vv. 24b-25,

---

[6]Note the distinction in spelling from "the LORD," the traditional designation when the divine name (Yahweh) appears in the text.

recall the empty words with which God taunts the king of Babylon in 14:3ff.

37:26-27 What these powerful (by human standards) rulers do not realize is that their place in history has been **ordained** by God long before their birth, and that in all of their success God has **brought it to pass**. As quickly as God has given them power, however, so quickly can he take it away when they abuse it or fail to acknowledge him. Other nations may have withered before Assyria **like plants in the field**, but the roles are reversed when the seemingly invincible conquerors oppose God.

37:28-29 God's omnipresence and omnipotence are somewhat overwhelming but ultimately comforting to those who seek him (cf. Psalm 139). For those who manifest **insolence** and **rage against** him, however, these same traits ensure unavoidable judgment. God's final words to Sennacherib are a promise to send him back home by putting **my hook in your nose and my bit in your mouth**. Both pictures provide perspective on the truth about the relative places of God and Sennacherib in the world. In the latter image Sennacherib is not the one who controls history but rather a domesticated creature appointed to carry out God's bidding. The former is an ironic twist on a cruel method by which the Assyrians would lead away their captives.

37:30 As with the oracles regarding the nations in 13–23, God's message to Sennacherib actually addresses Hezekiah and the people of Jerusalem. Whether or not the Assyrian king receives God's verbal response, he will get the message contained in these words. In light of this purpose, God speaks directly to Hezekiah in the remainder of his response. Since God knew the unbelieving heart of Ahaz, he exposed the king's lack of faith by inviting him to ask for a sign. In light of Hezekiah's openness to divine aid, God simply tells him what **will be the sign** that will confirm God's saving presence. At the outset Hezekiah's sign possesses some similarities to the one God gave to Ahaz whether he wanted it or not. The idea of eating **what grows by itself** for two years, followed by a **third year** in which the people will cultivate the land again, appears no more miraculous than giving birth to a child who will eat curds and honey (7:14ff.). The ability of the inhabitants of Jerusalem to survive that long, however, and the possibility that they will enjoy enough peace and security to leave the walls of the city to tend their fields again, will require miraculous intervention.

37:31-32 The sign given to Ahaz, though it contained elements of judgment due to unbelief,[7] also pointed to something much more significant in the birth of the greater Immanuel. So Hezekiah's sign looks beyond planting grain and vineyards to the time when **a remnant of the house of Judah will take root below and bear fruit above**. When Hezekiah first heard the Assyrian report, he sent his representatives to Isaiah to ask him to "pray for the remnant that still survives" (v. 4). God's promise is that the remnant will not only survive, but also go forth in keeping with the future envisioned in 2:1ff. As with the conclusion to the great messianic promise in 9:7, this deliverance from the enemy and continuation of God's purpose will occur through the **zeal of the LORD Almighty**. God has so supervised the events that no explanation for Jerusalem's survival remains other than his commitment to the covenant.

37:33-35 In case any doubt lingers regarding the meaning of God's promises, God states explicitly that he will not allow Sennacherib to do anything against Jerusalem and that the blasphemous invader **will return** without satisfying his destructive intent. In addition, God reiterates the reasons why he **will defend this city and save it**. He is zealous for Jerusalem, but why? When he states that he will act **for my sake**, he isolates the fundamental reason for all of God's actions. He does nothing through compulsion or coercion; he acts on the basis of his nature. Part of his nature is to be true to his promises, a trait that underlies the words **for the sake of David my servant**. God's covenant with David (cf. 2 Sam 7:8ff.) cannot be completely separated from his commitment to Jerusalem since David founded the city as Israel's capital and moved the ark of the covenant there.

7. God's Response to Sennacherib (37:36-38)

36Then the angel of the LORD went out and put to death a hundred and eighty-five thousand men in the Assyrian camp. When the people got up the next morning—there were all the dead bodies! 37So Sennacherib king of Assyria broke camp and withdrew. He returned to Nineveh and stayed there.

---

[7]See the comments on 7:14ff. in the first volume of this commentary.

38One day, while he was worshiping in the temple of his god Nisroch, his sons Adrammelech and Sharezer cut him down with the sword, and they escaped to the land of Ararat. And Esarhaddon his son succeeded him as king.

37:36-37 God answers Hezekiah's prayer in sudden and dramatic fashion.[8] The Egyptian resistance from Tirhakah may have distracted Sennacherib, but the devastating overnight losses within his army result in his return to **Nineveh**. Skeptics, of course, have attacked the notion that 185,000 men fell in a single night. Some have argued that the numbers are inflated, but Oswalt argues persuasively that this number is realistic in light of the overall size of the Assyrian army.[9] Others seek a naturalistic explanation for the losses, such as an outbreak of bubonic plague. When one adds up all such explanations that are necessary to remove God's miraculous acts for his people, the striking number of "coincidences" becomes almost as miraculous as the straightforward claims of the biblical text.

The fact remains that Sennacherib does not complete his assault against Hezekiah. His withdrawal is difficult to explain in light of the Judean king's act of rebellion. His own words proclaim that he has Hezekiah "trapped like a bird in a cage."[10] It is hardly surprising that the Assyrian annals do not explain why he left the job unfinished in the same way the biblical record does. Boasting of conquering nations and gods fits in well with the nature of ancient monarchs and their records; recording an event that points so obviously to the successful intervention of Judah's God does not. Only a presupposition that miracles do not occur would compel one to reject the biblical explanation for Sennacherib's retreat.

37:38 The completion of God's judgment against Sennacherib reveals something of God's purpose in sending the king home before bringing his life to an end. The contrast between Hezekiah's successful intercession for Jerusalem in the temple of Yahweh and Sennacherib's assassination at the hand of two of his sons in the temple of his god[11]

---

[8]According to 2 Kings 19:35, God attacked the Assyrian army the same night Hezekiah prayed for deliverance.

[9]Oswalt, *Isaiah* 1, pp. 669-670.

[10]J.B. Pritchard, *Ancient Near Eastern Texts* (Princeton, NJ: Princeton University Press, 1955), p. 288.

[11]Sennacherib's assassination occurred twenty years after he attacked Hezekiah in 701 B.C.

highlights the ultimate futility of idolatry. From a historical perspective, Motyer notes that the "names *Nisroch*, *Adrammelech* and *Sharezer* are not found outside the Bible, but the Babylon Chronicle records the assassination of Sennacherib and Esarhaddon's accession."[12]

---

[12]Motyer, *Prophecy*, p. 285.

ISAIAH 38

B. THE CHALLENGE OF HEZEKIAH'S ILLNESS (38:1-22)

Two related experiences in the life of Hezekiah help to prepare him for Sennacherib's invasion of Judah. As was pointed out earlier, Isaiah records those two experiences after his account of the Assyrian defeat in order to connect the downfall of Assyria with chapters 1–35 and the Babylonian threat with chapters 40–66. By facing an illness that would have been fatal without God's intervention and the temptation to ally with another hostile nation, Hezekiah learns that he can trust in God and God alone.

Hezekiah's human frailty shows through in these two events. Death comes to him as it does to everyone else, even if he receives a temporary reprieve. He cannot see through the apparent act of kindness by the Babylonian king to his ultimately hostile intentions. Even though God's extension of his life strengthens his faith, he fails to manifest that faith when he courts the favor of the Babylonians. Just as Hezekiah's righteous successor Josiah proves by his death on the battlefield that he is not Judah's ultimate hope for salvation, so Hezekiah falls short as well. Yet some interpreters go too far in their criticism of Hezekiah under these circumstances. Motyer, for example, states that the king's "first thoughts were for himself."[1] The comments below will hopefully demonstrate that, in spite of his human weaknesses, Hezekiah still stands as an outstanding example of faith under extremely difficult circumstances.

1. God's Announcement of Hezekiah's Imminent Death (38:1-3)

¹In those days Hezekiah became ill and was at the point of death. The prophet Isaiah son of Amoz went to him and said,

---

[1] Motyer, *Prophecy*, p. 290.

"This is what the LORD says: Put your house in order, because you are going to die; you will not recover."
²Hezekiah turned his face to the wall and prayed to the LORD, ³"Remember, O LORD, how I have walked before you faithfully and with wholehearted devotion and have done what is good in your eyes." And Hezekiah wept bitterly.

38:1 According to the context, the vague time reference, **in those days**, would appear to fix the time of Hezekiah's illness in proximity to Sennacherib's assassination. Other factors in this narrative, however, will indicate otherwise. The seemingly absolute proclamation by Isaiah, in which he tells the king **you are going to die; you will not recover**, proves in the unfolding events not to be so absolute after all. This example of conditional prophecy[2] points to Hezekiah's illness and recovery as a test of his faith. The situation resembles the occasions when, after the golden calf and other serious sins by Israel in the wilderness, God tells Moses that he intends to destroy Israel. Moses passes these challenges to his love for and leadership of his people when he effectively intercedes for them. Hezekiah will intercede for himself, and in the process learn that God has the power to overcome the threat of destruction for those who turn to him in trust.[3]

38:2-3 Hezekiah's brief prayer and his tears may suggest he is a somewhat pathetic figure. God's response to his prayer, however, along with Hezekiah's more detailed song of thanksgiving, points to a more positive interpretation. The king's prayer is a condensed version of the many laments one finds in Psalms. Any believer in distress faces the temptation to bargain with God on the basis of past faithfulness, even though no one can place God in a position of debt or obligation. As Jesus puts it in Luke 17:10, "So you also, when you have done everything you were told to do, should say, 'We are unworthy servants; we have only done our duty.'" When one reads a lament which reminds God of the person's past service, therefore, the tendency is to assume this individual is praying improperly. The

---

[2]Cf. "Special Study: Conditional Fulfillment of Prophecy" in the first volume of this commentary, pp. 59-61.

[3]Webb (*Message*, p. 155) observes that Hezekiah's crisis parallels the threat to Jerusalem by the Assyrians. Just as Hezekiah's deliverance is a temporary reprieve from death, so Jerusalem will escape Assyria only to be destroyed by Babylon.

favorable inclusion of many such prayers, however, indicates that a different dynamic is at work and that these faithful individuals deserve the benefit of the doubt.

The first words of Hezekiah's expression of thanksgiving recall that in facing death he had asked, "In the prime of my life must I go through the gates of death and be robbed of the rest of my years?" In the Old Testament context, with a limited view of an afterlife at best, the measurement of the covenant relationship leaned heavily upon factors such as long life, peace, and fruitfulness. For a faithful believer to die prematurely or without descendants thus constitutes a personal tragedy, and also calls into question God's reliability. According to 2 Kings 18:2, Hezekiah became king at age twenty-five and reigned twenty-nine years. Since God extended his life by fifteen years, he would have been thirty-nine at the opening of this chapter. The observation that one cannot praise God from the grave (v. 18; cf. Ps 6:5; 30:9; 88:11) does not indicate how indispensable the individual is to God as much as it points to the negative impact on others from the person's untimely death. Surely those who face an early death lament their personal situation, but the faithful focus even more on God's reputation.[4]

2. God's Response to Hezekiah's Prayer (38:4-8)

⁴Then the word of the LORD came to Isaiah: ⁵"Go and tell Hezekiah, 'This is what the LORD, the God of your father David, says: I have heard your prayer and seen your tears; I will add fifteen years to your life. ⁶And I will deliver you and this city from the hand of the king of Assyria. I will defend this city.

⁷"'This is the LORD's sign to you that the LORD will do what he has promised: ⁸I will make the shadow cast by the sun go back the ten steps it has gone down on the stairway of Ahaz.'" So the sunlight went back the ten steps it had gone down.

38:4-6 Just as God subtly reminded Ahaz of the confidence he should have as a result of the covenant relationship by referring to

---

[4]Cf. the so-called imprecatory psalms, in which a righteous sufferer calls forth curses from God against his enemies. These psalms appear to call for personal vengeance, but on closer examination seek the vindication of God (cf. Ps 58:11; 59:13; 79:9-10; 94:1-7).

him as "house of David" (7:2,13), so here God refers to himself as **the God of your father David**. God responds both to Hezekiah's **prayer** and to his **tears**. Rather than a sign of weakness, the king's tears reveal the heartfelt nature of his petition. God promises not only to **add fifteen years** to Hezekiah's life, but also to deliver him and Jerusalem **from the hand of the king of Assyria**. The close connection between these two promises substantiates the view that the announcement of Hezekiah's death serves as a test of the king's faith that prepares him to respond properly to Sennacherib's threats in chapters 36 and 37.

38:7 The **sign** God gives to affirm to Hezekiah **that the LORD will do what he has promised** constitutes an additional contrast between this king and his father. God offered Ahaz a sign that could be anything "in the deepest depths or in the highest heights" (7:11), an offer Ahaz rejected out of unbelief.[5] God now provides a sign for Hezekiah to strengthen his capacity to believe.[6] God does not call for blind faith. As in this case, he prepares individuals for great tests of faith by giving them a basis for trusting him prior to the major event. He provides Hezekiah with a miraculous sign that corresponds well with the promise to "turn back the clock" on the previously announced time of his death. God's power over life and death then prepares Hezekiah to trust in God's power over Sennacherib and the Assyrian army.

38:8 Precisely how God makes **the shadow cast by the sun go back the ten steps it has gone down** is not explained. Oswalt concludes that "Since reversing the rotation of the earth carries with it so many other implications, it seems likely that some sort of refraction of light was involved."[7] The method by which God makes the shadow go back is not as important as the message it conveys to Hezekiah: God has the power, whenever he chooses, to reverse the normal course of human events. To understand this message is to know the essence of the miraculous.

---

[5]The fact that the miracle takes place on "the stairway of Ahaz" surely represents an intentional irony.

[6]According to 2 Kgs 20:8-10, Hezekiah requested the sign and was given the option of the shadow moving forward or backward ten steps.

[7]Oswalt, *Isaiah* 1, p. 678.

3. Hezekiah's Song of Thanksgiving (38:9-20)

⁹A writing of Hezekiah king of Judah after his illness and recovery:
¹⁰I said, "In the prime of my life / must I go through the gates of death[a] / and be robbed of the rest of my years?" / ¹¹I said, "I will not again see the LORD, / the LORD, in the land of the living; / no longer will I look on mankind, / or be with those who now dwell in this world.[b] / ¹²Like a shepherd's tent my house / has been pulled down and taken from me. / Like a weaver I have rolled up my life, / and he has cut me off from the loom; / day and night you made an end of me. / ¹³I waited patiently till dawn, / but like a lion he broke all my bones; / day and night you made an end of me. / ¹⁴I cried like a swift or thrush, / I moaned like a mourning dove. / My eyes grew weak as I looked to the heavens. / I am troubled; O Lord, come to my aid!"

¹⁵But what can I say? / He has spoken to me, and he himself has done this. / I will walk humbly all my years / because of this anguish of my soul. / ¹⁶Lord, by such things men live; / and my spirit finds life in them too. / You restored me to health / and let me live. / ¹⁷Surely it was for my benefit / that I suffered such anguish. / In your love you kept me / from the pit of destruction; / you have put all my sins / behind your back. / ¹⁸For the grave[a] cannot praise you, / death cannot sing your praise; / those who go down to the pit / cannot hope for your faithfulness. / ¹⁹The living, the living— they praise you, / as I am doing today; / fathers tell their children / about your faithfulness.

²⁰The LORD will save me, / and we will sing with stringed instruments / all the days of our lives / in the temple of the LORD.

[a]*10,18* Hebrew Sheol   [b]*11* A few Hebrew manuscripts; most Hebrew manuscripts *in the place of cessation*

38:9 The context of this composition and the climactic expression of praise for deliverance qualify it loosely as a song of thanksgiving. It possesses a number of similarities to other songs of thanksgiving such as Psalm 30, but it also differs in two significant areas. First, it does not open with a note of thanksgiving (cf. Ps 30:1-5). In addition, the lament with which Hezekiah's song begins persists through most of the song. A thanksgiving song may contain an element of lament in the description of the prior distress (cf. Ps 30:6-10), but the lament normally constitutes a smaller portion of the whole. Psalm types frequently intermingle, however, and the key to a given work's classification is the perspective from which it is composed (in this case, **after his illness and recovery**).

38:10-12 Hezekiah uses typical poetic style and imagery to describe his illness and the prospect of his death. As noted earlier, he begins with a recognition of the tragedy of premature death and the uncertainty of the afterlife. Strictly speaking, he says that he will never see God **in the land of the living**, not that he will never see God again. Two similes from daily life describe the king's view of the way God is bringing an end to his life. In the first he sees himself as a **shepherd's tent** being taken down.[8] In the second he is both the **weaver** and the fabric on the **loom** that God decides is finished and cuts off.

38:13-14 In these verses Hezekiah expresses his frustration in the midst of his crisis. The words of Psalm 22:1 – "My God, My God, why have you forsaken me?" – express most poignantly the dilemma of the believer in such circumstances. God is sovereign and thus must have some role in the distress, even if it is merely permissive.[9] At the same time, he is still the only one to whom the believer can legitimately turn for help. Hezekiah repeatedly attributes his anguish to God, even comparing him to a **lion** who has broken his bones (cf. Ps 22:16-21). Yet he looks to the heavens so intently for help that his eyes grow weary.

38:15-17 As Hezekiah's focus begins to turn to the resolution of his crisis, he becomes aware of the positive purpose God has for his illness. Not every illness or loss has a precise disciplinary purpose, but the believer is always open to the possibility. In this case God has made clear to Hezekiah that he is to learn to **walk humbly**[10] as a result of his **anguish**. He has found **life** (v. 16) and **benefit** (שָׁלוֹם, *šālôm*; v. 17) and experienced God's **love**[11] through what he has suffered. Finally, this experience has resulted in the forgiveness of his **sins**.

---

[8]Contrast the positive overtones of the same image in 2 Corinthians 5:1ff. and 2 Peter 1:13-14.

[9]As in Psalm 22, however, a distinction frequently exists between a sufferer's perception of reality and the truth the person comes to understand later.

[10]The rare word used here (הדה, *ddh*) implies walking slowly, deliberately, cautiously.

[11]The Hebrew in v. 17 literally says, "You [emphatic] have loved my soul from the pit of destruction." A slight emendation of the pointing of the verb (חָשַׁקְתָּ, *ḥāśaqtā* instead of חָשַׂקְתָּ, *ḥāśaqtā*) would yield the more logical meaning "You held back."

The literary arrangement of chapters 36–39 points to Hezekiah's healing as a preparation for trusting God during Sennacherib's attack. Hezekiah's own interpretation of the event, however, points in a different direction. These two possibilities are not mutually exclusive. Pride or any other sin in Hezekiah could stand in the way of God's deliverance of Jerusalem as surely as a lack of faith. Immediately following his healing, Hezekiah would not likely understand its connection to the Assyrian crisis, despite God's promise in verse 6.

38:18-20 Hezekiah promises to celebrate his deliverance from death in a way the dead cannot. The language of verses 18-20 implies that to live is to **praise** God. Hezekiah intends to join this chorus so that generations to come will hand down the truth about God's **faithfulness**. On a corporate level, Hezekiah's story will become part of the worship at the **temple**. God's saving acts for his people become part of a vast reservoir from which all believers may draw for comfort and strength.

4. A Final Note on Hezekiah's Recovery (38:21-22)

²¹Isaiah had said, "Prepare a poultice of figs and apply it to the boil, and he will recover."
²²Hezekiah had asked, "What will be the sign that I will go up to the temple of the LORD?"

38:21-22 The placement of these verses in Isaiah is difficult to explain. They seem to fit more naturally between verses 6 and 7, which is where they appear in the parallel in 2 Kings 20. The awkward renderings **Isaiah had said** and **Hezekiah had asked** (rather than "said" and "asked") represent the NIV's attempt to connect these verses back to the earlier context. Verse 21 would thus provide the fulfillment of God's promise to heal the king and verse 22 would indicate Hezekiah's request for a sign that was granted in the moving of the shadow. In Isaiah these verses seem to hang in a disconnected fashion.

Theories about this placement must of necessity be tentative. One possibility is that Isaiah understands the healing of a boil on Hezekiah as an additional sign of his recovery from his more severe illness, or perhaps as the removal of an outward symptom of his more severe internal illness.[12] Isaiah may have made use of the Kings

---

[12]Many readers wonder how a "boil" could constitute an illness that brings Hezekiah to the point of death.

account, leading him to separate these verses to make that distinction clearer.[13] If that is the case, rather than connecting verse 21 with verses 4-6 and verse 22 with verses 7-8, verses 21 and 22 stand apart in relation to one another.

---

[13]Is the Kings account the original that Isaiah adapted? Is the Isaiah account the original that the author of Kings adapted? Did both writers use a third source? Scholars differ on this question.

ISAIAH 39

C. THE CHALLENGE OF THE BABYLONIAN ENVOYS (39:1-8)

1. Hezekiah's Reception of the Babylonian Envoys (39:1-2)

¹At that time Merodach-baladan son of Baladan king of Babylon sent Hezekiah letters and a gift, because he had heard of his illness and recovery. ²Hezekiah received the envoys gladly and showed them what was in his storehouses—the silver, the gold, the spices, the fine oil, his entire armory and everything found among his treasures. There was nothing in his palace or in all his kingdom that Hezekiah did not show them.

39:1-2 Sometimes adversity is easier to deal with than prosperity. The humbling effect of Hezekiah's illness appears to fade in the face of his **recovery** and a flattering visit from the **envoys** of a powerful distant king. **Merodach-Baladan** ruled as **king of Babylon** on two occasions between 721 and 703 B.C. and sought to overthrow Assyria.[1] The events of this chapter probably occur during the latter part of that period and provoke, at least in part, Sennacherib's retaliation against Hezekiah in 701 B.C. Hezekiah should not have been so naive as to think that Merodach-Baladan had no ulterior motives in celebrating the Judean king's return to good health. Yet he welcomes **the envoys gladly**[2] and shows them all of his treasures and armaments.

2. God's Warning Regarding the Babylonians (39:3-8)

³Then Isaiah the prophet went to King Hezekiah and asked, "What did those men say, and where did they come from?"

---

[1]Cf. Oswalt, *Isaiah* 1, pp. 693-694.
[2]Literally, he "rejoiced over them" (וַיִּשְׂמַח עֲלֵיהֶם, *wayyiśmaḥ 'ălêhem*).

"From a distant land," Hezekiah replied. "They came to me from Babylon."

⁴The prophet asked, "What did they see in your palace?"

"They saw everything in my palace," Hezekiah said. "There is nothing among my treasures that I did not show them."

⁵Then Isaiah said to Hezekiah, "Hear the word of the LORD Almighty: ⁶The time will surely come when everything in your palace, and all that your fathers have stored up until this day, will be carried off to Babylon. Nothing will be left, says the LORD. ⁷And some of your descendants, your own flesh and blood who will be born to you, will be taken away, and they will become eunuchs in the palace of the king of Babylon."

⁸"The word of the LORD you have spoken is good," Hezekiah replied. For he thought, "There will be peace and security in my lifetime."

39:3-7 Isaiah's questions to Hezekiah, as when God asked Cain, "Where is your brother Abel?" aim not to gain information but to expose sin. The king appears, however, to be oblivious to his serious failure. Isaiah's subsequent announcement of the role Babylon will play in Judah's future devastation does not describe the *consequence* of Hezekiah's sin. Instead, this message highlights how foolish Hezekiah has been to court the favor of the Babylonians by showing them what a valuable ally he would be.³

39:8 More bothersome to some than Hezekiah's foolish reception of the Babylonian envoys is his apparently selfish attitude regarding the calamity Isaiah describes. His words need not, however, be interpreted as callously as is frequently the case. The overall character of Hezekiah's life would lead one to expect that he cares about his people, not to mention his own descendants. Why else would he have enacted such extensive religious reforms during his reign? If Hezekiah's sin with the Babylonian visitors was the cause of the coming destruction, the perspective on his words might be different. Solomon's sins did cause the division of the kingdom, but God graciously waited until after his death to separate the tribes (1 Kgs 11:11-13). Surely Hezekiah would be thankful to be spared from witnessing the tragedies Isaiah predicts, but that is not the focus of verse 8. When Hezekiah remarks that God's message about the Babylonian exile is

---

³Second Chronicles 32:27-30 details Hezekiah's wealth and accomplishments.

good, his point is not that he is happy about what will happen. Nor does the word refer to his relief that he will not have to see these events unfold.[4] What he is saying is that he humbly accepts what God has decreed (cf. 1 Sam 3:18; 2 Sam 10:12; 15:26; Job 1:21).

Isaiah's concise account in chapter 39 does not provide the reader with much context for interpreting Hezekiah's reaction to the news he receives from God. Second Chronicles 32:24ff., on the other hand, fills in details that help to put Isaiah's account into perspective.[5] First, verses 25-26 explain that Hezekiah did not respond to his healing as he should have, but was instead filled with pride. He repented of this pride, however, which is why God did not pour out his wrath on his people during Hezekiah's days. Verse 31 subsequently describes the visit of the Babylonian envoys as a time when "God left [Hezekiah] to test him and to know everything that was in his heart." Hezekiah's failure of the test, like David's sinful numbering of Israel (2 Sam 24:1ff./ 1 Chr 14:1ff.), probably reflects a broader lack of faith among God's people. The postponement of God's judgment, therefore, because it constitutes a gracious response to Hezekiah's repentance, should be a cause for celebration by the whole nation.

In the end, in spite of all his efforts at reformation, Hezekiah learns that Babylonian destruction looms in his people's future. In recording this news Isaiah's primary aim is neither to condemn nor to commend Hezekiah. He sets before his audience a message that, though tragic, must be accepted by the nation with the same humility as Judah's righteous but flawed king. The critical unresolved issue, of course, centers upon whether or not God's grace extends to a future for the covenant people beyond exile, and if so, how it will be achieved. To these matters the final major section of the book speaks.

---

[4]The word "for" in the NIV translation of verse 8 is not explicit in the Hebrew text. The simple conjunction (ו) on וַיֹּאמֶר (*wayyō'mer*) is most often translated "and." No clear causal relationship exists in the text, therefore, between the "goodness" of what God has said and Hezekiah's awareness that he will enjoy peace and security in his lifetime.

[5]Whether or not Isaiah assumes his audience possesses knowledge from other sources, an example from chapter 7 illustrates the clarification that can result from consulting these sources. Isaiah 7 does not explain why Ahaz refuses to ask for a sign to help him trust God, but 2 Kings 16:7ff. fills in the important detail that Ahaz had already pursued an alliance with Assyria.

INTRODUCTION TO ISAIAH 40–66

The structure of Isaiah 40–66 is more complex and difficult to discern than that of the rest of the book. One common approach divides these chapters into two major sections: chapters 40–55 and 56–66. This division is frequently associated with the notion of a Deutero-Isaiah originating in the Babylonian exile and a postexilic Palestinian Trito-Isaiah.[1] Some, however, accept this division on the basis of stylistic and content considerations without advocating the multiple authorship of Isaiah.[2] The other leading alternative focuses on the refrain, "'There is no peace,' says the LORD, 'for the wicked'" in 48:22 and 57:21. The structural clue provided by this refrain yields three sections of nine chapters each. This commentary follows the latter approach to the structure of chapters 40–66.

One of the striking features of Isaiah 40–66 is its sustained focus on the future. Chapter 39 closes with the prospect of Babylonian exile and chapter 40 opens by jumping ahead to a message of comfort at the end of the exile. What is the purpose of this leap? The very prospect of a traumatic event like exile could have a devastating effect on the already questionable faith of the Israelites. The unpopular forecast of this kind of judgment serves after the fact to confirm the reliability of the prophets through whom God reveals the dark days ahead. Isaiah has already made it clear, however, that God knows the message of impending doom will not change the current generation. God's ultimate goal in establishing the credibility of prophets such as Isaiah, therefore, is to authenticate as well their

---

[1] For a discussion of the unity of Isaiah, cf. Volume 1 of this commentary, pp. 14-16.

[2] Oswalt sees a major break between chapters 40–55 and 56–66, but he further divides the first section into chapters 40–48 and 49–55. Motyer divides the entire book into three large sections: 1–37, 38–55, and 56–66. Neither writer, however, affirms the multiple authorship of Isaiah that stems from a denial of the prophet's ability to foresee God's future for his people.

message of hope for the future. This message of hope will sustain the faithful through the crisis. Although the extent of Isaiah's discussion of a more glorious future (which stretches beyond the return from exile) is unique among the biblical prophets, it serves a vital purpose during a critical time. With its goal of strengthening faith, it speaks not only to those who will be eligible to return from exile, but also to the faithful in Isaiah's day, to those who experience exile, and to every subsequent generation.

Isaiah accomplishes his goal in this section by some of the most beautiful and powerful language in all of Scripture. He presents an exalted view of God that affirms his sovereign power, his compassion, his faithfulness to his covenant promises, and his inscrutable wisdom. Paul's words in Romans 11:33 apply well to Isaiah's portrait of God: "Oh, the depth of the riches of the wisdom and knowledge of God! How unsearchable his judgments, and his paths beyond tracing out!"

In chapters 40–48 Isaiah vividly contrasts God with the pagan gods who prove to be impotent blocks of wood. Only God possesses the power to foresee and to control the future, a power he demonstrates most clearly by proclaiming his use of the later conqueror Cyrus to return the Israelite exiles to the land of promise. Isaiah also introduces in this section the figure of the "servant" through whom God will accomplish a purpose that transcends his mission for Cyrus. Although Isaiah explicitly identifies Israel as God's servant, he also recounts unsparingly Israel's failure to live up to that designation. The disparity between the ideal servant and Israel's shortcomings raises questions as to the identity of the servant who will carry out God's will.

The work of Cyrus recedes into the background and the servant assumes prominence in Isaiah 49–57. The servant is faithful, but like many previous faithful servants of God he suffers rejection, abuse, and ultimately death. Unlike previous servants, however, his sufferings accomplish a redemptive purpose as he bears the sins and sorrows of others. In this role he is further distinguished from Israel because he acts on behalf of Israel. As a result of the servant's work, great and gracious blessings become available from God that extend beyond Israel to those who have formerly been outcasts.

The final section of Isaiah's collected message revisits many of the themes in the rest of the book[3] and reemphasizes the choices people

---

[3]Specific instances will be cited in the commentary, but it should be noted

must make in light of God's redemption through the servant. Chapters 58–66 begin, as does the book as a whole, by exposing hypocritical and manipulative approaches to worship that insult the glorious God whom Isaiah has so powerfully portrayed. If the worship that is supposed to restore and sustain fellowship with God is itself sinful, how can the barrier of sin between God and his people be removed? The answer lies in God's commitment to his purpose and in his creative power. The God who created the world will not cease to work until he has defeated sin, turned hearts to him, and established new heavens and a new earth. All that remains is for people to recognize the true nature and work of God and to respond to him in faith.

---

that as this section synthesizes elements from the rest of Isaiah it affirms the unity of the book.

OUTLINE OF ISAIAH 40–66

I. **THE SOVEREIGNTY OF GOD AND THE FAILURE OF HIS SERVANT** — 40:1–48:22
   A. **The God Who Comforts His People** — 40:1-31
      1. His Word Stands Forever — 40:1-11
      2. To Whom Will You Compare Him? — 40:12-26
      3. He Gives Strength to the Weary — 40:27-31
   B. **The God Who Remains Faithful to His People** — 41:1-29
      1. He Stirs Up One from the East — 41:1-7
      2. He Reaffirms His Chosen People — 41:8-20
      3. He Challenges the Nations and Their Idols — 41:21-29
   C. **The God Who Confronts the Failures of His People** — 42:1-25
      1. He Calls His Servant to Accomplish His Purpose — 42:1-9
      2. He Merits the World's Praise — 42:10-17
      3. He Seeks to Purify His Disobedient Servant — 42:18-25
   D. **The God Who Redeems His People** — 43:1-28
      1. He Is with His People in Their Distress — 43:1-7
      2. He Establishes Witnesses from His People — 43:8-13
      3. He Makes a Way for His People — 43:14-21
      4. He Forgives the Sins of His People — 43:22-28
   E. **The God Who Glorifies Himself in His People** — 44:1-28
      1. He Pours His Spirit on His People — 44:1-5
      2. He Exposes Idolatry before His People — 44:6-20
      3. He Accomplishes His Purpose for His People — 44:21-28
   F. **The God Who Mystifies His People** — 45:1-25
      1. He Anoints a Deliverer on Behalf of His People — 45:1-8
      2. He Overrules the Objections of His People — 45:9-13
      3. He Reveals Himself to the Nations by His People — 45:14-25
   G. **The God Who Defeats the Enemies of His People** — 46:1–47:15
      1. He Exposes the Folly of Idolatry — 46:1-7

      2. He Brings His Salvation Near — 46:8-13
      3. He Shames the Merciless — 47:1-7
      4. He Bereaves the Self-Sufficient — 47:8-11
      5. He Wearies the Misguided — 47:12-15
   H. The God Who Seeks Peace for His People — 48:1-22
      1. He Preempts His People's Dependence on Idols — 48:1-7
      2. He Refines His People for His Name's Sake — 48:8-11
      3. He Delivers His People by Giving Cyrus Success — 48:12-15
      4. He Teaches His People What Is Best for Them — 48:16-22

II. THE GRACE OF GOD AND THE SUCCESS OF HIS SERVANT — 49:1–57:21
  A. The Nature of the Servant's Work — 49:1–53:12
     1. The Servant Experiences Frustration, but God Gives Him Success — 49:1-26
       a. The Servant's Confidence in God — 49:1-4
       b. God's Commitment to the Servant — 49:5-13
       c. God's Commitment to Zion — 49:14-26
     2. The Servant Experiences Rejection, but God Vindicates Him — 50:1-11
       a. Unresponsive Israel — 50:1-3
       b. The Responsive Servant — 50:4-9
       c. The Call to Walk in God's Light — 50:10-11
     3. Interlude: Israel Must Awaken to God's Redemption — 51:1–52:12
       a. Listen to God's Promise of Salvation — 51:1-8
       b. Awake, O God, to the Plight of Your People — 51:9-16
       c. Awake, O Jerusalem, to the End of Your Suffering — 51:17-23
       d. Awake, O Zion, to the Joy of Your Salvation — 52:1-10
       e. Depart from the Place of Your Bondage — 52:11-12
     4. The Servant Experiences Death, but God Exalts Him — 52:13–53:12
       a. An Overview of the Tension: Exaltation and Disfigurement — 52:13-15
       b. A Heightening of the Tension: The Power of God and the Rejection of Men — 53:1-3
       c. A Pivotal Moment for the Tension: Suffering and Substitution — 53:4-6
       d. A Resumption of the Tension: The Death of the Innocent Sufferer and the Future — 53:7-9

e. A Resolution of the Tension: The Will of God and
          the Triumph over Death — 53:10-12
*Special Study: Isaiah's Portrayal of the Servant of the LORD:
   Summary and Conclusions*
   B. The Consequences of the Servant's Work — 54:1–57:21
      1. God Renews the Covenant with His People — 54:1-17
         a. The Restored Marriage — 54:1-10
         b. The Rebuilt City — 54:11-17
      2. God Freely Pardons His People — 55:1-13
         a. The Gracious Banquet — 55:1-2
         b. The Everlasting Covenant — 55:3-5
         c. The Effective Word — 55:6-13
      3. God Clarifies the Definition of His People — 56:1-8
         a. The Basis of Blessing and Inclusion — 56:1-2
         b. The Object of Blessing and Inclusion — 56:3-8
      4. God Gives Peace to His People — 56:9–57:21
         a. Failed Leadership Jeopardizes Peace — 56:9-12
         b. Idolatry Jeopardizes Peace — 57:1-13
         c. Penitence Prepares the Way for Peace — 57:14-21
 **III. THE FAITHFULNESS OF GOD AND THE FUTURE OF
      HIS SERVANTS** — 58:1–66:24
   **A. God's Commitment to Renew His Relationship with His
      People** — 58:1–59:21
      1. Israel's Misguided Religion — 58:1-14
         a. Religion That Fails to Connect — 58:1-5
         b. Religion That Results in Blessing — 58:6-14
      2. Israel's Separation from God — 59:1-21
         a. God Accuses Israel of Sin — 59:1-8
         b. Israel Suffers Because of Sin — 59:9-15a
         c. God Intercedes for Israel's Sin — 59:15b-21
   **B. God's Commitment to Reveal His Glory through His
      People** — 60:1–61:11
      1. God's Light in a World of Darkness — 60:1-22
         a. The Light of God's Presence Attracts Those Who
            See His Glory in His People — 60:1-10
         b. The Light of God's Presence Protects from Those
            Who Oppose His Glory in His People — 60:11-22
      2. God's Light in Zion — 61:1-11
         a. The Agent of God's Light — 61:1-3
         b. The Effects of God's Light — 61:4-9
         c. The Response to God's Light — 60:11-11

C. God's Commitment to Defend the Cause of His People — 62:1–64:12
  1. God's Faithfulness to Zion — 62:1–63:6
     a. God Promises to Glorify Zion — 62:1-7
     b. God Promises to Restore Zion — 62:8-12
     c. God Promises to Avenge Zion — 63:1-6
  2. The Proper Response to God's Promises — 63:7–64:12
     a. Praise God for Past Mercies — 63:7-10
     b. Pray to God to Deliver As in the Past — 63:11–64:3
     c. Pray to God to Forgive As in the Past — 64:4-12

D. God's Commitment to Renew the Creation for His People — 65:1–66:24
  1. God's Response to Isaiah's Prayer — 65:1-25
     a. God Will Repay Those Who Defy Him — 65:1-7
     b. God Will Preserve Those Who Seek Him — 65:8-12
     c. God Will Distinguish between His Servants and the Unresponsive — 65:13-16
     d. God Will Create New Heavens and a New Earth — 65:17-25
  2. Two Approaches to God — 66:1-24
     a. The Futility of Hypocritical Religion — 66:1-6
     b. The Power of Relational Religion — 66:7-13
     c. The End of the Two Approaches — 66:14-24

ISAIAH 40

I. THE SOVEREIGNTY OF GOD AND THE FAILURE OF HIS SERVANT (40:1–48:22)

A. THE GOD WHO COMFORTS HIS PEOPLE (40:1-31)

The previous section closes with a small measure of comfort for Hezekiah in that he will not have to witness the Babylonian conquest of Judah. But what of those who will not enjoy "peace and security" in their lives? Is there a message of comfort for those who will experience defeat and exile? Before elaborating on the cause of this future suffering and how God will overcome it, Isaiah begins with a powerful word of comfort. He provides reassurance that is based on the incomparable nature of God.

1. His Word Stands Forever (40:1-11)

¹Comfort, comfort my people, / says your God. / ²Speak tenderly to Jerusalem, / and proclaim to her / that her hard service has been completed, / that her sin has been paid for, / that she has received from the LORD's hand / double for all her sins.
³A voice of one calling: / "In the desert prepare / the way for the LORD[a]; / make straight in the wilderness / a highway for our God.[b] / ⁴Every valley shall be raised up, / every mountain and hill made low; / the rough ground shall become level, / the rugged places a plain. / ⁵And the glory of the LORD will be revealed, / and all mankind together will see it. / For the mouth of the LORD has spoken."
⁶A voice says, "Cry out." / And I said, "What shall I cry?" / "All men are like grass, / and all their glory is like the flowers of the field. / ⁷The grass withers and the flowers fall, / because the breath of the LORD blows on them. / Surely the people are grass. / ⁸The grass withers and the flowers fall, / but the word of our God stands forever."

⁹**You who bring good tidings to Zion, / go up on a high mountain. / You who bring good tidings to Jerusalem,ᶜ / lift up your voice with a shout, / lift it up, do not be afraid; / say to the towns of Judah, / "Here is your God!" / ¹⁰See, the Sovereign LORD comes with power, / and his arm rules for him. / See, his reward is with him, / and his recompense accompanies him. / ¹¹He tends his flock like a shepherd: / He gathers the lambs in his arms / and carries them close to his heart; / he gently leads those that have young.**

ᵃ*3 Or A voice of one calling in the desert: / "Prepare the way for the LORD*
ᵇ*3 Hebrew; Septuagint make straight the paths of our God*   ᶜ*9 Or O Zion, bringer of good tidings, / Go up on a high mountain. / O Jerusalem, bringer of good tidings*

These verses, which are frequently viewed as introductory to this section of Isaiah, contain a series of brief messages that God wants to deliver to his people before they experience the bad news God has given to Hezekiah. They need to know that God's work in Jerusalem still has a future; that exile does not mark the end of God's purpose for Israel; and most of all, that Babylonian conquest does not invalidate God's promises. The emphasis on the reliability of God's word may explain why these messages are delivered by an unnamed speaker (vv. 1-2) and a series of voices (vv. 3,6,9).

40:1 The repetition of the exhortation to **comfort**, coupled with the call to **speak tenderly**¹ **to Jerusalem**, signals a compassionate tone that dominates the latter portion of Isaiah. Chapters 1–35 and chapters 40–66 contain significant elements of both grace and judgment. The proportions vary, however, based on the differing perspectives of the two major segments of the book. The first 35 chapters view Judah's situation in the midst of the Assyrian crisis. Sin and unbelief have precipitated the crisis, so Isaiah's message focuses on warning the people of impending destruction if they do not turn back to God. To a significant but lesser degree he also proclaims that Judah's sin will not keep God from bringing his glorious purpose to completion. Chapters 40–66, on the other hand, look to the future in light of the message God sends to Hezekiah about the Babylonian exile. From that perspective, the people most need to

---

¹The Hebrew is literally "speak to the heart (דַּבְּרוּ עַל־לֵב, *dabbᵉrû 'al-lēb*) of Jerusalem." This expression may be used in a romantic context (Gen 34:3; Hos 2:14 [v. 16 in the Hebrew text]). It also appears in 2 Chronicles 32:7 in Hezekiah's exhortation to those in Jerusalem during the Assyrian invasion.

receive reassurance that God will overcome their failures and resume his work through them. At the same time, they also need the reminder that they must respond to God's redemption and turn from their former ways.

The initial message of comfort is that a day will come when the sins that have caused Jerusalem's destruction will no longer hinder God's relationship with his people. Three parallel verbs emphasize the complete removal of the barrier of sin: **has been completed**; **has been paid for**; and **has received . . . double**. The NIV translation of the second phrase in terms of "payment" could be misleading. The word for **sin** in that phrase (עָוֹן, *'āwōn*) can refer either to the sin itself or the punishment for it. The verb (נִרְצָה, *nirṣāh*) would be more literally translated "has been accepted." The only other context in which this passive form of the verb appears is in God's acceptance of the sacrifices (Lev 1:4; 7:18; 19:7; 22:23,25,27).[2] In this context the picture of receiving double for sins should not be taken literally, but as a way of indicating fullness.

40:2-5 Since the promise of comfort follows the announcement of Babylonian exile and the end of a period of "hard service," the command of the first **voice** to **make straight in the wilderness a highway** points to the return from exile. Several details within the text, however, indicate that the command encompasses something even greater. The language referring to raising valleys and leveling mountains is figurative, far exceeding anything that would happen or even be necessary for the exiles' return. The text also focuses on God as the primary "traveler" for whom this road is being prepared, although in a very real sense he is the one preparing the way. The goal of this highway is to reveal God's **glory** to **all mankind**. The return from exile will be a significant event, but in itself will not capture worldwide attention.

The use of the imagery of the "way" in 35:8, 57:14, and 62:10-11 also indicates God is preparing for something much larger than the return from exile. Only in light of subsequent events for which the return is critical does one see the fulfillment of the words of the first voice. All four Gospels confirm the broader significance of this text by applying it to John the Baptist's preparatory work for Jesus (Matt 3:3; Mark 1:3; Luke 3:4; John 1:23). God will not only bring his people back from Babylon, but he will also fulfill his worldwide redemptive purpose through them.

---

[2]Motyer, *Prophecy,* p. 299.

40:6-8 The next two voices provide evidence to help God's people trust in his promise to restore them. The first basis for confidence derives from an understanding of that which truly endures. Human beings are so limited in perspective that whatever seems impressive at any given moment may appear to be the ultimate reality. **All men are like grass**, however, so the **glory** that they and their works seem to possess will quickly fade when **the breath of the LORD blows on them**. Since man's frail efforts wither before God's power, God's people need not fear that a hostile power like Babylon can thwart his purpose. Isaiah does not draw a contrast between mankind and God, but between mankind and **the word of our God**, which **stands forever** (cf. 1 Pet 1:24-25). The reliability of God's word is tied to God's nature and character, of course, but the purpose here is to recall God's unfailing promises.[3]

40:9-11 The final voice anticipates the day when the **good tidings**[4] of God's return reach Jerusalem. The emphasis in the return remains on God because his presence is the key to a positive future for Jerusalem.[5] He alone possesses the **power** to bring **reward**, an observation that points to the fact that God does not return alone. The same God whose powerful **arm rules for him** also **gathers the lambs in his arms** as he brings them home. The familiar image of God as the **shepherd** of his people combines the traits of strength and tender care. These traits, in addition to the reliability of God's word, provide comfort to those who look ahead to a treacherous future, as well as those who will experience exile personally. The rest of this chapter, as well as the remaining chapters of Isaiah, elaborates on this high view of God as the only sure basis of hope for the future.

---

[3]Isaiah may also intend to draw a connection between God's "breath" that withers and his "word" that sustains.

[4]The root for this word (בשׂר, *bśr*) serves as the Old Testament equivalent of εὐαγγελίζω (*euangelizō*), the New Testament term for proclaiming the gospel.

[5]Ezekiel depicts the glory of God departing from the temple and Jerusalem (Ezekiel 10) before the Babylonian destruction, and the closing verse of the book (48:35) proclaims that "The LORD is there" in the restored temple.

2. To Whom Will You Compare Him? (40:12-26)

¹²Who has measured the waters in the hollow of his hand, / or with the breadth of his hand marked off the heavens? / Who has held the dust of the earth in a basket, / or weighed the mountains on the scales / and the hills in a balance? / ¹³Who has understood the mind[a] of the LORD, / or instructed him as his counselor? / ¹⁴Whom did the LORD consult to enlighten him, / and who taught him the right way? / Who was it that taught him knowledge / or showed him the path of understanding?

¹⁵Surely the nations are like a drop in a bucket; / they are regarded as dust on the scales; / he weighs the islands as though they were fine dust. / ¹⁶Lebanon is not sufficient for altar fires, / nor its animals enough for burnt offerings. / ¹⁷Before him all the nations are as nothing; / they are regarded by him as worthless / and less than nothing.

¹⁸To whom, then, will you compare God? / What image will you compare him to? / ¹⁹As for an idol, a craftsman casts it, / and a goldsmith overlays it with gold / and fashions silver chains for it. / ²⁰A man too poor to present such an offering / selects wood that will not rot. / He looks for a skilled craftsman / to set up an idol that will not topple.

²¹Do you not know? / Have you not heard? / Has it not been told you from the beginning? / Have you not understood since the earth was founded? / ²²He sits enthroned above the circle of the earth, / and its people are like grasshoppers. / He stretches out the heavens like a canopy, / and spreads them out like a tent to live in. / ²³He brings princes to naught / and reduces the rulers of this world to nothing. / ²⁴No sooner are they planted, / no sooner are they sown, / no sooner do they take root in the ground, / than he blows on them and they wither, / and a whirlwind sweeps them away like chaff.

²⁵"To whom will you compare me? / Or who is my equal?" says the Holy One. / ²⁶Lift your eyes and look to the heavens: / Who created all these? / He who brings out the starry host one by one, / and calls them each by name. / Because of his great power and mighty strength, / not one of them is missing.

ᵃ*13* Or *Spirit*; or *spirit*

40:12-14 In language similar to that with which God confronted Job (Job 38–41), God reminds his people of his relationship to the entire creation and its daily operation. The point of this series of rhetorical questions becomes explicit in verse 25 — "To whom will you compare me? Or who is my equal?" Who else but God can handle the world's **waters** and **mountains** and even the **heavens** as if they were daily household items? The focus moves from God's vast power to his unsearchable wisdom. Job argued forcefully with his friends about the cause of his suffering, but God reminded him that the complexity of God's ways exceeds the capacity of finite human minds to comprehend. Israel's complaint in verse 27 that God is apathetic to their plight calls for the same divine response. God does not need anyone to teach him **the right way**.

40:15-17 The contrast between God and the **nations** in verses 15-17 does not refer to the worth of the citizens of those nations as human beings in his eyes. God's covenant purpose through Israel, after all, aims to bring salvation to them. When their alleged glory and might are compared to that of God, however, **all the nations are as nothing**. Not only do they fail to compare to God's glory, but they cannot even adequately acknowledge God's glory. All the mighty cedars of **Lebanon** and all of their sacrificial animals would not be enough to give God his due. Religious acts cannot place God in their debt.

40:18-22 The contrast shifts from the nations to their idols. God transcends his creation so greatly that no **image** compares favorably to him. According to verse 22, **He sits enthroned above the circle of the earth** and **the heavens** are **like a tent** to him. Any attempt to portray him, therefore, by an element of his creation can only insult him and compromise the way humans conceive of him. In the first of several sarcastic denunciations of idolatry in chapters 40–66, Isaiah describes idols as requiring a **skilled craftsman** to set them up securely enough that they **will not topple**. This picture illustrates one of the greatest dangers of idolatry — creating the illusion that God depends on man in any way.

40:23-24 Isaiah next contrasts God to **the rulers of this world**. As with the nations in verses 15-17, so their rulers ultimately amount to **nothing**. In spite of their grandiose appearance and claims, they meet the same end of all other human beings (vv. 6-8). No matter how secure and enduring they may appear to be, from God's perspective they **wither** away as soon as they are **planted**. In contrast to the plants, however, the brief span of these **princes** derives not so much from their normal life span as from the intervention of God when **he blows on them**. Like the wicked in Psalm 1:4, arrogant human leaders in the end are **like chaff**, lightweight and useless.

40:25-26 The concluding piece in Isaiah's portrait of God's sovereignty calls attention to **the heavens**. Contemplation of God's creation of the earth impresses, but consideration of the vastness of the heavens results in an even more overwhelming awe. Scripture emphasizes God's role as creator of all to combat the pagan tendency to deify aspects of the creation. In this passage, however, Isaiah focuses on God's personal knowledge of and care for the **starry host**. He brings the stars out each night **one by one, and calls them each by name**. He supervises them so closely that **not one of them is missing**. This thought once again pulls together the power and the love of God, setting the stage for God's direct response to his people's concerns at the end of the chapter.

3. He Gives Strength to the Weary (40:27-31)

²⁷Why do you say, O Jacob, /and complain, O Israel, / "My way is hidden from the LORD; /my cause is disregarded by my God"? / ²⁸Do you not know? / Have you not heard? / The LORD is the everlasting God, /the Creator of the ends of the earth. / He will not grow tired or weary, /and his understanding no one can fathom. / ²⁹He gives strength to the weary /and increases the power of the weak. / ³⁰Even youths grow tired and weary, /and young men stumble and fall; / ³¹but those who hope in the LORD / will renew their strength. / They will soar on wings like eagles; / they will run and not grow weary, / they will walk and not be faint.

40:27 If God so powerfully and meticulously sustains the universe, how can Israel ever fear that her **way is hidden from the LORD**? Whereas this complaint implies that God has overlooked his covenant people, the charge that Israel's **cause** [מִשְׁפָּט, *mišpāṭ*] **is disregarded** alleges that he has deliberately given them over to injustice. These conclusions, though misguided, are understandable responses by people who see their world crumbling around them. God knows that it will be difficult for those who face defeat, destruction, and exile to keep their eyes focused on him and his promises of restoration.

40:28-29 What God offers the discouraged above all is **strength**. He has never promised a way that is easy, but he assures his people that he will never place them in a position without providing them sufficient resources to endure. In this passage God first responds to the questions about his faithfulness with questions of his own. Do they not **know** historically how God has proven himself? Have they not **heard** what he has revealed about himself in the words of this chapter? He reminds them briefly of his limitless power and unfathomable wisdom. When Israel faces hardship, it will not be the result of either weakness or ignorance by God. Regardless of the outward circumstances, God's people can rest assured that their circumstances have a place in the wise, sovereign purpose of God.

Sometimes through hardship God aims to make his people **weary** and **weak**. God has revealed in this chapter that the greatest of human strength pales by comparison to his might. Unfortunately, when God's people feel strong in and of themselves, they forget their dependence on God, as the earlier chapters of the book of Isaiah have demonstrated. Under those circumstances, the most gracious act of God is to use his wisdom and power to expose human foolishness and weakness. In the classic statement of the principle, after God has refused to remove his "thorn in the flesh" Paul confesses "when I am weak, then I am strong" (2 Corinthians 12:10).

40:30-31 God's goal, therefore, in exposing human weakness is to provide true **strength** and power to his people. The seemingly inexhaustible energy of **youths** finally reaches a limit, but God's supply knows no bounds. The danger in shattering the delusions of the self-sufficient is the possibility that the discouragement will not lead to faith but, as in verse 27, to despair. Only **those who hope in the LORD will renew their strength**. The word for "hope" (קוה, *qwh*) basically refers to waiting for someone or something.[6] The word for "renew" (יַחֲלִיפוּ, *yaḥălîphû*) literally means "exchange" and is used, for example, of changing clothes.[7] Those who cling to God in faith, therefore, remembering his faithfulness, can exchange their limited strength for the limitless resources of God. Those who follow this path **will soar on wings like eagles**. This image not only captures the majesty and effortless flight of a powerful bird, but also calls to mind the exodus from Egypt, after which God reminded his people of "how I carried you on eagles' wings and brought you to myself" (Exod 19:4). Once again, God reveals himself to be both powerful and loving.

---

[6]The participial form of the verb implies a continual state (cf. Motyer, *Prophecy*, p. 308).

[7]Wolf, *Interpreting Isaiah*, p. 187.

ISAIAH 41

B. THE GOD WHO REMAINS FAITHFUL TO HIS PEOPLE (41:1-29)

This chapter builds on the themes of the previous one. God's sovereignty allows him to raise up a powerful conqueror who will do his bidding. All the other nations can do as he approaches is turn to their lifeless idols. At the end of the chapter, God contrasts his ability to tell what will happen ahead of time and then make what he foretells happen with the powerlessness of the nations and their gods. The heart of the chapter, however, reveals the purpose behind God's actions on the international scene. No matter how threatening the actions of other nations might appear, God maintains his commitment to his people. He will protect them and cause the movements of history to work for their ultimate benefit.

1. He Stirs Up One from the East (41:1-7)

¹"Be silent before me, you islands! / Let the nations renew their strength! / Let them come forward and speak; / let us meet together at the place of judgment.

²"Who has stirred up one from the east, / calling him in righteousness to his service[a]? / He hands nations over to him / and subdues kings before him. / He turns them to dust with his sword, / to windblown chaff with his bow. / ³He pursues them and moves on unscathed, / by a path his feet have not traveled before. / ⁴Who has done this and carried it through, / calling forth the generations from the beginning? / I, the LORD—with the first of them / and with the last—I am he."

⁵The islands have seen it and fear; / the ends of the earth tremble. / They approach and come forward; / ⁶each helps the other / and says to his brother, "Be strong!" / ⁷The craftsman encourages

the goldsmith, /and he who smooths with the hammer /spurs on him who strikes the anvil. /He says of the welding, "It is good." / He nails down the idol so it will not topple.

ᵃ2 Or / *whom victory meets at every step*

41:1 The prophets occasionally portray God as calling Israel into court for a covenant lawsuit. Although God does not maintain the same level of covenant relationship with the nations, he still rules over them and has the right to summon them to **the place of judgment**.[1] He first calls them to **be silent** because he has a message for them, but he will later give them the opportunity to **speak** in response (although they will have nothing to say). The exhortation to the nations to **renew their strength** uses the same language as the promise God gave Israel in 40:31. It is not clear if these words are intended to mock the nations and their vain resources or to offer them an opportunity to share in Israel's blessings from God.

41:2-4 Regardless of the identification of the conqueror **from the east**, the answer to the question about who raises him up and gives him victory is the same. Most consider this passage the first of several references in chapters 40–48 to Cyrus, the Medo-Persian ruler who came from the east, overthrew the Babylonian empire, and in 538 B.C. allowed a group of Judean exiles to return home (cf. Ezra 1:1ff.). God calls him by name in 44:28 and 45:1, but simply describing his victorious march suffices at this point. The **righteousness** of this conqueror resides in his accomplishment of the divine purpose rather than his personal character. The question in verse 2 may have been rhetorical, but verse 4 leaves no doubt as to who is responsible for Cyrus's success. Like John's "Alpha and Omega" (Rev 1:8) and "the First and the Last" (Rev 1:17), God is the all-encompassing One who alone possesses the ability to foretell events and to make them happen.

41:5-7 What can the nations do to prepare for this conqueror to come, even if they are forewarned about his rise? The description of their limited options exposes the futility of what is available to them. For one thing, they can encourage one another. Yet the exhortation to **be strong!** sounds rather hollow in the face of the relentless assault described in verse 2. Their other option is to call on their best craftsmen to fashion an effective idol to deliver them. As in 40:20, however, how can one trust in something that has to be nailed

---

[1]This phrase could also be translated "for judgment" (cf. NASB).

down **so it will not topple**? The same verb for "Be strong!" (חזק, *ḥzq*) in verse 6 recurs twice in verse 7 for **encourages** and **nails down** (literally, "makes it strong with nails"). Such "strength" is obviously insufficient.

2. He Reaffirms His Chosen People (41:8-20)

⁸"But you, O Israel, my servant, / Jacob, whom I have chosen, / you descendants of Abraham my friend, / ⁹I took you from the ends of the earth, / from its farthest corners I called you. / I said, 'You are my servant'; / I have chosen you and have not rejected you. / ¹⁰So do not fear, for I am with you; / do not be dismayed, for I am your God. / I will strengthen you and help you; / I will uphold you with my righteous right hand.

¹¹"All who rage against you / will surely be ashamed and disgraced; / those who oppose you / will be as nothing and perish. / ¹²Though you search for your enemies, / you will not find them. / Those who wage war against you / will be as nothing at all. / ¹³For I am the LORD, your God, / who takes hold of your right hand / and says to you, Do not fear; / I will help you. / ¹⁴Do not be afraid, O worm Jacob, / O little Israel, / for I myself will help you," declares the LORD, / your Redeemer, the Holy One of Israel. / ¹⁵"See, I will make you into a threshing sledge, / new and sharp, with many teeth. / You will thresh the mountains and crush them, / and reduce the hills to chaff. / ¹⁶You will winnow them, the wind will pick them up, / and a gale will blow them away. / But you will rejoice in the LORD / and glory in the Holy One of Israel.

¹⁷"The poor and needy search for water, / but there is none; / their tongues are parched with thirst. / But I the LORD will answer them; / I, the God of Israel, will not forsake them. / ¹⁸I will make rivers flow on barren heights, / and springs within the valleys. / I will turn the desert into pools of water, / and the parched ground into springs. / ¹⁹I will put in the desert / the cedar and the acacia, the myrtle and the olive. / I will set pines in the wasteland, / the fir and the cypress together, / ²⁰so that people may see and know, / may consider and understand, / that the hand of the LORD has done this, / that the Holy One of Israel has created it.

41:8a In undermining the misplaced pride of the nations, God aims to overthrow the misplaced fear of **Israel**. According to outward appearances, the nations have reason to be confident and Israel has reason to fear. The unseen factor, however, is God's commitment to the covenant he has with his people. God thus multiplies the reasons Israel should look beyond the surface and recall the basis of her relationship with him. He begins with the designation of Israel as **my servant**. This label will become increasingly significant in subsequent chapters, but it also hearkens back to the status of Moses (Exod 14:31), David (2 Sam 3:18), and the prophets (2 Kgs 17:13). Israel can be encouraged because God acknowledges that he has a purpose yet to be accomplished through this people.

41:8b-9 God next refers to Israel as the **chosen** people and the **descendants of Abraham my friend**. They are not chosen because they possess any inherent righteousness, but because they are heirs of the covenant promises rooted in God's special relationship with their father Abraham. God has also made a significant investment in this people. The reference to taking them **from the ends of the earth** probably alludes both to the exodus from Egypt and to the return from exile. He has not **rejected** those he plans to reassemble. None of these words of reassurance derives from any merit in Israel but only from the character of God.

41:10 The most important message God can offer to overcome Israel's fears is **I am with you**.[2] After the sin with the golden calf, God threatened to withdraw his presence so that he would not break out against his people and consume them. Moses interceded, however, recognizing that Israel had no chance for success without God in her midst (Exod 32–33). That incident highlights the dilemma created by bringing together a holy God and a sinful people. God's presence in one sense constitutes a danger, yet without the holy God's presence the sinful people have no hope. The exile represents God's response to a later generation's disregard for his holiness, but the promise to restore his presence acknowledges his commitment to the covenant with Israel. God renewed the covenant after the golden calf, and to those facing exile he promises **I am [still] your God**.

41:11-13 God's presence constitutes good news for Israel and bad news for Israel's enemies. God's **right hand** (vv. 10,13) is "righteous" in that it reflects his reliable character, and by it he powerfully and tenderly leads his people through any danger. Consequently, Israel need not **fear** when others **rage against** her because God will

---

[2]Cf. the "Immanuel" sign in chapters 7–8.

cause those hostile forces to **be ashamed and disgraced**. In the end, those who seem so powerful **will be as nothing at all**.

41:14-16 In these verses God makes it clear that he will not only act *on behalf of* Israel, but also that he will prevail over the opposition *through* Israel. That this victory will take place by the power of God is clear because Israel possesses no more inherent might than a **worm**. Yet God will transform this worm into a **threshing sledge**, a heavy piece of equipment used to break up and separate the grain from the **chaff**. This is no ordinary threshing sledge, however, because the worm's opponents are as powerful as **mountains**, but these mountains cannot stand before those whom God empowers. Since the power for this unlikely victory clearly derives from God, the victory provides an occasion for his people to **rejoice** and **glory** in him.

The purpose of the striking contrast between the worm and the threshing sledge that crushes mountains is to strike crippling fear from Israel's heart (v. 14). But to what event(s) does this imagery refer? Threshing and winnowing frequently refer to times of judgment. Webb points out that "From the moment God called Abraham, the fate of nations depended on their response to him and his descendants. . . . In this sense [the surviving remnant of Israel] will fulfill their calling by simply being there, in the world, as the people of God." The New Testament hints at a similar role for Christians (cf. Matt 19:28; Luke 22:30; Rev 20:4).

41:17-20 God changes the setting for his encouragement to Israel in the promises of verses 17-20. Isaiah often parallels the long and treacherous return from exile with Israel's exodus and wilderness experiences. The language of these verses contains a number of allusions to God's ability to sustain his people in a barren wilderness.[3] Such imagery inspires confidence on two levels. First, it reminds Israel that what God has done in the past he can do again. In addition, it lets Israel know that God will no more **forsake** his people in exile than he did when they became slaves in Egypt. Just as God's transformation of his people into victors over their opposition calls for praise (v. 16), so God's transformation of a desert into a place of sustenance for his people points to the fact that **the hand**

---

[3]Cf. Exod 15:22ff.; 17:1ff. (Motyer, *Prophecy*, p. 314). These verses also closely parallel the promises of Isaiah 35.

of the LORD has done this. God's redemptive work in Isaiah 40–66 represents not only a second exodus, but also a new creation.[4]

3. He Challenges the Nations and Their Idols (41:21-29)

²¹"Present your case," says the LORD. / "Set forth your arguments," says Jacob's King. / ²²"Bring in ⌐your idols⌐ to tell us / what is going to happen. / Tell us what the former things were, / so that we may consider them / and know their final outcome. / Or declare to us the things to come, / ²³tell us what the future holds, / so we may know that you are gods. / Do something, whether good or bad, / so that we will be dismayed and filled with fear. / ²⁴But you are less than nothing / and your works are utterly worthless; / he who chooses you is detestable.

²⁵"I have stirred up one from the north, and he comes— / one from the rising sun who calls on my name. / He treads on rulers as if they were mortar, / as if he were a potter treading the clay. / ²⁶Who told of this from the beginning, so we could know, / or beforehand, so we could say, 'He was right'? / No one told of this, / no one foretold it, / no one heard any words from you. / ²⁷I was the first to tell Zion, 'Look, here they are!' / I gave to Jerusalem a messenger of good tidings. / ²⁸I look but there is no one— / no one among them to give counsel, / no one to give answer when I ask them. / ²⁹See, they are all false! / Their deeds amount to nothing; / their images are but wind and confusion.

41:21-24 Jacob's King has presented his case, so he invites the nations to do the same. God has been present from the beginning and brings his work to its completion (v. 4). Can the gods of the nations describe either **the former things** or **their final outcome**? If they cannot foretell **what the future holds** or demonstrate their ability to do something, **whether good or bad**, why should anyone acknowledge that they are **gods**? The fact that so many choose to acknowledge these idols in spite of the lack of evidence of their power marks their devotees as **detestable** (תּוֹעֵבָה, *tôʿēbāh*). Verse 24 reveals that idolatry is a choice for which one is responsible, and that this choice puts the worshiper of idols in the same category as the

---

[4]The word translated "created" in verse 20 (ברא, *brʾ*) is the same word used in Genesis 1:1. Cf. 65:17-18; 66:22.

idol itself and other unclean and defiling items.⁵ One of the reasons Isaiah stresses worship (cf. chs. 1; 58) is the inevitable link between the object and nature of a person's worship and that person's character.⁶

41:25-29 If the one God **has stirred up . . .** "from the east" (v. 2) is Cyrus, he may also be described as coming **from the north**, the direction from which he would enter both Babylon and Palestine.⁷ His rise to power, foretold by God, brackets this chapter as the clearest demonstration in the immediate future of God's unique ability to tell what will happen **from the beginning**. The message that the nations cannot foresee (v. 26) will cause terror when it becomes reality (v. 5), but it will constitute **good tidings** (מְבַשֵּׂר, *mᵊbaśśēr*; cf. 40:9) for **Jerusalem** since Cyrus will initiate the return from exile. The closing note of the chapter reinforces the point that Isaiah's original audience, those who go into exile, and every subsequent generation of believers must recognize: the gods of the nations **are all false! Their deeds amount to nothing; their images are but wind and confusion**.⁸ Fear and futility await those who trust in these gods; confidence and victory lie in store for those who trust in the God who controls history.

---

⁵Cf. Deut 14:3; 18:9-12; 20:18; 27:15 for examples of what God labels "detestable."

⁶Cf. Ps 115:8; Jer 2:5 (Motyer, *Prophecy*, p. 316).

⁷Verse 25 actually refers to the conqueror coming from both "the north" and the east ("the rising sun").

⁸The word for "confusion" (תֹהוּ, *tōhû*) refers to the "formless" original state of the creation in Genesis 1:2 (cf. the "desolate" city under God's judgment in Isa 24:10).

ISAIAH 42

C. THE GOD WHO CONFRONTS THE FAILURES OF HIS PEOPLE (42:1-25)

Chapters 40 and 41 abound with encouragement for Israel in spite of (and because of) the backdrop of the Babylonian exile. Each of these chapters possesses an a-b-a structure in which the outer frame of encouragement surrounds the heart of the chapter that provides the real basis for Israel's confidence. In chapter 40 that basis is the incomparable majesty of God and in chapter 41 it is God's unwavering commitment to his servant Israel.

Chapter 42 also manifests an a-b-a structure, and at its heart once again Isaiah emphasizes the awesome nature of God. In this case, however, the outer frame develops the notion of the servant introduced in 41:8-9. The servant is a glorious figure in the opening of the chapter, but at the end he is deaf and blind. The tension created here will not be resolved until the climactic portrayal of the servant in 52:13–53:12.

SPECIAL NOTE ON HOW TO APPROACH THE SERVANT SONGS

Isaiah 42 introduces the first of the "servant songs," the passages in which most interpret the servant as a messianic figure. Scholars generally agree on four such servant songs, although they differ as to the precise textual boundaries of each one: 42:1-4 (some would extend it to verse 7 or verse 9); 49:1-6 (perhaps through verse 7 or verse 13); 50:4-9 (or 4-11); and 52:13–53:12.

A predisposition to interpret these passages in a messianic fashion (especially from a Christian perspective in which the identity of the Messiah is already known) can hinder one's ability to hear Isaiah's message clearly. Isaiah explicitly labels Israel as God's servant, yet he presents a dramatic contrast between Israel's spiritual condition and effectiveness and that of the one who appears in the servant songs. Every student of Isaiah needs to feel this tension in order to appreciate more fully Isaiah's message.

This commentary will strive to allow Isaiah's picture of the servant to unfold naturally. The cumulative material will be considered along the way, but no attempt will be made to draw final conclusions until after the final servant song is heard.

1. He Calls His Servant to Accomplish His Purpose (42:1-9)

¹"Here is my servant, whom I uphold, / my chosen one in whom I delight; / I will put my Spirit on him / and he will bring justice to the nations. / ²He will not shout or cry out, / or raise his voice in the streets. / ³A bruised reed he will not break, / and a smoldering wick he will not snuff out. / In faithfulness he will bring forth justice; / ⁴he will not falter or be discouraged / till he establishes justice on earth. / In his law the islands will put their hope."

⁵This is what God the LORD says— / he who created the heavens and stretched them out, / who spread out the earth and all that comes out of it, / who gives breath to its people, / and life to those who walk on it: / ⁶"I, the LORD, have called you in righteousness; / I will take hold of your hand. / I will keep you and will make you / to be a covenant for the people / and a light for the Gentiles, / ⁷to open eyes that are blind, / to free captives from prison / and to release from the dungeon those who sit in darkness.

⁸"I am the LORD; that is my name! / I will not give my glory to another / or my praise to idols. / ⁹See, the former things have taken place, / and new things I declare; / before they spring into being / I announce them to you."

42:1-4 Although this passage does not specifically equate the **servant** with Israel as in 41:8, several connections with chapter 41 point in that direction.[1] First, God promises to **uphold** him (v. 1), using

---

[1]It should be pointed out that the use of a singular term like "servant," or singular pronouns like "he" or "him," when referring to the nation Israel is not a problem. God sent Moses to tell Pharaoh, "Let my people go" (Exod

the same root (תמך, *tmk*) that he does in the promise to Israel in 41:10. Second, he parallels the servant with **my chosen one**, repeating the root (בחר, *bḥr*) found in the parallelism of 41:8. The allusion in 41:8 to Abraham, the one through whom all peoples on earth will be blessed (Gen 12:3), links Israel with the servant's role as "a covenant for the people and a light for the Gentiles" in verse 6. Finally, the reassuring note that the One who upholds the servant foretells and controls history (v. 9) repeats one of the dominant themes of chapter 41.

God's commitment to and purpose for the servant parallel God's relationship with Israel, but the character of the servant does not resemble the Israel of Isaiah's day (cf. vv. 18ff.). The servant is one in whom God can **delight**. He is one whom God considers fit to empower with his **Spirit**. Like the description of God in chapter 42, he is powerful enough to **bring justice to the nations**, yet he is also tender and compassionate. Verses 2-3 indicate that he is not interested in making noise and calling attention to himself, nor in leaving behind the weak and wounded as he marches to victory. The **bruised reed** and **smoldering wick** represent that which has been weakened and has almost come to an end. The **justice** that the servant will establish is not like the savage imposition of order by a totalitarian regime, but the kind of just and compassionate society that God has sought to model in Israel. Where Israel has failed, the servant will by his **faithfulness** and endurance lead the **islands** (i.e., the distant nations) to **put their hope** in the **law**, fulfilling the vision of 2:2-4.

Proponents of the divided authorship of Isaiah point out the contrast between the critical role of the Davidic messiah in the first part of the book (cf. 9:6-7; 11:1ff.) and the emphasis on the servant in the later chapters. Isaiah does not abandon the notion of the Davidic covenant, however (cf. 55:3), and the description of the servant bears numerous parallels to the descriptions of the Davidic messiah. Two notable examples from chapter 42 are his empowerment by God's Spirit (cf. 11:2), his righteous and faithful character (cf. 11:5), and his role in establishing justice on the earth (cf. 9:7; 11:3-4).

5:1; 7:16), but he also said, "Let my *son* go" (Exod 4:23). Even the designation "Israel" refers both to an individual and to a nation.

42:5-7 The servant's faithfulness and effectiveness do not overshadow the fact that he owes his success to the God **who created the heavens and . . . the earth** and **gives breath to its people**. The one who gives and sustains life guarantees the servant's success because God's plan to give **light** to the **Gentiles** in their blindness and freedom to the **captives** in the **prison** of **darkness** hinges on the work of the servant. In a sense God intends to create a new world through the work of the servant because the present order holds little hope of life for the Gentiles.

42:8 Life is found in relationship with God. Israel has been blessed with the opportunity to experience this life through the covenant relationship (cf. Deut 30:15ff.), but to this point the other nations have for the most part not enjoyed the same opportunity. God will not simply *establish* a covenant relationship with the Gentiles through the servant; he will cause him "to *be* a covenant for the people." He will be "the means through whom people will come into a covenant relation with the Lord."[2] God cares about the nations, but he also acts for the sake of his **name**. In their darkness the Gentiles worship impersonal aspects of the creation rather than the personal Creator. God's promise that **I will not give my glory to another or my praise to idols** is closely connected to his promise to defeat Sennacherib. God will no more allow nonexistent gods to usurp his place than he allowed the Assyrian king to overstep his bounds. God defends his name by destroying those who blaspheme it, but he also does so by making it possible for the nations to call on his name for salvation rather than turn to empty idols.

2. He Merits the World's Praise (42:10-17)

¹⁰**Sing to the LORD a new song, / his praise from the ends of the earth, / you who go down to the sea, and all that is in it, / you islands, and all who live in them. /** ¹¹**Let the desert and its towns raise their voices; / let the settlements where Kedar lives rejoice. / Let the people of Sela sing for joy; / let them shout from the mountaintops. /** ¹²**Let them give glory to the LORD / and proclaim his praise in the islands. /** ¹³**The LORD will march out like a mighty man, / like a warrior he will stir up his zeal; / with a shout he will raise the battle cry / and will triumph over his enemies.**

---

[2]Motyer, *Prophecy*, p. 322.

¹⁴"For a long time I have kept silent, / I have been quiet and held myself back. / But now, like a woman in childbirth, / I cry out, I gasp and pant. / ¹⁵I will lay waste the mountains and hills / and dry up all their vegetation; / I will turn rivers into islands / and dry up the pools. / ¹⁶I will lead the blind by ways they have not known, / along unfamiliar paths I will guide them; / I will turn the darkness into light before them / and make the rough places smooth. / These are the things I will do; / I will not forsake them. / ¹⁷But those who trust in idols, / who say to images, 'You are our gods,' / will be turned back in utter shame.

42:10-12 What new act of God calls forth this **new song**? The promise to extend the covenant blessings to all nations goes back at least to Abraham. The work of Cyrus and the ministry of the servant, however, bring new clarity and a greater sense of imminence to God's promise. They also cause him to receive **praise from the ends of the earth**, fulfilling verses 8-9. The call for praise from earth's most remote bounds makes the mention of **Kedar** and **Sela** in the **desert** of Edom seem anticlimactic by comparison. The explanation may be that Edom's inclusion "shows that the Lord's triumph is triumph indeed, even over inveterate hostility. . . ."[3]

42:13-14 Isaiah uses two pairs of images in verses 13-17 to describe God's work for which he is worthy of praise. In the first pair he is a **warrior** who **will triumph over his enemies**, but also a **woman in childbirth**. Although these pictures appear incompatible, they actually complement each other. Perhaps they point to the two agents through whom God will move his purpose forward. Cyrus conquers in the military sense, a necessary work to restore Israel to the land of promise. The servant restores the covenant relationship, thus extending life to the nations. The long period of silence in verse 14 links the two pictures together. It fits better with the gestation period of the pregnant woman, but it provides important insights into the warrior God and his "delays" as well. The verb for **held myself back** (אתאפק, 'eth'appaq) appears in Genesis 43:31 and 45:1 for Joseph's struggle to withhold his identity from his brothers in Egypt.[4] Just as there is a proper time to give birth, so there is a proper time for God to act. He is eager to act on behalf of his pur-

---

[3] Ibid., p. 324.
[4] Cf. Wolf, *Interpreting Isaiah*, pp. 192-193.

pose in the world, but his restraint reflects his wisdom and self-control and should therefore call for praise.

42:15-16 The second pair of seemingly incompatible pictures appears in verses 15-16. In verse 15 God destroys everything in the landscape before him,[5] whereas in verse 16 he is making **the rough places smooth** in order to **lead the blind by ways they have not known**. Once again, however, there is a destructive as well as a constructive side to building roads. It may not be necessary to choose here whether God is working on behalf of the blind of the nations (vv. 6-7) or the blind in Israel (vv. 18-20).[6] As in 40:3-5, God will remove all obstacles that stand in the way of the accomplishment of his purpose.

42:17 God promises in 41:17 that he will not forsake the poor and needy. At the end of 42:16, he promises that he "will not forsake" the things he has committed to do. He is compassionate and powerful and reliable. The song of praise ends with a note of contrast between God and the **images** that many acknowledge as their **gods**. Since there is no reality behind these images, **those who trust in idols . . . will be turned back in utter shame**. God does not sing his own praises out of vanity, but out of a deep desire to help lead the blind to the light. His radical commitment to this task makes the plight of those who choose idols instead all the more tragic.

3. He Seeks to Purify His Disobedient Servant (42:18-25)

[18]"Hear, you deaf; / look, you blind, and see! / [19]Who is blind but my servant, / and deaf like the messenger I send? / Who is blind like the one committed to me, / blind like the servant of the LORD? / [20]You have seen many things, but have paid no attention; / your ears are open, but you hear nothing." / [21]It pleased the LORD / for the sake of his righteousness / to make his law great and glorious. / [22]But this is a people plundered and looted, / all of them trapped in pits / or hidden away in prisons. / They have become

---

[5]The contrast between verse 15 and 41:18-19 illustrates the highly figurative nature of this language.

[6]A close connection is established between the servant's work on behalf of the blind in vv. 6-7 and God's work in leading the blind in verse 16. Cf. Motyer, *Prophecy*, pp. 324-325; Oswalt, *Isaiah* 2, pp. 126-127.

plunder, / with no one to rescue them; / they have been made loot, / with no one to say, "Send them back."

²³Which of you will listen to this / or pay close attention in time to come? / ²⁴Who handed Jacob over to become loot, / and Israel to the plunderers? / Was it not the LORD, / against whom we have sinned? / For they would not follow his ways; / they did not obey his law. / ²⁵So he poured out on them his burning anger, / the violence of war. / It enveloped them in flames, yet they did not understand; / it consumed them, but they did not take it to heart.

42:18-21 The last section of the chapter introduces a significant challenge to the great work of God described in the previous sections. In 41:8 God identifies Israel as his servant. In 42:1-7 God calls his servant to serve as a light for the Gentiles. Yet how can the servant fulfill his calling when his blindness and deafness exceed that of all others? At Isaiah's calling, God informed him of Israel's disturbing lack of spiritual perception (6:9-10). There as here, Israel's condition is described as self-imposed. Their eyes and ears have been exposed to **many things**, but they **have paid no attention**.[7] For his own sake God has made **his law great and glorious** before Israel, but his people have not embraced God's ways and thus have not confirmed them before the rest of the world.[8]

42:22-25 As a result of this failure, Israel has not become a light to the nations, but instead **a people plundered and looted**. They have **no one to rescue them** because God is the only one who can do so and he is the very one who has **handed Jacob over to become loot**. God has not permanently abandoned Israel, but he is using the hardships he has imposed to overcome his people's blindness and deafness. Unfortunately, however, even though their distress **enveloped them in flames** to the point that **it consumed them**, they still **did not understand** or **take it to heart**.

Both Israel's hardness of heart and God's "alien work" (28:21) of warring against his people to turn them back are familiar concepts in Isaiah. Here again God highlights the gap between the ideal

---

[7]Literally, they have not "kept" or "guarded" (שׁמר, *šmr*) what they have seen.

[8]Cf. Deuteronomy 4, especially verses 5-8, wherein Israel's observance of God's laws would show their "wisdom and understanding to the nations, who will hear about all these decrees and say, 'Surely this great nation is a wise and understanding people.'"

servant and the reality of Israel as God's servant. God's immediate response in chapter 43 is to reaffirm his commitment to Israel, but the ultimate question remains: How can God accomplish the great work he has assigned to the servant when his servant Israel is oblivious to the consuming flames of God's discipline?

ISAIAH 43

D. THE GOD WHO REDEEMS HIS PEOPLE (43:1-28)

In reassuring the "worm Jacob" that he will help his people in their weakness, God refers to himself as their "Redeemer" (41:14). The concept of redemption recurs frequently throughout Isaiah 40–66.[1] Perhaps nowhere does it strike a more welcome chord than at the outset of this chapter, following the painful reminder of Israel's miserable failure in 42:18-25. An understanding of God's redemptive nature plays a vital role in maintaining Israel's belief that God still intends to work through his people. Isaiah 43 details several implications of God's role as Israel's Redeemer.

1. He Is with His People in Their Distress (43:1-7)

¹But now, this is what the LORD says— / he who created you, O Jacob, / he who formed you, O Israel: / "Fear not, for I have redeemed you; / I have summoned you by name; you are mine. / ²When you pass through the waters, / I will be with you; / and when you pass through the rivers, / they will not sweep over you. / When you walk through the fire, / you will not be burned; / the flames will not set you ablaze. / ³For I am the LORD, your God, / the Holy One of Israel, your Savior; / I give Egypt for your ransom, / Cush[a] and Seba in your stead. / ⁴Since you are precious and honored in my sight, / and because I love you, / I will give men in exchange for you, / and people in exchange for your life. / ⁵Do not be afraid, for I am with you; / I will bring your children from the east / and gather you from the west. / ⁶I will say to the north, 'Give them up!' / and to the south, 'Do not

---

[1] Cf. 43:1,14; 44:6,22-24; 47:4; 48:17,20; 49:7,26; 50:2; 51:10; 52:3,9; 54:5,8; 59:20; 60:16; 62:12; 63:4,9,16.

hold them back.' /Bring my sons from afar /and my daughters from the ends of the earth— /⁷everyone who is called by my name, /whom I created for my glory, /whom I formed and made."

ᵃ3 That is, the upper Nile region

43:1 But now links these verses to the end of the previous chapter and also signals a welcome contrast to the seemingly hopeless situation described there. Israel's hope derives from God's commitment to his people as evidenced in his works of creation and redemption. God's creation of the world was a loving act that established his status as owner of all he made. Yet humanity rebelled against God and introduced sin, decay, and death into his creation. God showed even greater love by breaking into his creation to overturn the effects of sin and restore humanity to a right relationship with him. A key element of that work was his "creation" of Israel as a covenant people, which involved redeeming and calling them. The verbs **created**, **formed**, **have redeemed**, and **have summoned** all refer to a completed action in the past. The primary historical referent is the exodus, the central redemptive event of the Old Testament. God calls Israel back to this event, not as a mere history lesson, but as a reminder of the investment he has made in them. Additionally, the exodus and Israel's subsequent history reveal that redemption is not a one-time event at the center of the nature of God.

If the original creation established God's ownership of all, his work of redemption doubly affirms his claim. After God delivered Israel from Egypt, he invited them into the covenant relationship, promising them that if they would be faithful, "then out of all nations you will be my treasured possession. Although the whole earth is mine, you will be for me a kingdom of priests and a holy nation" (Exod 19:3; cf. 1 Cor 6:19-20). In Isaiah 43:1 God reminds Israel that **you are mine**.[2] The concept of ownership, however, does not fully convey the context of redemption. God expresses his goal of personal presence and mutual relationship in Leviticus 26:12 – "I will walk among you and be your God, and you will be my people." Israel can see this personal context in the role of the kinsman redeemer, the one who is responsible for helping a relative who faces slavery or loss of property due to debt, or a married brother who dies childless. God thus provides an opening word of reassurance to Israel that is rich with historical significance.

---

[2]"Mine" is in an emphatic position in the Hebrew: "Mine you are."

43:2 God's redemptive nature does not mean that his people will not **pass through the waters** or **walk through the fire**, but his promise that **I will be with you** assures them that they will survive. The mention of fire may look back to the flames of God's burning anger in 42:25 although it would have a broader reference as well. Fire and flood figuratively describe various calamities, but the experience of Shadrach, Meshach, and Abednego in Daniel 3 provides a more literal application of God's promise of protection.

43:3-4 Redemption involves the payment of a price to effect someone's release, so the related notion of **ransom** raises the issue of the price for Israel's redemption. In the original exodus the Egyptians paid a heavy price due to Pharaoh's stubbornness, culminating with the death of their firstborn.[3] God promises that his **love** for his people is so great that he will pay any price to save them again. The reference here may be to the nations God will give over to Cyrus in exchange for his role in returning Israel from exile. This tactic may seem unfair, but God is able to bring about the judgment the wicked deserve in such a way that it coincides with and benefits God's redemptive purpose.[4] He did so in his judgment of the Pharaoh of the exodus and the Canaanites during the conquest. Any "favoritism" God manifests toward Israel stems from Israel's calling to bring God's salvation to all nations. Oswalt points out that God's redemption "was ultimately worked out in him who knew no sin becoming sin for our sakes (2 Cor. 5:21) and giving 'his life as a ransom for many' (Matt. 20:28). It was ultimately not Egypt and Nubia that God gave in ransom, but his own Son. . . ."[5] Even in the original context of Isaiah the extent of God's love for Israel in light of his knowledge of her true nature reveals his grace powerfully.[6]

43:5-7 The prophesied exile will result in a scattering of the descendants of Isaiah's original audience. God therefore promises to regather them from all points of the compass and **the ends of the earth**. God speaks first of **your children**, but then he refers to them as **my sons** and **my daughters**, reflecting again the personal nature of the covenant relationship. The fact that these children bear God's **name** says even more about his commitment to them. He **created** a

---

[3]The NIV's "I give" in verse 3 is more accurately "I gave" (נָתַתִּי, *nāthattî*).
[4]Cf. Prov 21:18 — The wicked become a ransom for the righteous.
[5]Oswalt, *Isaiah* 2, p. 140.
[6]Ibid.

covenant people for his **glory**, a theme to which Isaiah returns in the next chapter. For the sake of his name (i.e., reputation), God will not allow his people to languish in exile but will return them to a position where they can fulfill his purpose for them. This basis for God's actions does not invalidate the personal relationship he seeks with his people, but it does bring together his sovereignty (he will accomplish his will in spite of Israel's sinfulness) and his grace (he extends favor to his people that they do not deserve).

2. He Establishes Witnesses from His People (43:8-13)

⁸Lead out those who have eyes but are blind, / who have ears but are deaf. / ⁹All the nations gather together / and the peoples assemble. / Which of them foretold this / and proclaimed to us the former things? / Let them bring in their witnesses to prove they were right, / so that others may hear and say, "It is true." / ¹⁰"You are my witnesses," declares the LORD, / "and my servant whom I have chosen, / so that you may know and believe me / and understand that I am he. / Before me no god was formed, / nor will there be one after me. / ¹¹I, even I, am the LORD, / and apart from me there is no savior. / ¹²I have revealed and saved and proclaimed— / I, and not some foreign god among you. / You are my witnesses," declares the LORD, "that I am God. / ¹³Yes, and from ancient days I am he. / No one can deliver out of my hand. / When I act, who can reverse it?"

43:8-10 God's ability both to make use of his frail people for his purposes and to bless them in the process emerges in this section. As he once again summons the **nations** into a courtroom scene, God and the nations are to call **witnesses** to testify as to who controls history. The fact that God can win his case with **blind** and **deaf** witnesses reveals the strength of his case and the utter lack of evidence on the other side. God parallels **my witnesses** with **my servant** in verse 10, reinforcing the identification of the witnesses as Israel. Even though Israel lacks spiritual perception, the continued existence of God's people, especially in the return from exile, bears witness to God's work on their behalf.[7] A major purpose of this work, in fact, is not to bear witness *through* Israel but *to* Israel (**so that you may know and believe and understand that I am he**).

---

[7]Israel never actually gives verbal testimony regarding God's salvation.

43:11-13 God's activity on behalf of Israel is described by three verbs — **revealed and saved and proclaimed**. Motyer sees the sequence of these verbs as significant in that "divine speech comes first, setting out what the coming events will be and what they will mean."[8] No **foreign god**[9] can provide evidence of any such activity. Moreover, neither the nations nor their gods can **deliver** anyone from God (cf. Deut 32:39) or **reverse** his actions. In light of the total imbalance of this evidence and God's obvious commitment to his people, why would any Israelite turn to idols?

3. He Makes a Way for His People (43:14-21)

¹⁴This is what the LORD says— / your Redeemer, the Holy One of Israel: / "For your sake I will send to Babylon / and bring down as fugitives all the Babylonians,ª / in the ships in which they took pride. / ¹⁵I am the LORD, your Holy One, / Israel's Creator, your King."
¹⁶This is what the LORD says— / he who made a way through the sea, / a path through the mighty waters, / ¹⁷who drew out the chariots and horses, / the army and reinforcements together, / and they lay there, never to rise again, / extinguished, snuffed out like a wick: / ¹⁸"Forget the former things; / do not dwell on the past. / ¹⁹See, I am doing a new thing! / Now it springs up; do you not perceive it? / I am making a way in the desert / and streams in the wasteland. / ²⁰The wild animals honor me, / the jackals and the owls, / because I provide water in the desert / and streams in the wasteland, / to give drink to my people, my chosen, / ²¹the people I formed for myself / that they may proclaim my praise.

ª*14* Or *Chaldeans*

43:14-21 The reference to God as Israel's **Redeemer** sets the stage for a return to an exodus motif as God looks to the next phase of his long history of deliverance. He first describes the flight of the **Babylonians**[10] in **ships** down the Euphrates at the approach of

---

[8]Motyer, *Prophecy,* p. 335.
[9]The NIV adds the word "god;" the Hebrew simply has "foreign" (זָר, *zār*).
[10]As the NIV footnote indicates, the Hebrew literally says "Chaldeans," the name of a ruling dynasty in Babylon (which includes Nebuchadnezzar, the king who destroyed Jerusalem and the temple). Sometimes this designation is used as a synonym for "Babylonians."

Cyrus. The fall of Babylon, however, only prepares for Israel's return from exile. God promises that just as he **made a way through the sea** for the departure from Egypt, so now he will make **a way in the desert** for the exiles to return to Jerusalem.

God calls attention to the "first exodus" to reassure Israel of his ability to bring about a second. God's past actions provide the foundation for his present and future works because his nature is unchanging. In another sense, however, he wants Israel to **forget the former things** so that they can **perceive** the **new thing** he is about to do. Knowledge of the past can limit the imagination, and God's capacity to act knows no limits.[11] In the exodus from Egypt, God created a dry **path through the mighty waters**; in the return from exile he will **provide water in the desert**. The latter description not only anticipates God's provision for the travelers from Babylon, but also points figuratively to something even greater. Israel's return from exile is related to God's larger purpose of restoring life to a barren world (cf. 35:1-10; 44:2-5). **The wild animals honor** God for the way he provides for his chosen people. The question is whether or not the people God created **that they may proclaim [his] praise** will recognize what he has done and fulfill the purpose for which they were made.

4. He Forgives the Sins of His People (43:22-28)

²²**"Yet you have not called upon me, O Jacob, / you have not wearied yourselves for me, O Israel. / ²³You have not brought me sheep for burnt offerings, / nor honored me with your sacrifices.**

I have not burdened you with grain offerings / nor wearied you with demands for incense. / ²⁴You have not bought any fragrant calamus for me, / or lavished on me the fat of your sacrifices. / But you have burdened me with your sins / and wearied me with your offenses.

²⁵**"I, even I, am he who blots out / your transgressions, for my own sake, / and remembers your sins no more. / ²⁶Review the past for me, / let us argue the matter together; / state the case for your innocence. / ²⁷Your first father sinned; / your spokesmen rebelled**

---

[11]Jesus' teaching about the danger of putting new wine in old wineskins (Matt 9:16-17) addresses the resistance he faced by those who were so bound by the past that they could not see God at work in his ministry.

against me. / ²⁸So I will disgrace the dignitaries of your temple, / and I will consign Jacob to destruction^a /and Israel to scorn.

^a*28* The Hebrew term refers to the irrevocable giving over of things or persons to the LORD, often by totally destroying them.

43:22-24 These verses answer the question raised at the end of the previous section in the negative. Just as chapter 42 concludes with a description of Israel's spiritual insensitivity, so this chapter closes with an indictment of Israel's worship. Praise, the purpose for which God formed his people (v. 21), lies at the heart of true worship, but Israel's worship fails to accomplish that purpose. The wild animals may honor God, but Israel's sacrifices do not.

A superficial reading of these verses would imply that the problem is Israel's failure to bring offerings to God. As in 1:10-20, however, the problem is neither the quantity nor the quality of the sacrifices, but the quality of the relationship between the alleged worshipers and God (cf. also 58:1-14). The emphatic placement of the pronoun **me** in verse 22 ("*me* you have not called upon") hints at the outset that the issue here is the failure of the offerings to please God.[12] Two verbs that recur in verses 22-24 further confirm this interpretation: burden (יָגַע, *yḡʿ*) and weary (הֶעֱבִיד, *heʿĕḇîd*). The first verb could be translated "enslave." God says that he has not **burdened** Israel with **grain offerings**, but Israel has **burdened** God with her **sins**.[13] The sacrifices have never been intended by God as enforced labor, but rather a means of grace. Israel has grown weary of God (v. 22),[14] but God never intended to weary Israel **with demands for incense**.[15] In the end, Israel has **wearied** God with her **offenses**.

---

[12]Motyer, *Prophecy*, p. 338. Motyer provides an excellent treatment of the issues involved in this passage and their implications for a proper view of worship.

[13]Ibid. Perhaps it is placing too much weight on the basic notion of the verb here to speak of Israel's worship as an attempt to "enslave" God. As the following comments will indicate, however, Israel's approach to God constitutes an attempt to manipulate him and is thus labeled a sin.

[14]There is no negative in the second line of verse 22 in the Hebrew. Perhaps the NIV translators inserted the word "not" to make the second line parallel with the first. Without the negative the verse would indicate that Israel has not (truly/effectively) called upon God because she has grown weary of him.

[15]Incense and calamus (a fragrant spice added to the anointing oil) and fat represent some of the choicest elements of offerings made to God.

Religious practices that arise out of anything other than a meaningful relationship with God inevitably become burdensome and wearying to the worshiper. Such practices have the same effect on God, because they miss God's goal for them — the nurturing and sustaining of relationship. In addition, empty rituals attempt to manipulate God for the worshiper's ends. This approach dishonors God and transforms something intended as a blessing into the **sins** and **offenses** of verse 24.

43:25 Isaiah occasionally uses the technique of an abrupt transition to highlight God's intervention at the darkest hour or when it appears least deserved.[16] Verse 25 certainly qualifies for that category. The two dramatic images of blotting out sin and remembering it no more emphasize the total removal of past transgressions from further consideration in the relationship. Nothing in the context has created any expectation of this good news. That lack of foundation, however, points even more clearly to what the text itself states. The repetition of the emphatic pronoun **I** and the words **for my own sake** root Israel's forgiveness solely in the grace of God.

43:26-27 Many readers of Scripture fail to see evidence of God's grace in the Old Testament. As God now calls Israel into court, he challenges his people to examine their **past** to see if they can argue their **innocence**. The result of the search is that their sin extends back to their **first father** (either Abraham or Jacob) and has even infected their **spokesmen**[17] (priests and prophets). God is remarkably patient and loving toward the patriarchs and then Israel throughout the Old Testament. God's offer of pardon in verse 25 is not extended to a generation that has departed from a prevailing standard of faithfulness; it is offered to those who fit Israel's historic profile. For God to maintain his faithfulness to such a people and to work through them to redeem the nations is truly an act of grace that overarches the entire Old Testament (and continues throughout the church age as well).

43:28 God graciously maintains his relationship with Israel in the Old Testament, but as an aspect of his grace he steps in to bring judgment upon the impenitent in order to limit the effects of their

---

[16]Cf. the transition in chapter 8 between verses 5-8 and verses 9-10.
[17]The NIV translates the same word (מֵלִיץ, *mēlîṣ*) as "mediator" in Job 33:23.

evil. In the same way in verse 28 he speaks of disgracing[18] **the dignitaries of your temple** and consigning **Jacob to destruction**.[19] Not even the catastrophic desecration of the temple and destruction of Jerusalem by the Babylonians will thwart God's determination to be gracious to his people. In fact, apart from those painful events one could argue that Israel would never become sufficiently humble to receive grace. These challenging ideas cry out for greater elaboration, which Isaiah supplies to some extent as his message continues to unfold.

---

[18]The word (חלל, *ḥll*) literally refers to profaning or defiling, a particularly disturbing prospect for priests.

[19]In another painful image, God applies the term to Israel that was used of the ritual destruction of the Canaanites (חרם, *ḥērem*).

ISAIAH 44

E. THE GOD WHO GLORIFIES HIMSELF IN HIS PEOPLE (44:1-28)

Isaiah has reminded Israel of God's determination to forgive her, but he also points out how deeply ingrained her sins are. The conflict between Israel's calling as God's servant/witness and the blindness and deafness that block the fulfillment of her calling remains unresolved. If Israel is going to bring God glory, God must do something to break through this impasse.

1. He Pours His Spirit on His People (44:1-5)

¹"But now listen, O Jacob, my servant, / Israel, whom I have chosen. /²This is what the LORD says— / he who made you, who formed you in the womb, / and who will help you: / Do not be afraid, O Jacob, my servant, / Jeshurun, whom I have chosen. /³For I will pour water on the thirsty land, / and streams on the dry ground; / I will pour out my Spirit on your offspring, / and my blessing on your descendants. /⁴They will spring up like grass in a meadow, / like poplar trees by flowing streams. /⁵One will say, 'I belong to the LORD'; / another will call himself by the name of Jacob; / still another will write on his hand, 'The LORD's,' / and will take the name Israel.

Some view these verses as the conclusion to the preceding section. They fit equally well, however, as part of an a-b-a pattern in chapter 44, as is true of chapters 40–42. In verses 1-5 God promises to renew his people by his Spirit, and in verses 21-28 he promises to fulfill what he has said through the prophets about his purpose for Israel. At the center of the chapter is an extended sarcastic dismissal of idolatry. The structure of the chapter thus dramatically contrasts the impotence of idolatry with God's ability to do the seemingly impossible through Israel.

44:1-2 God begins this opening message of encouragement (**Do not be afraid**) by multiplying now-familiar descriptors of his relationship with Israel (**my servant, . . . whom I have chosen, . . . who made you, who formed you in the womb, and who will help you**). He adds a new label for Israel, however, in **Jeshurun**, a name drawn from the song of Moses (Deut 32:15) and Moses' blessing of the tribes (33:5,26). The name derives from the root for "upright," but the true significance of its use here more likely lies in its association with the exodus. God has created, saved, called, and sustained his people in the past, so he possesses the love and the power to revive them in the future.

44:3-4 These verses confirm the figurative interpretation of 43:19-21. God's promise to **pour water on the thirsty land** parallels his commitment to **pour out my Spirit on your offspring, and my blessing on your descendants**. He wants those who face the prospect of exile to know that he still cares about and has a purpose for them and their children. Ezekiel also associates the gathering of the exiles into a faithful and obedient people with the granting of God's Spirit that will replace hearts of stone with hearts of flesh (Ezek 36:24ff.).[1] Only the God who "breathed the breath of life" into the first human being (Gen 2:7) can by his Spirit revive those who are spiritually dead.[2]

In spite of God's promises, Israel's struggles before the time of renewal will lead many to experience discouragement and disillusionment. Feeling that the great promises made to their fathers lack credibility, they will be tempted to distance themselves from their identity. In that better day, however, those who experience God's blessings will be eager to say **I belong to the LORD**. Once again, only God can accomplish such a reversal of circumstances on behalf of those who are hopelessly weak and discouraged.

---

[1]Webb (*Message*, p. 179, n. 63) refers to the idea of "pouring" in Isaiah 32:15; Ezekiel 39:29; Joel 2:28f.; and Zechariah 12:10 and their fulfillment in the outpouring of the Holy Spirit on the day of Pentecost (Acts 2:16-17).

[2]Cf. Ezekiel 37 and the vision of the dry bones that come to life.

2. He Exposes Idolatry before His People (44:6-20)

⁶"This is what the LORD says— / Israel's King and Redeemer, the LORD Almighty: / I am the first and I am the last; / apart from me there is no God. / ⁷Who then is like me? Let him proclaim it. / Let him declare and lay out before me / what has happened since I established my ancient people, / and what is yet to come— / yes, let him foretell what will come. / ⁸Do not tremble, do not be afraid. / Did I not proclaim this and foretell it long ago? / You are my witnesses. Is there any God besides me? / No, there is no other Rock; I know not one."

⁹All who make idols are nothing, / and the things they treasure are worthless. / Those who would speak up for them are blind; / they are ignorant, to their own shame. / ¹⁰Who shapes a god and casts an idol, / which can profit him nothing? / ¹¹He and his kind will be put to shame; / craftsmen are nothing but men. / Let them all come together and take their stand; / they will be brought down to terror and infamy.

¹²The blacksmith takes a tool / and works with it in the coals; / he shapes an idol with hammers, / he forges it with the might of his arm. / He gets hungry and loses his strength; / he drinks no water and grows faint. / ¹³The carpenter measures with a line / and makes an outline with a marker; / he roughs it out with chisels / and marks it with compasses. / He shapes it in the form of man, / of man in all his glory, / that it may dwell in a shrine. / ¹⁴He cut down cedars, / or perhaps took a cypress or oak. / He let it grow among the trees of the forest, / or planted a pine, and the rain made it grow. / ¹⁵It is man's fuel for burning; / some of it he takes and warms himself, / he kindles a fire and bakes bread. / But he also fashions a god and worships it; / he makes an idol and bows down to it. / ¹⁶Half of the wood he burns in the fire; / over it he prepares his meal, / he roasts his meat and eats his fill. / He also warms himself and says, / "Ah! I am warm; I see the fire." / ¹⁷From the rest he makes a god, his idol; / he bows down to it and worships. / He prays to it and says, / "Save me; you are my god." / ¹⁸They know nothing, they understand nothing; / their eyes are plastered over so they cannot see, / and their minds closed so they cannot understand. / ¹⁹No one stops to think, / no one has the knowledge or understanding to say, / "Half of it I used for fuel; / I even baked bread over its coals, / I roasted meat and I ate. / Shall

I make a detestable thing from what is left? / Shall I bow down to a block of wood?" / ²⁰He feeds on ashes, a deluded heart misleads him; /he cannot save himself, or say, / "Is not this thing in my right hand a lie?"

44:6 After another description of his status in relation to Israel (**Israel's King and Redeemer, the LORD Almighty**), God once more demonstrates his superiority over the idol gods who, though they are nonexistent, still exert great power over those too blind to see the truth. God's attacks may appear to be harsh and cruel, but they are actually loving if they allow the blind to see and be healed.

44:7-8 God begins his assault by calling for evidence that anyone else in the past had foretold **what has happened since I established my ancient people**, or if anyone else can **foretell what will come**. Israel can testify to what God has done, but the absence of other witnesses leads to the conclusion that **there is no other Rock**[3] upon whom anyone can rely for strength and stability.

44:9-11 Much of the emphasis in this passage falls on those **who make idols**. By contrast, in verse 21 God points out to Israel that "I have made you." These idols are thus dependent upon man for their very existence. "There would be no god if the would-be worshiper had not made it!"[4] Those who craft the idols suffer from delusion and fail to grasp the irony of the situation.[5] Their creations are **worthless**; in fact, they can bring only **shame** to their makers. This shame comes when time and circumstance verify what God is saying here, but the passage hints that God brings them to shame (**they will be brought down to terror and infamy**) due to their rejection of him.

44:12-13a Verses 12-17 further expose the folly of idolatry by elaborating on the process by which the **blacksmith** and the **carpenter** do their "creative" work in metal and wood, respectively. The activity of the blacksmith reveals that the idol he forges owes its origin to **the might of his arm**, yet the creator suffers from hunger and

---

[3]The picture of God as the "Rock" is common in Psalms, but this reference may be another allusion (like Jeshurun) to the song of Moses in Deuteronomy 32 (cf. vv. 4,15,18,30,31,37).

[4]Motyer, *Prophecy*, p. 345.

[5]While the focus in this text seems to be on the pagan nations, the point is directed to Israel in her dangerous tendency to walk in the blind ways of the idolaters.

thirst so that he **loses his strength** and **grows faint**. Can that which is made be more powerful than the one who made it? By contrast, God sustains his people by the power of his arm (cf. 40:10), and he gives strength to his people because he never grows weary (cf. 40:28-31). Perhaps this picture also anticipates the burdensome nature of idolatry for its adherents (cf. 46:1-7).

44:13b Two ironic features emerge in the work of the carpenter. Verse 13 describes his creation as a human product that in the end looks like **man in all his glory**. God has in fact glorified man in the order and nature of creation (cf. Psalm 8). When man seeks to become God, that glory turns into shame. God created man in his image, but in every form of idolatry man inevitably creates a god in his image. One of the marks of the inspiration of the Bible is the fact that the God it reveals stands apart from what he has made. He is not like a god that man would create. The Bible clearly prohibits worshiping the creation rather than the Creator, but approaching the Creator as if he possesses the limitations of the creation is equally serious. In Psalm 50:21 God rebukes those who think he cannot see or does not care about their hypocritical worship by saying, "You thought I was altogether like you."

44:14-17 The second irony related to the carpenter involves the material with which he works. The raw material of the blacksmith ultimately derives from God as well, but the fact that the carpenter cuts down living **trees** that have been nurtured by the **rain** emphasizes how he takes what God has created and from it crafts a god to which he **bows down** in worship. God made the trees for the benefit of humanity, so there is nothing wrong with using them as **fuel for burning**. They may provide warmth and a means for preparing food. Yet to fashion a god from the same tree from which one has received God's blessing is both illogical and sinful. When the carpenter prays to the piece of wood, **"Save me; you are my god,"** he does not realize that he has made it impossible for the only true and living God to save him.

44:18-20 This section closes with a reiteration of the tragically deluded state of the idolater. Verse 18 maintains a deliberate ambiguity as to whether the **plastered over** eyes and **closed** minds refer to the idols or their worshipers. In fact, they refer to both, because people inevitably become like that which they worship. Idolatry thus has a debilitating effect so that the person does not realize that making a god out of leftover wood yields a **detestable thing** and a **lie**.

How **deluded** must a person be if he **feeds on ashes** and does not realize how unsatisfying they are? (Cf. 55:1-2). The word for "feeds" (רעה, *r'h*) could be translated "grazes" since its background is that of tending sheep. "Instead of the rich grass of the messianic kingdom, the idolaters are pictured as trying to find food in a field that has been burned to ashes. Such is the empty reality of the worship of this world."[6] The ashes may also allude back to the portion of the wood that has been burned in the fire. Wood can serve as a beneficial means to an end by providing fuel for cooking nourishing food. If, however, it becomes a god, it yields only ashes for food.

Since idolatry consists of a self-perpetuating delusion, the person caught in it **cannot save himself** because he is unable to see that **this thing in my right hand [is] a lie**. The situation becomes even more disturbing in light of Israel's inclination to idolatry and subsequent blindness. The need for God to intervene becomes more obvious. In hindsight, the need for exile as part of the intervention also emerges. What God cannot accomplish by words, by patience and kindness, or even by lesser acts of discipline, he has brought about by the exile. Through that process God has purged idolatry from his people.

3. He Accomplishes His Purpose for His People (44:21-28)

[21]"Remember these things, O Jacob, / for you are my servant, O Israel. / I have made you, you are my servant; / O Israel, I will not forget you. / [22]I have swept away your offenses like a cloud, / your sins like the morning mist. / Return to me, / for I have redeemed you."

[23]Sing for joy, O heavens, for the LORD has done this; / shout aloud, O earth beneath. / Burst into song, you mountains, / you forests and all your trees, / for the LORD has redeemed Jacob, / he displays his glory in Israel.

[24]"This is what the LORD says— / your Redeemer, who formed you in the womb:

I am the LORD, / who has made all things, / who alone stretched out the heavens, / who spread out the earth by myself,

[25]who foils the signs of false prophets / and makes fools of diviners, / who overthrows the learning of the wise / and turns it

---

[6]Oswalt, *Isaiah* 2, p. 186.

into nonsense, / ²⁶who carries out the words of his servants / and fulfills the predictions of his messengers,
who says of Jerusalem, 'It shall be inhabited,' / of the towns of Judah, 'They shall be built,' / and of their ruins, 'I will restore them,' / ²⁷who says to the watery deep, 'Be dry, / and I will dry up your streams,' / ²⁸who says of Cyrus, 'He is my shepherd / and will accomplish all that I please; / he will say of Jerusalem, "Let it be rebuilt," / and of the temple, "Let its foundations be laid."'

44:21-23 The call for Israel to **Remember these things** connects the encouragement of this final section with the preceding attack against idolatry. Motyer detects four contrasts between verses 9-20 and verses 21-23.[7] The idolaters make their idols (vv. 9-10,12), but God **made** Israel (v. 21). The idolater is in bondage to his idol (vv. 18-20), but Israel is bound as a **servant** to God (v. 21). The idolater vainly prays for his idol to save him (v. 17), but God says that he has **redeemed** Israel. The idolater bows down to a piece of wood (v. 19), but the **trees** join in the celebration of God's salvation of Israel.

How can these contrasts come about? God does not simply *tell* the blind to see; he speaks of a time when he will *make it possible* for his people to see. The promise that **I will not forget you** encourages patient endurance while God provides purification from idolatry through the experience of exile. The message of consolation begun in chapter 40 comes as a result of completing Israel's time of "hard service" (40:2). That is why God's call to **Return to me** is based on his claim that **I have redeemed you**. He does not wait for Israel to come to her senses on her own, for such a time will never come. He brings about defeat and exile, but he also redeems his people from exile as he had redeemed them from Egyptian bondage. In that earlier act of redemption as well, God acted first and then called his people into covenant relationship with him (cf. Exod 19:3-6). If Israel had truly repented of her sins prior to the exile, atonement through sacrifice was available and meaningful conversion could have occurred. Since that did not happen, Israel "received from the LORD's hand double for all her sins" (40:2) in exile. In either case, the result is that these sins have evaporated **like a cloud** or **the morning mist** so that Israel can become God's servant.

Just as the entire creation shares in the corruption and decay that human sin has introduced, so the creation also shares in the

---

[7]Motyer, *Prophecy*, p. 349.

celebration of God's work of redemption (cf. Rom 8:19-22). The particular cause for celebration in verse 23 is the anticipation of God's certain work (**the LORD has done this**) with the result that **he displays his glory in Israel**. God has chosen to reveal himself through his people to a world afflicted by blindness. His entire work of redemption hinges on achieving this goal, which explains his unwavering commitment to forging at least a faithful remnant in Israel. The church now bears the same awesome responsibility to reveal God's glory to the world, but with the same reassurance that God will not give up on his people.

44:24-26 Verses 24-28 connect God's significant but vague promises about Israel's future with his repudiation of idolatry by means of a very specific prophecy. God sets the stage by affirming himself as the sole creator, thus distancing himself from paganism in two ways. Paganism is polytheistic, and it holds that multiple aspects of creation are gods. Rather than being trapped as part of the system in the impersonal, mechanical cosmology of paganism, God is free to act as he sees fit.[8] He can thus foil the attempts by **false prophets** to mislead people with their counterfeit **signs**; he can expose the folly of **diviners** who seek to discover the future by tapping into the set laws of the universe; and he can overthrow the efforts of the **wise** to figure out by human reason what will happen. These human efforts typically aim not so much to *know* the future as they do to *control* the future. God alone both knows and controls what will happen.

44:27-28 One thing God confidently asserts about the future: Judah and Jerusalem will be rebuilt. The reference to drying up the **watery deep** roots God's future activity once again in his past actions in the exodus.[9] What is most striking about this prediction is the fact that God calls **Cyrus**, the agent for fulfilling the prophecy, by name. For the original audience, the most unsettling aspect of the prophecy is God's labeling of this pagan king as **my shepherd**. For many more recent readers, the challenge has been the naming of an individual 150 years before his time. Such specificity is not common in the Bible, but neither is it unprecedented.[10]

---

[8]Cf. Oswalt, *Isaiah* 2, p. 194.

[9]The word for the "watery deep" is from the same root (צוּלָה, *ṣûlāh*) as the word used for the Red Sea in Exodus 15:5 (Motyer, *Prophecy*, p. 358).

[10]Cf. the unnamed prophet in 1 Kings 13 who mentioned Josiah by name as the Davidic king who would desecrate Jeroboam's golden calves.

If one rejects the possibility of divine revelation and predictive prophecy outright, then even the more general references to a rising power who will liberate the Judean exiles (41:2-3,25) must be dismissed as later additions. If one accepts God's revelation to the prophets, however, no compelling reason remains to question the mention of Cyrus by name. This issue is not an incidental detail because God's ability to foretell events and bring them to pass stands at the heart of Isaiah's argument throughout chapters 40–48. The eighth-century prophets parallel the writers of the Gospels in at least one important aspect. Just as the faith of the persecuted early church depends on the credibility of the Gospel accounts of Jesus as the Son of God who is risen from the dead, so the survival of Israelite faith after the destruction of the temple depends on the credibility of the prophets who foretell both God's judgment and his restoration.

ISAIAH 45

F. THE GOD WHO MYSTIFIES HIS PEOPLE (45:1-25)

In the New Testament, Paul speaks frequently about the "mystery" of God and his ways. Although the Old Testament does not use the same terminology, the concept appears there as well. In Deuteronomy 29:29 Moses tells Israel that "The secret things belong to the LORD our God, but the things revealed belong to us and to our children forever, that we may follow all the words of this law." In other words, God has revealed to his people what they need to know, but the "secret things" remain. Many individuals have struggled to understand or accept God's hidden ways. Abraham could not figure out how God would provide him an heir, why God delayed so long, or why God commanded him to sacrifice the heir once he was born. Job wrestled with the reason for the suffering he experienced as did the psalmists in their laments. Sometimes the struggle was not with what remained hidden, but with that which God had already made known. Habakkuk originally could not grasp how God could allow wickedness to persist in Judah, but when God revealed his plan to punish his people by the Babylonians, the prophet had even more difficulty comprehending how God could work through those more wicked than his people.

God's dramatic announcement of Cyrus as his "shepherd" at the end of chapter 44 apparently prompts questions about God's ways similar to those raised by Habakkuk. Although chapter 45 does not state specific objections to God's use of Cyrus, God's response makes it clear that such reservations exist. God's message to his people, as with his response to Job, affirms his sovereignty and the goodness of his purpose more than it provides the rationale for his actions.

1. He Anoints a Deliverer on Behalf of His People (45:1-8)

¹"This is what the LORD says to his anointed, / to Cyrus, whose right hand I take hold of / to subdue nations before him / and to

strip kings of their armor, / to open doors before him / so that gates will not be shut: / ²I will go before you / and will level the mountains[a]; / I will break down gates of bronze / and cut through bars of iron. / ³I will give you the treasures of darkness, / riches stored in secret places, / so that you may know that I am the LORD, / the God of Israel, who summons you by name. / ⁴For the sake of Jacob my servant, / of Israel my chosen, / I summon you by name / and bestow on you a title of honor, / though you do not acknowledge me. / ⁵I am the LORD, and there is no other; / apart from me there is no God. / I will strengthen you, / though you have not acknowledged me, / ⁶so that from the rising of the sun / to the place of its setting / men may know there is none besides me. / I am the LORD, and there is no other. / ⁷I form the light and create darkness, / I bring prosperity and create disaster; / I, the LORD, do all these things.

⁸"You heavens above, rain down righteousness; / let the clouds shower it down. / Let the earth open wide, / let salvation spring up, / let righteousness grow with it; / I, the LORD, have created it.

[a]2 Dead Sea Scrolls and Septuagint; the meaning of the word in the Masoretic Text is uncertain.

45:1 God's designation of Cyrus as his shepherd associates this foreign conqueror with the Davidic king (cf. Ezekiel 34, esp. v. 23). When Isaiah calls Cyrus God's **anointed**, the association becomes even clearer (1 Sam 16:13; Ps 2:2). God's promise **to open doors before him so that gates will not be shut** also calls to mind the language used of "the key to the house of David" given to Eliakim in 22:22. Using a non-Israelite to deliver Israel and implying that he will assume the role promised to David and his descendants would be enough to arouse serious concerns among the covenant people. As God presents his case at the outset, however, the tone is altogether positive. God's use of "Davidic language" in referring to Cyrus aims solely to assure Cyrus's success in his divinely appointed task, not to overturn the Davidic covenant.

45:2-3 God has a threefold purpose in giving Cyrus such success. The first relates to Cyrus himself: **so that you may know that I am the LORD, the God of Israel, who summons you by name.**[1] This purpose appears to find its fulfillment in Ezra 1:2, as Cyrus confesses

---

[1]God mentions summoning Cyrus "by name" again in verse 4. This language highlights the importance of predictive prophecy for Isaiah's message and forces the reader to decide whether the book is inspired or a deception.

that "The LORD, the God of heaven, has given me all the kingdoms of the earth and he has appointed me to build a temple for him at Jerusalem in Judah." Those words likely represent political expediency, however, since Cyrus granted the same privileges to other nations and their gods. Some conclude that Isaiah 45:3 prophesies a true conversion on the part of Cyrus, but there is no more indication that such a conversion occurred than with Nebuchadnezzar, who made similar confessions (cf. Dan 2:46-47; 3:28-29; 4:34-37). Twice in this passage God states that Cyrus does not "acknowledge" (literally, "know") him (vv. 4,5). Cyrus has the opportunity to know God, and it is God's purpose that he do so. Cyrus also has the same freedom to reject the knowledge available to him, however, as Israel and the rest of the world do.

45:4 God's second purpose in working through Cyrus relates to Israel: **For the sake of Jacob my servant, of Israel my chosen, I summon you by name**. Israel stands in need of a deliverer, but God can still refer to his people as his "servant." Cyrus will not fill that role but will be used by God on behalf of his servant. Cyrus's failure to **acknowledge** God does not mean that God cannot in his sovereignty accomplish his purpose through Cyrus. What his failure does mean is that he should be seen only as an agent of God and not as the fulfillment of the covenant promises given to David.

4:5-6 The final purpose God has for Cyrus relates to the whole world: **that from the rising of the sun to the place of its setting men may know there is none besides me**. Perhaps God considers it fitting to use a non-Israelite as a key figure in making it possible for Israel to fulfill her ultimate purpose to draw all nations to God. The vital link between the return from exile that Cyrus will enable and the fulfillment of that larger purpose explains how the return from exile will receive worldwide notice. The return itself will not have that effect, but it will open the door to greater works of God that will gain the world's attention.

45:7 This verse proclaims God's total sovereignty by means of two absolute contrasts. In both contrasts God claims to **create** (ברא, *br'*). He is thus "ultimately responsible for everything"[2] in his creation. Whereas the light-and-darkness contrast is well known, the second one is less clear. On one end of the spectrum is **prosperity**, and on the other is **disaster**. The first word (שָׁלוֹם, *šālôm*), frequently trans-

---

[2]Oswalt, *Isaiah* 2, p. 204.

lated "peace," refers to the wholeness or completeness that exists in the creation when God's will prevails. The opposite term (רַע, *ra‘*) is a broad word which at the most basic level means "bad" or "evil." The NIV translation captures the intent of the passage well. Motyer points out that of the 640 occurrences of this word in the Old Testament, "there are 275 instances where 'trouble' or 'calamity' is the meaning."[3] The point for Israel and the world is that God is in control of all circumstances. Israel should not interpret her experience of "disaster," therefore, as weakness or failure by God.

45:8 The final verse of this section builds on the theme of God's creative activity and draws a parallel between the life-giving rains and the righteous works of God. Just as God **created** the world so that life will be sustained and revived, so he sustains and revives his people even if he does so through an agent like Cyrus. God's goal is **righteousness**, or making things right.[4] In this case, the righteousness that will grow is paralleled with **salvation**. God's use of Cyrus aims to make right the plight of the exiles by liberating them from their foreign bondage.

2. He Overrules the Objections of His People (45:9-13)

⁹"Woe to him who quarrels with his Maker, / to him who is but a potsherd among the potsherds on the ground. / Does the clay say to the potter, / 'What are you making?' / Does your work say, / 'He has no hands'? / ¹⁰Woe to him who says to his father, / 'What have you begotten?' / or to his mother, / 'What have you brought to birth?'

¹¹"This is what the LORD says— / the Holy One of Israel, and its Maker: / Concerning things to come, / do you question me about my children, / or give me orders about the work of my hands? / ¹²It is I who made the earth / and created mankind upon it. / My own hands stretched out the heavens; / I marshaled their starry hosts. / ¹³I will raise up Cyrusᵃ in my righteousness: / I will make all his ways straight. / He will rebuild my city / and set my exiles free, / but not for a price or reward, / says the LORD Almighty."

ᵃ*13* Hebrew *him*

---

[3]Motyer, *Prophecy*, p. 359.
[4]Oswalt, *Isaiah* 2, p. 204.

45:9-10 Although using a foreigner like Cyrus as his "shepherd" and "anointed" might be unorthodox, surely no one could complain about God's intentions! Yet the text begins a vigorous defense of God's right to accomplish his purpose by whatever methods he chooses. God has previously rebuked the Assyrians for forgetting who is the tool and who is the one who wields it (10:15). He has also made the same case against Israel by the analogy of the **clay** and the **potter** (29:16). At the beginning of the present passage Isaiah highlights the disparity between the two parties by contrasting the **Maker** with a pot that cries out from among the other pots (**a potsherd among the potsherds**). In other words, the one who **quarrels** with God is limited to the perspective of those around him. The principle here is that a stream cannot rise above its source. By changing the image to that of a child questioning his **father** and his **mother** about their offspring, the picture of inappropriateness, disrespect, and ingratitude becomes more personal.

45:11-13 God's response to those who contend with him reveals their central concern. For what "wrong" do they dare to challenge the creator of all,[5] the one who cares about his **children** who are his handiwork as well? The reaffirmation of God's promise to **raise up Cyrus**[6] indicates that this method of operation is the point of contention. The additional words **in my righteousness** confirm that at least some question whether Cyrus can or should be the one used by God to make things right. God promises Cyrus that he will **make all his ways straight** (cf. the promises to Israel in 40:3-4) so that Cyrus can accomplish God's work of restoration for the **exiles**. This transaction, however, involves no **price or reward**. God does not favor Cyrus so much that he will sell Israel into his hands. As the sovereign creator, God owes his agent of deliverance nothing. God is about to reveal, in fact, what gifts the nations will bring to Israel and the even greater gift that Israel will make available to the nations.

3. He Reveals Himself to the Nations by His People (45:14-25)

¹⁴**This is what the LORD says:**

---

[5]Three times in verses 12-13 the emphatic first person pronoun ("I") appears in order to stress God's claim to act independently.

[6]The Hebrew text does not call Cyrus by name here. The NIV has specified the simple pronoun "him," by substituting Cyrus, but that identification of the pronoun is certainly correct.

"The products of Egypt and the merchandise of Cush,ᵃ /and those tall Sabeans— /they will come over to you /and will be yours; /they will trudge behind you, /coming over to you in chains. /They will bow down before you /and plead with you, saying, / 'Surely God is with you, and there is no other; /there is no other god.'"

¹⁵Truly you are a God who hides himself, /O God and Savior of Israel. / ¹⁶All the makers of idols will be put to shame and disgraced; /they will go off into disgrace together. / ¹⁷But Israel will be saved by the LORD / with an everlasting salvation; / you will never be put to shame or disgraced, /to ages everlasting.

¹⁸For this is what the LORD says— /he who created the heavens, /he is God; /he who fashioned and made the earth, /he founded it; /he did not create it to be empty, /but formed it to be inhabited— /he says: / "I am the LORD, /and there is no other. / ¹⁹I have not spoken in secret, /from somewhere in a land of darkness; / I have not said to Jacob's descendants, / 'Seek me in vain.' / I, the LORD, speak the truth; /I declare what is right.

²⁰"Gather together and come; /assemble, you fugitives from the nations. /Ignorant are those who carry about idols of wood, /who pray to gods that cannot save. / ²¹Declare what is to be, present it— / let them take counsel together. / Who foretold this long ago, / who declared it from the distant past? / Was it not I, the LORD? / And there is no God apart from me, / a righteous God and a Savior; / there is none but me.

²²"Turn to me and be saved, /all you ends of the earth; /for I am God, and there is no other. / ²³By myself I have sworn, /my mouth has uttered in all integrity /a word that will not be revoked: /Before me every knee will bow; /by me every tongue will swear. / ²⁴They will say of me, 'In the LORD alone /are righteousness and strength.'" /All who have raged against him /will come to him and be put to shame. / ²⁵But in the LORD all the descendants of Israel /will be found righteous and will exult.

ᵃ*14* That is, the upper Nile region

45:14-17 In 43:3 God promises to give Egypt, Cush, and Seba as a ransom for Israel.⁷ In 45:17 the inhabitants of those same three areas willingly submit to Israel because they recognize that the only

---

⁷In chapter 43, as here, the mention of these nations in particular may reflect an exodus background.

true God is with Israel.⁸ What a dramatic turn of events from the time of exile! Should not Israel humbly accept God's use of Cyrus if this scenario is the result? These nations that discover the way to the true God is through Israel have become aware of the mystery of God's ways, leading them to confess **a God who hides himself**. These words do not contradict the references in subsequent verses to God's revelation of himself. Rather, they reflect the true nature of mystery: the fact that God remains hidden unless and until he reveals himself. Once the nations become aware of the truth about God, however, they quickly overcome their former blindness and see the contrast between the **disgrace** that will come to the **idols** and the **everlasting salvation** that God has in store for **Israel**.⁹

45:18 The mention of Israel's salvation returns the emphasis once again to the numerous implications of God's creative activity. God will save in the end because he created both the world and Israel for a positive purpose. Just as God **did not create** the world **to be empty** (תֹהוּ, *tōhû*; cf. Gen 1:2), neither did he say to Israel, **Seek me in vain** (*tōhû*). Nor has he **spoken in secret**¹⁰ so that Israel would have to grope about in the darkness like the idol worshipers. God made the way of life clear and accessible to his people, according to Deuteronomy 30:11-14.

> Now what I am commanding you today is not too difficult for you or beyond your reach. It is not up in heaven, so that you have to ask, "Who will ascend into heaven to get it and proclaim it to us so we may obey it?" Nor is it beyond the sea, so that you have to ask, "Who will cross the sea to get it and proclaim it to us so we may obey it?" No, the word is very near you; it is in your mouth and in your heart so you may obey it.

45:20-21 Another implication of God's nature as sole creator is that he controls human history. As God assembles the converts who formerly had been in bondage to idolatry, he refers to them as **fugitives** or those who have escaped. He reminds them of the ignorance

---

⁸Motyer (*Prophecy*, p. 363) notes that in the imagery of conquest and surrender as it is applied to the conversion of the nations, "we need to be careful not to confuse the motif with the reality."

⁹In light of Motyer's understanding of the speakers in verse 15, he concludes that in verse 17 "The great name Israel must now include the saved of the Gentile world" (*Prophecy*, p. 364).

¹⁰סתר, *str*; the same root as "hides himself" in verse 15.

of praying to a god made of a block of **wood** that its worshipers have to **carry about**. By contrast, God is the one **Who foretold this long ago** and made it happen without any human assistance.

45:22-25 The final implication of God's creative work is his position as the judge of all humanity. He is able to say, **Turn to me and be saved, all you ends of the earth**. Because everyone will not respond to this offer, he also announces that in the end **Before me every knee will bow; by me every tongue will swear** (cf. Rom 14:11; Phil 2:10-11). Those who refuse to acknowledge God willingly will **be put to shame. But in the LORD all the descendants of Israel will be found righteous and will exult**.[11] God's authority to condemn those **who have raged against him** flows naturally from his status as creator. The language of verse 25, however, sounds remarkably similar to Paul's teaching on justification by faith, and Isaiah has not yet revealed the basis for God's acquittal of believers.

---

[11]Cf. verses 16-17. As with verse 17, Motyer holds that "A merely national significance of *Israel* would make nonsense of the whole argument of this passage" (*Prophecy*, p. 367). His case appears stronger here because the qualifier "all the descendants of Israel" is difficult to take in a literal, national sense.

ISAIAH 46

G. THE GOD WHO DEFEATS THE ENEMIES OF HIS PEOPLE (46:1-47:15)

The section of Isaiah beginning with chapter 40 emphasizes Israel's future return from Babylonian exile. God's sovereignty in general and his promise to raise up Cyrus in particular explain how he will bring about this deliverance. Isaiah 46-47 elaborates on the other side of Israel's rescue from Babylon. For Cyrus to conquer and the exiles to return home, Babylon must fall. When Israel entered Canaan after the exodus from Egypt, God brought together in time his judgment of the Canaanites and the fulfillment of his promise to give the land to Abraham's descendants. God works in a similar fashion in his judgment of Babylon, but this time the fulfillment of the promise to return Abraham's descendants to the land occurs through the victory God gives to Cyrus. Although chapters 46-47 focus on Babylon's fall, the underlying theme remains God's redemption of his people (cf. 46:3-4,8-13; 47:4).

1. He Exposes the Folly of Idolatry (46:1-7)

¹Bel bows down, Nebo stoops low; / their idols are borne by beasts of burden.ᵃ / The images that are carried about are burdensome, / a burden for the weary. / ²They stoop and bow down together; / unable to rescue the burden, / they themselves go off into captivity.

³"Listen to me, O house of Jacob, / all you who remain of the house of Israel, / you whom I have upheld since you were conceived, / and have carried since your birth. / ⁴Even to your old age and gray hairs / I am he, I am he who will sustain you. / I have made you and I will carry you; / I will sustain you and I will rescue you.

⁵"To whom will you compare me or count me equal? / To whom will you liken me that we may be compared? / ⁶Some pour out gold from their bags / and weigh out silver on the scales; / they hire a goldsmith to make it into a god, / and they bow down and worship it. / ⁷They lift it to their shoulders and carry it; / they set it up in its place, and there it stands. / From that spot it cannot move. / Though one cries out to it, it does not answer; / it cannot save him from his troubles.

ᵃ*1 Or are but beasts and cattle*

46:1-2 In 45:20 God rebukes the ignorance of "those who carry about idols of wood." The opening of chapter 46 elaborates on the way the **idols** are **burdensome** rather than liberating. Not only does the need to carry them about reveal their impotence, but it also demonstrates that the idols **weary** their worshipers. Isaiah singles out the two most prominent gods of Babylon. **Bel**, which corresponds to the Canaanite Baal ("lord, master"), is a title given to Marduk. **Nebo** (Nabu) is the son of Marduk. They are pictured here as bowed down in sorrow and shame when they are carried away to **captivity** because they are **unable to rescue**. When God empowers Babylon to serve as his agent of judgment against Judah and Jerusalem, many will conclude that the gods of Babylon are more powerful than Yahweh. What will they think when these same gods are carted off to their own exile?

46:3-7 In contrast to the gods of Babylon, Yahweh reassures the remnant after the exile (**all you who remain of the house of Israel**) that just as he has **carried** them since their conception, so he **will carry** them until their **old age**. The one who is truly God carries his people rather than being carried by them. The reference to God's lifelong care of the remnant reveals that he is sustaining them even when he must put them through the experience of exile. Once Babylon falls, no future remains for that nation. God brings about the fall of his people in order to purify a remnant that he will raise up again to fulfill his purpose. No other gods can **compare** to him. Even if the images of these gods are made from **gold** or **silver**, they have no ultimate worth because they **cannot move** or **answer** or **save**. The precious metals only make an idol heavier and more of a burden for those who have to **lift it to their shoulders and carry it**.

2. He Brings His Salvation Near (46:8-13)

⁸"Remember this, fix it in mind, / take it to heart, you rebels. / ⁹Remember the former things, those of long ago; / I am God, and there is no other; / I am God, and there is none like me. / ¹⁰I make known the end from the beginning, / from ancient times, what is still to come. / I say: My purpose will stand, / and I will do all that I please. / ¹¹From the east I summon a bird of prey; / from a far-off land, a man to fulfill my purpose. / What I have said, that will I bring about; / what I have planned, that will I do. / ¹²Listen to me, you stubborn-hearted, / you who are far from righteousness. / ¹³I am bringing my righteousness near, / it is not far away; / and my salvation will not be delayed. / I will grant salvation to Zion, / my splendor to Israel.

46:8-10 Neither the nations nor their gods can thwart Yahweh's purpose for his people. The biggest obstacle God faces is the lack of perception by the very people he is working to save. Because they are **rebels** and "stubborn-hearted" (v. 12), God calls them to take note of what he has done and what he is about to do. He holds the nations accountable for recognizing his works, but only Israel possesses the larger framework within which to understand and rejoice in God's works.

46:11 God is free to do as he pleases, in the present situation summoning a **bird of prey** from the **east**. This image refers to Cyrus, the **man to fulfill my purpose**. God's displeasure with Israel's rebellion may be general in nature but in this context probably refers back to a resistance to God's use of Cyrus. Webb concludes that "such a response is tantamount to rebellion against God, for it calls into question not just his sovereign freedom, but his goodness — and that is to strike at the very heart of the covenant relationship."[1]

46:12-13 The chapter thus concludes with an exhortation for Israel to recognize what God is about to do. Israel at present is **far from righteousness** while God promises that **I am bringing my righteousness near**. In the parallelism of verse 13, God's righteousness once again refers to his **salvation**. God will make things right by saving his people, but his people have distanced themselves from him and his work in their rejection of his methods.

---

[1]Webb, *Message*, p. 188.

When God brings **salvation to Zion** his **splendor** will be manifest. Israel must take care or she will miss it due to the blindness of stubborn unbelief.[2]

---

[2]The difficult situation described here sets the stage for the gap between Israel and the servant that emerges in chapters 49–57. It may also anticipate the inability by many Jews to see God at work in the son of the carpenter from Nazareth in the New Testament.

ISAIAH 47

3. He Shames the Merciless (47:1-7)

¹"Go down, sit in the dust, / Virgin Daughter of Babylon; / sit on the ground without a throne, / Daughter of the Babylonians.ᵃ / No more will you be called / tender or delicate. / ²Take millstones and grind flour; / take off your veil. / Lift up your skirts, bare your legs, / and wade through the streams. / ³Your nakedness will be exposed / and your shame uncovered. / I will take vengeance; / I will spare no one."

⁴Our Redeemer—the LORD Almighty is his name— / is the Holy One of Israel.

⁵"Sit in silence, go into darkness, / Daughter of the Babylonians; / no more will you be called / queen of kingdoms. / ⁶I was angry with my people / and desecrated my inheritance; / I gave them into your hand, / and you showed them no mercy. / Even on the aged / you laid a very heavy yoke. / ⁷You said, 'I will continue forever— / the eternal queen!' / But you did not consider these things / or reflect on what might happen.

ᵃ*1* Or *Chaldeans*; also in verse 5

47:1-3a In his response to Sennacherib's blasphemous boasts, God describes Jerusalem as "The Virgin Daughter of Zion" (37:21) who mocks the Assyrian king. By contrast, the **Virgin Daughter of Babylon** will forfeit her privileged status. She will lose her **throne** and **sit in the dust** in mourning over what she has lost. Rather than being pampered, she will have to **grind flour** as a peasant woman does. Rather than sitting on her throne or being carried about, she will have to **wade through the streams** as she goes into exile with her gods (46:2). Rather than wearing her royal finery (**take off your veil**), she will have her **nakedness . . . exposed** to her **shame**. This act refers to the humiliation imposed upon exiles (cf. 20:4), or perhaps even to the treatment of a prostitute (cf. Ezek 16:37).

47:3b-6a Verses 3b-4 make clear what has been implied to this point: God's judgment on behalf of Israel brings about Babylon's downfall. Babylon's fundamental sin is pride,[1] but a particular manifestation of that pride demands God's judgment. Babylon will be demoted from her status as **queen of kingdoms** because of her mistreatment of the Judean exiles. The sovereign God who plants and uproots kingdoms takes action against his own people through the Babylonians. Both Babylon and Israel need to understand, however, that the Babylonian victory over Judah and the desecration of God's **inheritance** result solely from God's anger with his people.

47:6b-7 Babylon's sin is not the conquest of Judah or even the destruction of the temple, because these actions carry out God's will. The sin occurs in the failure to show any **mercy**, even imposing heavy burdens on the **aged**. Even those who have not received God's revealed law should recognize the evil of such cruel insensitivity. This sin derives from Babylon's assumption that she **will continue forever—the eternal queen!** With this outlook, a human kingdom considers itself the ultimate authority and answerable to no one. The rise and fall of so many kingdoms before her should lead Babylon to **reflect on what might happen**, but pride rules out such reflection. From a pagan perspective, success vindicates one's actions.

> This is the problem of a people whose gods are simply themselves written large. They have no one outside themselves, over against themselves, to remind them that even if they are the greatest the world has ever seen, they are not the standard of greatness. God is the standard, and all of us, from the greatest human to the least, are measured against him, not ourselves.[2]

4. He Bereaves the Self-Sufficient (47:8-11)

[8]"Now then, listen, you wanton creature, / lounging in your security /and saying to yourself, / 'I am, and there is none besides me. /I will never be a widow /or suffer the loss of children.' /[9]Both of these will overtake you / in a moment, on a single day: / loss of

---

[1] The sin of pride dominates God's assessment of the nations in chapters 13–23 as well.
[2] Oswalt, *Isaiah* 2, p. 247.

children and widowhood. / They will come upon you in full measure, / in spite of your many sorceries / and all your potent spells. / ¹⁰You have trusted in your wickedness / and have said, 'No one sees me.' / Your wisdom and knowledge mislead you / when you say to yourself, / 'I am, and there is none besides me.' / ¹¹Disaster will come upon you, / and you will not know how to conjure it away. / A calamity will fall upon you / that you cannot ward off with a ransom; / a catastrophe you cannot foresee / will suddenly come upon you.

47:8-9 The pampered queen imagery continues as Babylon enjoys her riches[3] and revels in her sense of **security**. She assumes that she **will never be a widow or suffer the loss of children**. In other words, she will never feel the vulnerability of a woman without a husband or children. By assuming the attitude that **I am, and there is none besides me**, however, Babylon makes the same mistake Sennacherib made of usurping the place of God (cf. 45:5-6,18,22; 46:9). As a result, the very losses Babylon cannot conceive for herself will come upon her suddenly and **in full measure**.

47:10-11 God will expose the various bases of Babylon's false confidence. Babylon takes great pride in her expertise in astrology, the magical arts, and wisdom (cf. Dan 4:6; 5:7); but when God's judgment comes, she will not be able to **conjure it away** by her **many sorceries** and her **potent spells**. Her astrologers will not be able to **foresee**[4] the **catastrophe** that **will suddenly come upon** her. She trusts in her **wickedness** that deludes her into thinking **No one sees me**, but God sees her and will bring **Disaster**[5] upon her. Her limited **wisdom and knowledge mislead** her into thinking that she is equal to God. Even her great wealth cannot pay the **ransom** to free her from God's intention.

5. He Wearies the Misguided (47:12-15)

¹²"**Keep on, then, with your magic spells / and with your many sorceries, / which you have labored at since childhood. / Perhaps

---

[3]The word translated "wanton creature" in verse 8 (עֲדִינָה, *ʿădînāh*) derives from a root associated with luxury (cf. NRSV, "you lover of pleasures").

[4]Literally, "know."

[5]The same word for "wickedness" in verse 10 (רָעָה, *rāʿāh*) lies behind "Disaster" in verse 11.

you will succeed, /perhaps you will cause terror. /¹³All the counsel you have received has only worn you out! / Let your astrologers come forward, / those stargazers who make predictions month by month, / let them save you from what is coming upon you. / ¹⁴Surely they are like stubble; / the fire will burn them up. / They cannot even save themselves / from the power of the flame. / Here are no coals to warm anyone; / here is no fire to sit by. / ¹⁵That is all they can do for you— / these you have labored with / and trafficked with since childhood. / Each of them goes on in his error; / there is not one that can save you.

47:12-15 God finally taunts Babylon much as Elijah did with the prophets of Baal at Mt. Carmel (1 Kgs 18:27ff.). He exposes the great lie the professional religious experts in Babylon have foisted upon the people.[6] Their **counsel** has only brought Babylon labor[7] and **worn her out**.[8] "Commitment, discipline and effort are a true part of religion, but when allied to the worthless they are only a weariness."[9] Once the crisis comes, the true worth of these experts emerges: **Surely they are like stubble; the fire will burn them up**. They cannot **save** Babylon because **they cannot even save themselves**.

Webb rightly points out that

> Babylon here is not merely the ancient city of that name, and the poem does not simply look forward to what was to happen to it in 539 when Cyrus conquered it. Like Jerusalem, with which it is contrasted, it is both a concrete historical reality and a symbol.... Babylon represents humankind organized in defiance of God — the kingdom of mere mortals, in contrast to the kingdom of God. In this sense, 'Babylon' is still with us, and still stands under the judgment of God. The historical Babylon of the sixth century BC was merely one manifestation of it.[10]

---

[6]The root translated "trafficked" in verse 15 (סחר, *sḥr*) refers to those who wander about trading their wares. The same root is translated "merchants" in describing Tyre in 23:2,8.

[7]The word for "labored" (יגע, *ygʻ*) in verse 12 is used for wearisome toil (cf. v. 15; 40:28,30,31; 43:22).

[8]This verb (לאה, *lʼh*) appears in 1:14 for God's weariness with Israel's hypocritical worship.

[9]Motyer, *Prophecy*, p. 374.

[10]Webb, *Message*, p. 190.

John's use of Babylon in Revelation confirms this view. Apocalyptic writings typically take significant historical persons, places, or events and use them as paradigmatic examples of the way God operates. Isaiah uses this approach in his references to the exodus, for example, and he establishes Babylon as a new paradigm for rebellious humanity (although it could be argued that Isaiah merely builds on the events at the tower of Babel in Genesis 11). The significance of this observation is that believers of every generation can be confident in the knowledge that the Babylons of the world will never prevail over the purpose of God.

ISAIAH 48

H. THE GOD WHO SEEKS PEACE FOR HIS PEOPLE (48:1-22)

Chapter 48 stands as more than simply the final chapter in the opening section of Isaiah 40–66. It summarizes and intensifies the major themes that have emerged in chapters 40–47. Yahweh has been presented as the only being worthy to be designated God. He stands above his creation and supervises the workings of human history in such a way that he preserves his covenant people and enables them to fulfill their redemptive purpose. The idols and the proud nations that worship them are as nothing compared to God in terms of who controls what happens in the world. Cyrus will do God's bidding; Babylon will fall. God proclaims these events before they happen so that his people will know who brings them to pass. Yet Israel, God's chosen servant, remains blind and deaf, stubbornly persisting in questioning and violating God's ways. Consequently, God sets forth his nature and his purpose again in chapter 48, not to the nations but to Israel.

1. He Preempts His People's Dependence on Idols (48:1-7)

¹"Listen to this, O house of Jacob, /you who are called by the name of Israel /and come from the line of Judah, /you who take oaths in the name of the LORD /and invoke the God of Israel— /but not in truth or righteousness— /²you who call yourselves citizens of the holy city /and rely on the God of Israel— /the LORD Almighty is his name: / ³I foretold the former things long ago, / my mouth announced them and I made them known; /then suddenly I acted, and they came to pass. / ⁴For I knew how stubborn you were; / the sinews of your neck were iron, /your forehead was bronze. /⁵Therefore I told you these things long ago; / before they happened I

announced them to you /so that you could not say, / 'My idols did them; /my wooden image and metal god ordained them.' / ⁶You have heard these things; look at them all. / Will you not admit them?

"From now on I will tell you of new things, /of hidden things unknown to you. / ⁷They are created now, and not long ago; /you have not heard of them before today. /So you cannot say, / 'Yes, I knew of them.'

48:1-2 In verses 1-2 God presents the self-image of his people (**house of Jacob, called by the name of Israel, from the line of Judah, citizens of the holy city**) and their outward expressions of faith (**take oaths in the name of the L**ORD **and invoke the God of Israel, rely on the God of Israel**). He also reveals, however, his knowledge of how hollow are those claims (**but not in truth or righteousness**). From the opening chapter of the book, Israel has been exposed as a people whose religiosity exceeds the sincerity of their commitment to God. The **L**ORD **Almighty** can neither be deceived by nor tolerate such hypocrisy, so he must attack the problem.

48:3-7 God has been aware of the **stubborn** nature of his people from the beginning. To speak of their **neck** of **iron** and **forehead** of **bronze** characterizes them as exceedingly difficult to turn from their ways (cf. Deut 9:6; Ezek 3:7-9). The most dangerous manifestation of their stubbornness is their refusal to take to heart God's many powerful and compassionate actions on their behalf. Their inclination is to see his works and say, **My idols did them**. God fights that deadly tendency by foretelling events and then **suddenly** fulfilling his words before anyone can give the idols credit. Sadly, God must challenge Israel to face the facts and draw the proper conclusion (**Will you not admit them?**). He promises to "create" (ברא, *br'*) even more **new things** that have remained **hidden**[1] to convince his people of his love and power. These new things may relate to the work of the servant that is about to be unfolded.

2. He Refines His People for His Name's Sake (48:8-11)

⁸You have neither heard nor understood; /from of old your ear has not been open. / Well do I know how treacherous you are; /you

---

[1]This word (נצר, *nṣr*) is used in 27:3 in reference to God "watching over" his vineyard. God has guarded this information for the proper time.

were called a rebel from birth. / ⁹For my own name's sake I delay my wrath; / for the sake of my praise I hold it back from you, / so as not to cut you off. / ¹⁰See, I have refined you, though not as silver; / I have tested you in the furnace of affliction. / ¹¹For my own sake, for my own sake, I do this. / How can I let myself be defamed? / I will not yield my glory to another.

48:8 In the previous verses, God raises the subject of Israel's stubbornness to explain why he sometimes announces and brings to pass suddenly plans that he has kept secret. In this section he again speaks of Israel's **treacherous**[2] ways and the fact that she was **called a rebel from birth**. The latter description does not refer to the concept of original sin, but serves as an example of hyperbole as in Psalm 58:3, where the wicked speak lies from birth (cf. Ps 51:5). The point is that God has known about and dealt with Israel's faithlessness from the beginning of their relationship. This fact leads to a couple of understandable questions. Why did God choose this nation in the first place? Why has he maintained his relationship with Israel for so long under these circumstances?

48:9-11 The answer to the first question remains shrouded in the mystery of God's choice of Abraham. It is possible to answer the question with another question. Could God have chosen any individual and raised up a nation that would be faithful to him? God clearly answers the second question. Once he committed to accomplish his redemptive work through Abraham's seed, his reputation was tied to those descendants. By the use of three parallel phrases (**For my own name's sake**; **for the sake of my praise**; **For my own sake**), God makes clear that the continuity of his relationship with Israel is rooted solely in his nature and not in any goodness in Israel. God will not allow himself to **be defamed** or surrender his **glory to another** by giving up on the people with whom he has entered into a covenant relationship (cf. Exod 32:11-14).

God's commitment to the covenant does not mean that Israel faces no accountability for her lack of faithfulness to the covenant. God's reputation suffers not only if he abandons the people to whom he has committed, but also if he allows his people to remain rebellious and unbelieving. God holds back his consuming **wrath**,

---

[2]The root, which appears in an emphatic construction here (בָּגוֹד תִּבְגּוֹד, *bāgôd tibgôd*), refers to acting deceptively or breaking faith with someone (cf. 24:16; 33:1).

but he still applies the **furnace of affliction**[3] to purify Israel. It is not clear in what sense Israel's refinement is **not as silver**. Oswalt cites Calvin's view, "that if God had refined them like silver, there would be nothing left of them, because they are all dross."[4] Motyer follows this interpretation as well, referring to the statement in 1:22 that Israel's "silver has become dross."[5] The result is that God limits the extent of the refinement to avoid destroying his people, with the implication that a significant amount of impurity remains.

3. He Delivers His People by Giving Cyrus Success (48:12-15)

¹²"Listen to me, O Jacob, / Israel, whom I have called: / I am he; / I am the first and I am the last. / ¹³My own hand laid the foundations of the earth, / and my right hand spread out the heavens; / when I summon them, / they all stand up together.

¹⁴"Come together, all of you, and listen: / Which of ⌊the idols⌋ has foretold these things? / The LORD's chosen ally / will carry out his purpose against Babylon; / his arm will be against the Babylonians.ᵃ / ¹⁵I, even I, have spoken; / yes, I have called him. / I will bring him, / and he will succeed in his mission.

ᵃ*14 Or Chaldeans*

48:12-15 These verses return to the theme of the God who created and commands (**when I summon them, they all stand up together**) the heavens and the earth. The same God who can summon the elements of creation and has **called** the one who will deliver from Babylon (v. 15) has also **called** Israel to be his people.[6] Israel, however, is not as responsive as the inanimate creation or even the pagan conqueror. God exercises his sovereignty to foretell "the one he loves"[7] who **will carry out his purpose against Babylon**, but Israel's reluctance to accept God's work through Cyrus has already

---

[3]The NIV reads that God "tested" Israel in this furnace. This reading is based on an emending of the Hebrew text from בְּחַרְתִּיךָ (*bᵊḥartîkā*, I have chosen) to בְּחַנְתִּיךָ (*bᵊḥantîkā*) based on the 1QIsᵃ scroll from Qumran.

[4]Oswalt, *Isaiah* 2, p. 270. He acknowledges that this view is possible, but not necessary.

[5]Motyer, *Prophecy*, p. 379.

[6]All of these verbs are from the root קרא (*qrʾ*).

[7]This translation is a more literal rendering of אֲהֵבוֹ (*ʾăhēbô*), which the NIV translates "chosen ally."

been noted. This reluctance sets the stage for the lament in verses 18-19, because the success of Cyrus's **mission** brings about Israel's release from exile. Israel's failure to appreciate what God is doing for her in this situation typifies the way the covenant people have missed out on a multitude of opportunities for blessing.

4. He Teaches His People What Is Best for Them (48:16-22)

¹⁶"Come near me and listen to this:
"From the first announcement I have not spoken in secret; / at the time it happens, I am there."
And now the Sovereign LORD has sent me, / with his Spirit.
¹⁷This is what the LORD says— / your Redeemer, the Holy One of Israel: / "I am the LORD your God, / who teaches you what is best for you, / who directs you in the way you should go. / ¹⁸If only you had paid attention to my commands, / your peace would have been like a river, / your righteousness like the waves of the sea. / ¹⁹Your descendants would have been like the sand, / your children like its numberless grains; / their name would never be cut off / nor destroyed from before me."
²⁰Leave Babylon, / flee from the Babylonians[a]! / Announce this with shouts of joy / and proclaim it. / Send it out to the ends of the earth; / say, "The LORD has redeemed his servant Jacob." / ²¹They did not thirst when he led them through the deserts; / he made water flow for them from the rock; / he split the rock and water gushed out.
²²"There is no peace," says the LORD, "for the wicked."

[a]*20 Or* Chaldeans

48:16 Verse 16 transitions to the concluding thoughts of this chapter and of the larger section of chapters 40–48. The **first announcement** may refer to Cyrus's mission (vv. 14-15), or it may be a general statement about God's revelation of his work in the world. In either case, God's purpose has been to bless his people that they might fulfill their redemptive purpose. He has spoken openly, therefore (cf. 45:19), so that they will recognize his presence in his saving acts. Without this presence, Israel will enjoy no success. Moses understood this principle from the beginning of Israel's existence (cf. Exod 33:15-16). The words **I am there** (שָׁם אָנִי, *šām 'ānî*) recall the final note of Ezekiel. God's removal of his presence from Jerusalem results in the destruction of the city, but the name of the restored Jerusalem in Ezekiel 48:35 is **THE LORD IS THERE** (יְהוָה שָׁמָּה, *YHWH šāmmāh*).

The identity of the one whom God has sent **with his Spirit** is unclear. Perhaps this vagueness is intentional, creating anticipation for that which Isaiah 49–57 clarifies. This person could simply be Isaiah, but the endowment of God's Spirit in the prophet's message sometimes signals an even more significant agent of God. In 11:2 it is the Davidic Messiah upon whom the Spirit rests, and in 42:1 God puts his Spirit on his servant. Since the servant is about to reemerge in renewed significance in the next chapter, the reference to the Spirit in verse 16 may prepare for this new direction.

48:17-19 The two titles for God in the opening of verse 17 convey the dilemma he faces in his relationship with Israel. On the one hand, he is the **Redeemer**, the one who identifies with his people and seeks to rescue them from their distress. On the other hand, Israel's God is **the Holy One** who cannot simply dismiss his people's sin.[8] Despite his ongoing efforts to **teach** them **what is best**[9] and to point them to the right paths, Israel has consistently refused to listen to God's **commands**. These commandments have never been intended as a burden, but rather as a path to blessing (cf. Ps 19:7-11). By ignoring them, Israel has failed to receive the abundant **peace** and **righteousness** that God makes available. Rather than fulfilling the covenant promises to Abraham of a multitude of **descendants** (cf. Gen 15:5; 22:17), the exile will refine Israel so that only a remnant remains.

The tragic tone of verses 17-19, against the backdrop of verses 9-11, illustrates the relationship between the unconditional and the conditional elements of the covenant relationship between God and his people. The unconditional element has to do with the accomplishment of God's redemptive purpose through his people. The fulfillment of this purpose depends on the character of God, and he will do whatever is necessary to bring it about. The conditional element has to do with the degree of blessing the covenant people enjoy in the process of fulfilling God's purpose. Israel has forfeited a large measure of that blessing, but God's ongoing faithfulness will

---

[8]Motyer, *Prophecy*, p. 381.
[9]The word here (לְהוֹעִיל, *lᵉhôʿîl*) literally means "to profit/benefit."

redeem his people again and give them a fresh opportunity to be both blessed and a blessing.

48:20-21 Chapter 40 begins with God's great message of comfort that the way through the wilderness is being prepared for the exiles' journey home from Babylon. No matter how resistant Israel may have been to God's use of Cyrus, the survivors of exile must **flee from the Babylonians** when God opens that door to them through the Medo-Persian conquest. They will not need to "leave in haste" (52:12) as their ancestors did when leaving Egypt. The sense of urgency here is more akin to the message delivered to Lot and his family about leaving Sodom. Babylon, like Sodom, faces God's judgment. As the remnant leaves, they also must proclaim **to the ends of the earth** that **The LORD** [not Cyrus] **has redeemed his servant Jacob**. God's redemption involves more than allowing the exiles to leave Babylon; just as he **led them through the deserts** after the exodus from Egypt, so he will provide for them in the journey from Babylon to the land of promise.

48:22 This last verse, which seems somewhat disconnected from the preceding context, serves as a refrain concluding both chapters 40–48 and chapters 49–57 (cf. 57:21). The last verse of chapters 58–66 (66:24) does not contain the same refrain, but it also closes on a somber note, referring to the corpses of those who have rebelled against God. These conclusions, though negative, are appropriate to the context of Isaiah's message. In light of God's certain completion of his work and Israel's general failure to cooperate with God, these closing references stand as an exhortation to realize what is at stake for each individual and each generation as they consider their response. Verse 18 laments Israel's failure to enjoy the "peace" of God that "would have been like a river." No one need make the same mistake and be saddled with the lot of the **wicked**.

Isaiah makes it clear that God will accomplish his work of redemption even if his servant Israel is at present blind and deaf and rebellious. What he has not yet revealed is how God will overcome the problem of sin in his servant. If "there is no peace for the wicked," sin is clearly a more fundamental problem than exile. "A change of scene does not bring a change of heart. Leaving Babylon, the people do not escape from their own character."[10] Although idolatry seems to have been largely eradicated by the experience of

---

[10] Motyer, *Prophecy,* p. 382.

exile, those who will return to the land are not characterized by righteousness. Neither do they immediately become a magnet drawing the nations to Zion (2:2-4). Chapters 49–57 will make clearer the relationship of the servant to sin and the fulfillment of God's purpose.

ISAIAH 49

II. THE GRACE OF GOD AND THE SUCCESS OF HIS SERVANT (49:1–57:21)

A. THE NATURE OF THE SERVANT'S WORK (49:1–53:12)

1. The Servant Experiences Frustration, but God Gives Him Success (49:1-26)

Chapters 40–48 contain one servant song (42:1ff.). The focus of those chapters, however, falls on God's sovereign power as he foretells the rise of Cyrus and his use of this conqueror to liberate Israel from Babylonian exile. Chapters 49–57 begin with a servant song and bring the role of the servant to a climax. If Israel struggles to accept God's use of the foreigner Cyrus as an agent of deliverance, the developing portrait of the servant will raise even more questions. In fact, the servant will face frustration in his own perception of the way God works through him.

The Servant's Confidence in God (49:1-4)

¹Listen to me, you islands; / hear this, you distant nations: / Before I was born the Lord called me; / from my birth he has made mention of my name. / ²He made my mouth like a sharpened sword, / in the shadow of his hand he hid me; / he made me into a polished arrow / and concealed me in his quiver. / ³He said to me, "You are my servant, / Israel, in whom I will display my splendor." / ⁴But I said, "I have labored to no purpose; / I have spent my strength in vain and for nothing. / Yet what is due me is in the Lord's hand, / and my reward is with my God."

49:1 The parallelism of the first two lines of verse 1 clarifies that Isaiah's references to the **islands** indicate faraway lands (= **distant nations**). At the outset of this chapter and this section, therefore, the worldwide scope of the servant's work emerges as he calls the nations to give attention to his divinely appointed mission. The servant recognizes that God is with him because God has **called** him from his mother's womb.[1] Such references in poetic imagery indicate a trait so closely identified with an individual's identity that it must go back to the beginning of the person's existence (cf. Ps 51:5; 58:3).

49:2 The servant sees himself as a weapon at God's disposal. He remains hidden away until the time of God's choosing. As a **sharpened sword** and a **polished arrow**, he is well prepared for the task. The identification of his **mouth** as the weapon implies that his message will be an important part of his function (cf. the cleansing of Isaiah's lips as preparation for his commission as a prophet). Although the following verses reveal the positive function of the servant, the imagery of God's word as a sword points to its power to judge (cf. Heb 4:12-13; Rev 1:16; 19:15). Just as the revelation of God either saves or condemns, so the rest of this chapter demonstrates that the future of the nations depends on how they respond to God's revelation of himself in the servant/Israel.

49:3-4 Verse 3 explicitly identifies the **servant** as **Israel** again (cf. 41:8), but his subsequent description connects him more to the picture in 42:1ff. than to the blind and deaf servant in the rest of chapters 40–48. God's desire to manifest his **splendor** in Israel (cf. 44:23)[2] will find its fulfillment in the servant. At present, however, the servant confesses a sense of frustration.[3] The expressions **to no purpose** (לְרִיק, *lᵉrîq*), **in vain** (לְתֹהוּ, *lᵉthōhû*), and **for nothing** (וְהֶבֶל, *wᵉhebel*) strongly convey the apparent failure of his efforts. Isaiah applies a similar frustration to Israel in 26:18, in which the nation laments its failure to bring "salvation to the earth." Yet in this case the servant expresses confidence in God's ultimate vindication.

God's Commitment to the Servant (49:5-13)

⁵**And now the LORD says— / he who formed me in the womb to be his servant / to bring Jacob back to him / and gather Israel to**

---

[1]Cf. Jer 1:5. The phrases translated "before I was born" and "from my birth" both refer literally to the time when he was in his mother's womb.

[2]Although the NIV reads "he displays his *glory*" in 44:23 and "I will display my *splendor*" in 49:3, both verbs are from the same root (פאר, *p'r*).

[3]The use of the personal pronoun (וַאֲנִי, *waʾănî*) in "but I said" at the beginning of verse 4 indicates a strong contrast between God's acknowledgment of the servant and the servant's feelings about what he has accomplished.

himself, / for I am honored in the eyes of the LORD / and my God has been my strength—
⁶he says:
"It is too small a thing for you to be my servant / to restore the tribes of Jacob / and bring back those of Israel I have kept. / I will also make you a light for the Gentiles, / that you may bring my salvation to the ends of the earth."
⁷This is what the LORD says— / the Redeemer and Holy One of Israel— / to him who was despised and abhorred by the nation, / to the servant of rulers: / "Kings will see you and rise up, / princes will see and bow down, / because of the LORD, who is faithful, / the Holy One of Israel, who has chosen you."
⁸This is what the LORD says:
"In the time of my favor I will answer you, / and in the day of salvation I will help you; / I will keep you and will make you / to be a covenant for the people, / to restore the land / and to reassign its desolate inheritances, / ⁹to say to the captives, 'Come out,' / and to those in darkness, 'Be free!'
"They will feed beside the roads / and find pasture on every barren hill. / ¹⁰They will neither hunger nor thirst, / nor will the desert heat or the sun beat upon them. / He who has compassion on them will guide them / and lead them beside springs of water. / ¹¹I will turn all my mountains into roads, / and my highways will be raised up. / ¹²See, they will come from afar— / some from the north, some from the west, / some from the region of Aswan.ᵃ"
¹³Shout for joy, O heavens; / rejoice, O earth; / burst into song, O mountains! / For the LORD comforts his people / and will have compassion on his afflicted ones.

ᵃ*12* Dead Sea Scrolls; Masoretic Text *Sinim*

49:5 To this point Isaiah has presented a perplexing dual portrait of the servant. On the one hand, he has equated the servant with Israel, including all of Israel's shortcomings. On the other hand, he has presented the servant as God's faithful and capable means of accomplishing his purpose in 42:1ff. and 49:1-2. Is the contrast between Israel at present and Israel in the future? Does Isaiah distinguish between the nation as a whole and the righteous remnant? Verses 5-6 begin to reveal a solution to the paradox. God has appointed the servant **in the womb** with a purpose *on behalf of* the unresponsive nation. He is Israel, yet at the same time God calls him **to bring Jacob back to him and gather Israel to himself.** How this duality is possible calls for greater clarification, but this text requires some distinction to be made between the servant and Israel.[4]

49:6 As difficult as the task of turning Israel back to God will surely be, God considers this task **too small a thing** for the **servant**. The servant will not only turn Israel back to God but will also serve as **a light for the Gentiles**, making it possible to bring God's **salvation to the ends of the earth**. This role of illuminating the way for the Gentiles has already been assigned to the servant in 42:6, although at that point the distinction between the servant and Israel had not been established. Isaiah has demonstrated that Israel shares the darkness with the Gentile world (cf. 5:20, 30; 8:22). God has promised to shine his light into the darkness of the "Galilee of the Gentiles" (9:1-2), a necessary event for both Israel and the nations, and one in which the servant will play a prominent role.

Scholars disagree as to whether verses 7-13 continue the servant song or not. The ambiguity at this point stems from the close connection between Israel and the servant. The clearest indicator that these verses represent a continuation of verses 1-6 is the relationship between verses 8b-9a and 42:6-7. In both passages the servant is described as "a covenant for the people" and as one who sets the captives free. The significance of this connection emerges in the new element introduced by verse 7. For the first time (though not the last), the servant appears as one who experiences humiliation yet is vindicated by God. This dimension of the servant's portrayal fits well with the frustration he expresses in verse 4.

49:7 Verse 7 presents a radical contrast between the servant's initial reception by humanity and the response to him once God reveals his true importance. That he will be **despised and abhorred by the nation** points to his lack of appeal according to outward human standards. The word for "the nation" (גוֹי, *gôy*, literally, "a nation") does not typically refer to Israel and may deliberately indicate a general human response. For God's chosen one to be **the servant of rulers** means that he will not wield great power. Because God is **faithful**,

---

[4]The parallelism in the first half of verse 6 could be helpful in narrowing the options for this distinction. The initial task of the servant is "to restore the tribes of Jacob." Parallel to "the tribes of Jacob" are "those of Israel I have kept." The word translated "kept" (נצר, *nṣr*) is not a customary term for the remnant. If "the remnant" is its intended meaning here, however, the servant could not be the remnant because that group stands as the initial focus of his ministry. Cf. Motyer, *Prophecy*, p. 388.

however, the servant of the LORD will not remain in that subservient role. If the mightiest of the world's inhabitants will ultimately either **rise up** in respect in his presence or **bow down** out of reverence before him, the whole world will acknowledge him. The means of this reversal is not the important point, but rather the one who guarantees that it will occur. As with the servant, Israel should not expect triumph without struggle. The servant's experience demonstrates that "to be the chosen of God does not mean glory along the way, but it does mean glory at the end of the way."[5]

49:8 The **day of salvation** God promises to his servant is parallel to the time of God's **favor** (רָצוֹן, rāṣôn).[6] This "favor" refers to that which pleases God and accords with his will.[7] In the context of Isaiah's emphasis on divine sovereignty, God maintains control over the time of the servant's rejection as much as he does the day of his "salvation." God will **keep**[8] him from perishing and **make** him **a covenant for the people**. These active verbs further demonstrate God's control of history as he accomplishes his purpose through his servant. As in 42:6, the servant embodies the covenant, but here his role is not parallel to his function as "a light for the Gentiles." Instead, his covenant role is **to restore the land and to reassign its desolate inheritances**. This allusion to the division of Canaan among the Israelites (cf. Num 34:13), when considered in conjunction with the parallelism of 42:6, hints that the allusion should be understood figuratively.

49:9-13 The description of God's work through the servant continues in verses 9-12 through the kind of language that has been used since chapter 40 for the return from exile. As in 43:5-6, however, the fact that God promises to bring his people from all points of the compass[9] (v. 12) also indicates that God has in mind some-

---

[5]Oswalt, *Isaiah* 2, p. 295.
[6]Paul applies verse 8 to the need to accept God's grace in 2 Corinthians 6:2.
[7]Cf. the use of the same word for "acceptable" worship in 56:7; 58:5
[8]This word (*nṣr*) appears in the parallel phrase in 42:6 and also lies behind "those of Israel I have kept" in verse 6.
[9]Webb (*Message*, p. 195, n. 124) explains the absence of reference to "the east" by "the fact that direct approach from the east was blocked by the north Arabian desert." Motyer (*Prophecy*, p. 392), on the other hand, suggests that "Isaiah did not want this journey to be confused with the return from Babylon." **Aswan** (סִינִים, *sînîm*) is a city in the south of Egypt. In Ezekiel 29:10 and 30:6, the expression "from Migdol to Aswan" appears to be a reference to Egypt's northern and southern borders.

thing greater than the return from Babylon. The call for heaven and earth to celebrate the comfort God extends to his people (cf. 44:23) further signals a work of God that has universal implications. The return from exile represents a component of God's work, but Cyrus is the primary agent for that aspect of the divine purpose. God's work through the servant goes beyond the return from exile and results in extending "salvation to the ends of the earth."

God's Commitment to Zion (49:14-26)

¹⁴But Zion said, "The LORD has forsaken me, / the Lord has forgotten me."
¹⁵"Can a mother forget the baby at her breast / and have no compassion on the child she has borne? / Though she may forget, / I will not forget you! / ¹⁶See, I have engraved you on the palms of my hands; / your walls are ever before me. / ¹⁷Your sons hasten back, / and those who laid you waste depart from you. / ¹⁸Lift up your eyes and look around; / all your sons gather and come to you. / As surely as I live," declares the LORD, / "you will wear them all as ornaments; / you will put them on, like a bride.
¹⁹"Though you were ruined and made desolate / and your land laid waste, / now you will be too small for your people, / and those who devoured you will be far away. / ²⁰The children born during your bereavement / will yet say in your hearing, / 'This place is too small for us; / give us more space to live in.' / ²¹Then you will say in your heart, / 'Who bore me these? / I was bereaved and barren; / I was exiled and rejected. / Who brought these up? / I was left all alone, but these—where have they come from?'"
²²This is what the Sovereign LORD says:
"See, I will beckon to the Gentiles, / I will lift up my banner to the peoples; / they will bring your sons in their arms / and carry your daughters on their shoulders. / ²³Kings will be your foster fathers, / and their queens your nursing mothers. / They will bow down before you with their faces to the ground; / they will lick the dust at your feet. / Then you will know that I am the LORD; / those who hope in me will not be disappointed."
²⁴Can plunder be taken from warriors, / or captives rescued from the fierce[a]?
²⁵But this is what the LORD says:
"Yes, captives will be taken from warriors, / and plunder retrieved from the fierce; / I will contend with those who contend

with you, / and your children I will save. / ²⁶I will make your oppressors eat their own flesh; / they will be drunk on their own blood, as with wine. / Then all mankind will know / that I, the LORD, am your Savior, / your Redeemer, the Mighty One of Jacob."

ᵃ*24* Dead Sea Scrolls, Vulgate and Syriac (see also Septuagint and verse 25); Masoretic Text *righteous*

49:14 With verse 14 the focus shifts from God's perspective on the future to Israel's perspective on the present. The portrait of the future in the preceding verses may transcend the return from Babylon, but at this point the people of Zion doubt that God is even aware of their plight. The opening cry recalls Psalm 22:1 as Zion feels **forgotten** and **forsaken** by God. Whereas the psalmist comes to realize how mistaken his initial perceptions were when he experiences God's deliverance, Zion at this point receives a message of reassurance based on God's love for his people.

49:15-16 As unthinkable as it might be that a nursing **mother** would **forget the baby at her breast**, such a tragedy has occurred on occasion. The bond between God and his people, however, is so unbreakable that he can confidently promise **I will not forget you** (cf. 44:21; Ps 27:10). Just as verse 14 parallels "forgotten" with "forsaken," so verse 15 parallels **forget** with **have no compassion on**. In the strictly literal sense God cannot forget. When he "remembers" as he did with Noah during the flood (Gen 8:1), this image refers to the time when he steps in to act on behalf of Noah. God will not forsake or fail to show compassion toward his people even when he must submit them to great hardships. Far from forgetting Zion, she is (figuratively) **engraved** on God's **palms**. "Instead of the master's name being written on the servant's hand, the servant's name is written on the master's hand."[10] Similarly, even though Zion's **walls** will fall, they are **ever before** God as he envisions their rebuilding.

49:17-21 Not only does God keep Zion in mind, he also foretells a day when her **children** will return to adorn her again. The reversal will be so total that the traditional boundaries of Zion will be **too small** to hold the masses who return. The fact that Zion will be so **desolate** as to be considered **bereaved and barren** during the exile raises the question of the origin of these children. In light of the relatively small number that Scripture records as returning from

---

[10]Oswalt, *Isaiah* 2, p. 306.

Babylon, the broader context points again to a larger gathering that perhaps incorporates the vision of 2:2-4.

49:22-23 It should come as no surprise that **the Sovereign LORD** has brought about the great reversal. The transformation of the **Gentiles** from faithless allies and enemies to **foster fathers** and **nursing mothers** who **will bow down** and **lick the dust** before Israel can only occur by the power of God. In 5:26 God "lifted up a banner" to signal the nations to come and attack his sinful people. Here God's **banner to the peoples** calls them to aid in bringing his children to Zion. Isaiah has also spoken of the work of the Messiah in 11:10,12 in terms of raising a banner to rally the nations to himself and return Israel's exiles.[11] As was pointed out earlier, the imagery of humble service and submission by Gentile rulers results not from military defeat but a recognition of God's activity on behalf of his people. Conversion rather than conquest confirms God's promise that **those who hope in me will not be disappointed**.

49:24-26 Not all, however, will respond favorably to God's work on behalf of his people. In addition to God's reassurance of his love, he offers his commitment to defeat those who oppose him. Verse 24 may represent something of a proverbial statement, but God directly contradicts it in the following verse. At this point the power of the hostile **warriors** is more real in the eyes of Israel than the power of God. Yet when God promises that **I will contend with those who contend with you**, he identifies himself squarely with his people and commits to come to their aid. Jerusalem will know the horrors of a long siege that will lead to cannibalism (Jer 19:9; Lam 4:10), but their **oppressors** will **eat their own flesh** and **will be drunk on their own blood** as an expression of retributive justice. By the fulfillment of God's positive purpose toward the Gentiles, Israel can know that God is true; by his judgment of the enemies of his people, **all mankind will know** that he is the **Savior**, the **Redeemer, the Mighty One of Jacob**. Based on God's history with Israel as evidenced in these great titles, his reassurances should be enough to inspire his people to "hope in him" (v. 23).

---

[11]As Oswalt notes (ibid., p. 310), "The connection between that passage [11:10,12] and this one, sandwiched as it is between two Servant passages, confirms that the Servant is indeed to be identified with the Messiah."

ISAIAH 50

2. The Servant Experiences Rejection, but God Vindicates Him (50:1-11)

Chapter 49 builds on the original portrayal of the servant in chapter 42. In the latter chapter Isaiah more clearly distinguishes the servant from Israel and elaborates on his role in restoring Israel and extending God's salvation to all nations. Chapter 50 continues to unfold the picture of the servant by filling out the nature of the contrast between the servant and Israel. In the end, both Israel and the nations must decide whether they will accept and imitate the servant or pursue their own path.

Unresponsive Israel (50:1-3)

¹**This is what the LORD says:**
"Where is your mother's certificate of divorce / with which I sent her away? / Or to which of my creditors / did I sell you? / Because of your sins you were sold; / because of your transgressions your mother was sent away. / ²When I came, why was there no one? / When I called, why was there no one to answer? / Was my arm too short to ransom you? / Do I lack the strength to rescue you? / By a mere rebuke I dry up the sea, / I turn rivers into a desert; / their fish rot for lack of water / and die of thirst. / ³I clothe the sky with darkness / and make sackcloth its covering."

Prior to the third servant song (vv. 4-9), God returns to a message of reassurance to his exiled people. If they respond to God's judgment with total despair, they will not be open to the greater future he has in store for them. The glimpses into life in the exile in Daniel 1-6 demonstrate God's presence with his people in a foreign land and what he can do through those who acknowledge his continued concern for them. God has already affirmed that his love and commitment to Israel exceed that of a mother for her nursing child

(49:15); now he seeks to overcome two false perspectives on the nature of his relationship with his people.

50:1 In 49:14ff. Zion is portrayed as a mother whose children (the exiles) return to her. In 50:1 the children, assessing their future in light of the exile, fear that God has given their mother a **certificate of divorce** (cf. Deut 24:1ff.) that has permanently severed their relationship. The second image in the minds of the exiles is that of children who have been sold into slavery because of the sins of their mother (cf. Lev 25:39-41; 2 Kgs 4:1; Neh 5:5). Both images are dangerous on two counts. First, God will deny that they accurately convey his relationship to Zion. In addition, they reflect a shifting of blame from themselves to their "mother" that removes their responsibility for their plight. Ezekiel 18 attacks this same fatalism on the part of the exiles.

God responds first by demanding that the certificate of divorce which would be given to a wife who had been sent away be presented. He had given a certificate of divorce to the northern tribes, and since Judah has continued in the same faithless ways, one might assume that a second divorce is inevitable (Jer 3:8). God holds open the possibility of return even for those he has divorced, however, and commits to preserve a remnant in Jerusalem (Jer 3:11ff.). Isaiah 54:6-7 indicates that God has abandoned his wife due to her sins, but not permanently.

In a similar vein, God demands to know the **creditors** to whom he has sold his children. The very mention of God's creditors reveals the flaw in the exiles' case, for God cannot be indebted to man. As in the previous analogy, there is an element of truth in the picture of God's selling his people. On several occasions the book of Judges claims that God sold his people to their enemies (cf. 3:8; 4:2; 10:7). In the first instance, however (Judg 2:14), selling is equated with handing over. In each case the "transaction," as with God abandoning his wife, marks a temporary situation for the purpose of discipline. Isaiah 52:3 claims that God's selling of his people does not constitute a financial exchange.

The use of the passive verbs in God's reply (**you were sold/your mother was sent away**) makes it clear that the children's **sins** are responsible for their plight, not God's divorce of their mother or his indebtedness to other nations. Their situation compares to that of Ahab, who "sold himself to do evil" (1 Kgs 21:25). Just as Exodus can speak of God's hardening Pharaoh's heart and Pharaoh's hardening his own heart, God acts here in accordance with the direction his people have chosen for themselves.

50:2-3 The rest of God's response clarifies why those who experience exile must accept accountability for their plight. God has **called** to his people through his prophets and his actions, but there was **no one to answer**. The people have been given the opportunity to end their estrangement from God but have turned a deaf ear to the invitation. God has the capacity to **ransom** his people (i.e., pay *their* debts, not his) and **rescue** them, but only those who are more committed to him than to their sins (cf. 59:1-2). The references to God's power to **dry up the sea** and **clothe the sky with darkness** should call to mind the power and commitment God manifested in bringing Israel out of Egypt.

The Responsive Servant (50:4-9)

⁴The Sovereign LORD has given me an instructed tongue, / to know the word that sustains the weary. / He wakens me morning by morning, /wakens my ear to listen like one being taught. / ⁵The Sovereign LORD has opened my ears, /and I have not been rebellious; / I have not drawn back. / ⁶I offered my back to those who beat me, /my cheeks to those who pulled out my beard; /I did not hide my face /from mocking and spitting. / ⁷Because the Sovereign LORD helps me, / I will not be disgraced. / Therefore have I set my face like flint, /and I know I will not be put to shame. / ⁸He who vindicates me is near. / Who then will bring charges against me? / Let us face each other! / Who is my accuser? / Let him confront me! / ⁹It is the Sovereign LORD who helps me. / Who is he that will condemn me? / They will all wear out like a garment; / the moths will eat them up.

50:4-5 In stark contrast to the preceding portrayal of rebellious, self-pitying Israel stands the figure described in these verses. This figure is the servant though he does not call himself by that name. Verse 10 makes the connection explicitly. This song does not pursue the mission of the servant to Israel or to the Gentiles but focuses instead on the intimacy of his relationship with God. The servant refers to God four times in these six verses as the **Sovereign LORD**, a designation that combines the word for "Lord" (אֲדֹנָי, *'ădōnāy*) with the divine name (יהוה, *YHWH*). This mode of reference reflects the servant's high regard for God's authority and power.

Isaiah has frequently pointed out the serious problem of Israel's lack of godly leadership. If Israel's leaders do not listen to God and guide them accordingly, little hope remains for a stable and faithful society (cf. Hos 4:5-6). The servant, on the other hand, possesses an **instructed tongue** with which he **sustains the weary** (cf. 40:29). The knowledge by which he provides comfort to others results from a combination of divine initiative (God **has given**, he **wakens**, he **has opened**) and the servant's responsiveness (**I have not been rebellious; I have not drawn back**). God has also called out to Israel as a whole, but no one has answered (v. 2).

50:6-9 Israel is suffering and will continue to suffer as a result of a lack of responsiveness to God. Ironically, the responsive servant suffers as well. The perpetrators of his suffering may be inferred from Israel's history of mistreating those who faithfully serve God, including the prophets. As one who suffers rejection and contempt, he is reminiscent of the one "who was despised and abhorred by the nation" in 49:7. Not only do **mocking and spitting** obviously show contempt, but the removal of someone's **beard** also expresses great disrespect, the kind typically associated with prisoners of war (2 Sam 10:4; Isa 15:2; Jer 41:5; Ezek 5:1).

Although both Israel and the servant suffer, the similarity ends there. The servant is an innocent sufferer, yet he willingly submits to it (**I offered my back . . . I did not hide my face**). Without complaint, he faces his hardships with courage and determination. To **set [his] face like flint** means to meet those hardened by sin with an equal determination to do God's will (cf. Jer 1:17-19; Ezek 3:7-9). He fully trusts that he **will not be disgraced** because the one **who vindicates [him] is near**.[1] Because of the presence of God, the ultimate judge, human beings cannot **condemn** him (cf. Rom 8:31ff.). He also does not fear men because he knows they are as transient and fragile as a **garment** that will either **wear out** or be eaten by **moths**.

This song thus declares the servant's innocence and implies that he will suffer like the prophets at the hands of his own people. It also affirms that God will vindicate him as a righteous sufferer. What remains to be revealed is the place of this suffering in God's purpose for the servant.

---

[1]The word for "vindicate" (מַצְדִּיק, *maṣdîq*) conveys the idea of declaring righteous or justifying.

The Call to Walk in God's Light (50:10-11)

¹⁰**Who among you fears the LORD /and obeys the word of his servant? /Let him who walks in the dark, /who has no light, /trust in the name of the LORD /and rely on his God. /¹¹But now, all you who light fires /and provide yourselves with flaming torches, /go, walk in the light of your fires /and of the torches you have set ablaze. /This is what you shall receive from my hand: /You will lie down in torment.**

The contrasting pictures of rebellious Israel and the servant who listens **like one being taught** (v. 4) result in a call to decision. The one who **fears the LORD and obeys the word of his servant** trusts in God to illuminate his way through the darkness. Such a person may not always be able to see the way from the struggles of the present to the end of the journey, but he has heard the testimony of the servant and believes God will vindicate all who trust in him. The only alternative to this path is for people to **light fires** and seek to discern the way of life by their own wisdom or to construct it themselves. Such efforts are futile, however, and doomed to failure. God therefore sarcastically exhorts those who refuse to trust him to pursue this approach and to see where it leads—to **torment**.[2]

---

[2]The word for "torment" (מַעֲצֵבָה, *ma'ăṣēbāh*) refers to a place where one experiences pain (cf. 66:24).

ISAIAH 51

3. Interlude: Israel Must Awaken to God's Redemption (51:1–52:12)

This section connects the third and fourth servant songs. The question in 50:10 (Who "obeys (שֹׁמֵעַ, šōmēaʻ) the word of [God's] servant?") is answered in part in 51:1 as the faithful are called to "listen" (שִׁמְעוּ, šimʻû) to God's message in preparation for the climactic revelation of the servant's nature and function. The emphasis on Israel's "comfort" (51:3,12,19; 52:9) brings Isaiah's message full circle from 40:1ff. Throughout these chapters the consolation God offers is connected to the return from exile, which God will accomplish through Cyrus. Isaiah has not elucidated the relationship of the return to the servant and God's greater redemptive purpose, but the question certainly begs for an answer as the final servant song looms just ahead. Perhaps this fact explains the numerous calls for attention and alertness in this section.

Listen to God's Promise of Salvation (51:1-8)

¹"Listen to me, you who pursue righteousness / and who seek the LORD: / Look to the rock from which you were cut / and to the quarry from which you were hewn; / ²look to Abraham, your father, / and to Sarah, who gave you birth. / When I called him he was but one, / and I blessed him and made him many. / ³The LORD will surely comfort Zion / and will look with compassion on all her ruins; / he will make her deserts like Eden, / her wastelands like the garden of the LORD. / Joy and gladness will be found in her, / thanksgiving and the sound of singing.

⁴"Listen to me, my people; / hear me, my nation: / The law will go out from me; / my justice will become a light to the nations. / ⁵My righteousness draws near speedily, / my salvation is on the way, / and my arm will bring justice to the nations. / The islands

will look to me /and wait in hope for my arm. / ⁶**Lift up your eyes to the heavens, / look at the earth beneath; / the heavens will vanish like smoke, / the earth will wear out like a garment / and its inhabitants die like flies. / But my salvation will last forever, / my righteousness will never fail.**

⁷**"Hear me, you who know what is right, / you people who have my law in your hearts: / Do not fear the reproach of men / or be terrified by their insults. / ⁸For the moth will eat them up like a garment; / the worm will devour them like wool. / But my righteousness will last forever, my salvation through all generations."**

51:1-3 The group addressed in these verses appears to be the faithful remnant. Unlike the majority in Israel, they possess a true and life-changing relationship with God. The parallelism of verse 1 describes them as the ones who **pursue righteousness** and **seek the LORD**. Verse 7 characterizes them as those who "know what is right" and "have my law in your hearts." They neither pursue idols nor present to God a religion of mere outward compliance. For them, righteousness is rooted in a desire for a relationship with God and in the internalization of his truth (cf. Deut 6:5-6).

An additional indicator that God addresses the remnant here is his identification of them as the true descendants of **Abraham** and **Sarah**. These individuals are **hewn** from the **quarry** of Abraham in that they share the same faith in God. Abraham's belief that God could make a great nation from him when **he was but one** must characterize the small group that will eventually survive the exile (cf. 1:8; 30:17; 49:21) and continue God's work.[1] Out of his **compassion** God promises to turn the **wastelands** of Zion's **ruins** into an **Eden** (cf. chapter 35) so that the city will be filled with **gladness** and **singing**. Such a transformation comes only from God and calls for a faith comparable to that of Abraham.[2]

51:4-5 God's promise to send out his **law** so that his **justice** will come to the **nations** recalls the great hope first proclaimed in 2:2-4. The same mission applies to the servant, who will serve as **a light to the nations** in extending God's justice to the world (42:1-6). In a subtle way, therefore, this passage points to the unity of Isaiah's mes-

---

[1]Motyer (*Prophecy*, p. 403) understands the use of inanimate stone as an illustration to indicate that there is no "inherent life" in the remnant.

[2]The reference to "Eden" anticipates God's promise of "new heavens and a new earth" in 65:17 (cf. 11:6ff.).

sage. These verses also indicate that the scope of Isaiah's message extends beyond the return from exile. God's work consists of more than the rebuilding of Zion's ruins. His **righteousness** (v. 5), which is parallel to his **salvation**, ultimately extends to the distant lands who **wait in hope for my arm** (= power).[3]

51:6-8 Once again God parallels **salvation** and **righteousness** in verses 6 and 8 as he contrasts the permanence and reliability of his redemptive purpose with lesser realities. The **heavens** and the **earth** might appear to be permanent, but they will **vanish like smoke** and **wear out like a garment**. The **reproach of men** might appear to be a constant and threatening fact of life, but **the moth will eat them up like a garment**. God himself is the ultimate reality. Anyone who understands his nature should be confident that his commitment to save **will last forever**.

Awake, O God, to the Plight of Your People (51:9-16)

⁹**Awake, awake! Clothe yourself with strength, / O arm of the LORD; / awake, as in days gone by, / as in generations of old. / Was it not you who cut Rahab to pieces, / who pierced that monster through? /** ¹⁰**Was it not you who dried up the sea, / the waters of the great deep, / who made a road in the depths of the sea / so that the redeemed might cross over? /** ¹¹**The ransomed of the LORD will return. / They will enter Zion with singing; / everlasting joy will crown their heads. / Gladness and joy will overtake them, / and sorrow and sighing will flee away.**

¹²**"I, even I, am he who comforts you. / Who are you that you fear mortal men, / the sons of men, who are but grass, /** ¹³**that you forget the LORD your Maker, / who stretched out the heavens / and laid the foundations of the earth, / that you live in constant terror every day / because of the wrath of the oppressor, / who is bent on destruction? / For where is the wrath of the oppressor? /** ¹⁴**The cowering prisoners will soon be set free; / they will not die in their dungeon, / nor will they lack bread. /** ¹⁵**For I am the LORD your God, / who churns up the sea so that its waves roar— / the LORD Almighty is his name. /** ¹⁶**I have put my words in your mouth / and covered you with the shadow of my hand— / I who set the heavens in place,**

---

[3]The beginning of verse 5 literally reads, "My righteousness is near, my salvation goes forth." God is establishing a connection between his restoration of Zion and his salvation of the nations.

/who laid the foundations of the earth, /and who say to Zion, 'You are my people.'"

51:9-10 The double imperative of verse 9 shifts the focus from God's reassurances to the perspective of his uncertain people. Their words may reflect a response to verses 1-8, or they may simply be placed here as a contrast. Regardless, Israel clearly knows of God's past actions on behalf of his people and calls for him to return to those ways. The call for God to **awake!** reflects a measure of impatience with his apparent inactivity. The nations may "wait in hope for [God's] arm" (v. 5), but Israel eagerly cries for the **arm of the LORD** to appear. Such impatience is not a bad thing unless it is rooted in doubt or a failure to acknowledge the impact of their sins on their situation. Israel's past frame of reference, appropriately enough, is the exodus from Egypt. **Rahab**, the mythical Canaanite sea monster, is equated with Egypt in 30:7. If God could make **a road in the depths of the sea** to allow the **redeemed** to escape from their Egyptian pursuers, why does he not do so at present?

51:11-16 God's response to Israel's impatience begins in 51:11 and continues through 52:12. Most of what he says is structured around his own double imperatives to Israel (51:17; 52:1,11). In these exhortations God calls for Israel to recognize what he is doing and to respond appropriately. Initially, however, God reaffirms what he has already said through Isaiah. Verse 11 is a direct quote from 35:10, the closing note of God's promise to transform the barren wilderness that had become his people's figurative habitation. Verses 12-16 reflect the themes begun in chapter 40. God **comforts** Israel (40:1) with the contrast between frail mortals and God the Creator (40:6-8,12ff.). Israel should not **live in constant terror every day** since they have such a powerful God and one who says **to Zion, "You are my people."** He promises that the **cowering prisoners will soon be set free** (42:7).

God says to Israel, **I have put my words in your mouth**,[4] a claim that is parallel with his covering them **with the shadow of [his] hand**. God's word protects his people if they will take refuge in its promises. For this reason the permanence of the word of God is contrasted with the impermanence of men who are like grass (40:7-8) as part of God's earlier message of comfort. In 59:21 God promises

---

[4]In Deut 18:18 God promises to put his words in the mouth of the prophet like Moses that he will raise up.

that his words will not depart from the mouths of present and future generations as part of his "covenant" with them.

Awake, O Jerusalem, to the End of Your Suffering (51:17-23)

¹⁷Awake, awake! / Rise up, O Jerusalem, / you who have drunk from the hand of the LORD / the cup of his wrath, / you who have drained to its dregs / the goblet that makes men stagger. / ¹⁸Of all the sons she bore / there was none to guide her; / of all the sons she reared / there was none to take her by the hand. / ¹⁹These double calamities have come upon you— / who can comfort you?— / ruin and destruction, famine and sword— / who can[a] console you? / ²⁰Your sons have fainted; / they lie at the head of every street, / like antelope caught in a net. / They are filled with the wrath of the LORD / and the rebuke of your God.

²¹Therefore hear this, you afflicted one, / made drunk, but not with wine. / ²²This is what your Sovereign LORD says, / your God, who defends his people: / "See, I have taken out of your hand / the cup that made you stagger; / from that cup, the goblet of my wrath, / you will never drink again. / ²³I will put it into the hands of your tormentors, / who said to you, / 'Fall prostrate that we may walk over you.' / And you made your back like the ground, / like a street to be walked over."

[a]*19* Dead Sea Scrolls, Setuagint, Vulgate and Syriac; Masoretic Text / *how can I*

51:17-21 Isaiah describes Israel's judgment in terms of drinking **the cup of [God's] wrath**. This bitter brew represents an accumulation of sins which, when the cup is full, must be **drained to its dregs** by those who have filled it (cf. Jer 23:15ff.; Ezek 23:32-34). The situation in which Jerusalem's **sons** have failed **to guide her** may refer to the ostensible leaders who suffer from their own drunkenness (29:9-10; cf. 5:22-23; 28:7-8). Consequently, they also **are filled with the wrath of the LORD**. How can Jerusalem recover from the **double calamities** (cf. 40:2) that have placed her in such a drunken stupor?

51:22-23 The only hope for Jerusalem is God's call for her to "Awake, awake!" and to "rise up" (v. 1). The need is not for God to awaken himself but to awaken his people. Thankfully, the God **who defends his people** has graciously taken the cup of his wrath from Israel and given it instead to Israel's **tormentors**. These harsh enemies, though they may have accomplished God's purpose in disciplining Israel, deserve God's judgment. Their practice of walking on the backs of those they conquer (cf. Josh 10:24) illustrates the cruelty for which they are justly condemned.

God's cup of wrath can be fatal, but his purpose for his people precludes that possibility in this case. By removing the cup God allows Israel to regain her senses and resume a place in God's work of redemption. It is vital, however, that Israel accept this message. "The problem is that she is still labouring under a sense of condemnation, and it is like a drug which stupefies her. 'Awake,' says Isaiah. 'Rise up. You are not condemned, and you must not go on behaving as though you are!"[5]

---

[5]Webb, *Message*, p. 205.

ISAIAH 52

Awake, O Zion, to the Joy of Your Salvation (52:1-10)

¹Awake, awake, O Zion, /clothe yourself with strength. /Put on your garments of splendor, /O Jerusalem, the holy city. / The uncircumcised and defiled /will not enter you again. /²Shake off your dust; /rise up, sit enthroned, O Jerusalem. / Free yourself from the chains on your neck, /O captive Daughter of Zion.

³For this is what the LORD says:

"You were sold for nothing, /and without money you will be redeemed."

⁴For this is what the Sovereign LORD says:

"At first my people went down to Egypt to live; /lately, Assyria has oppressed them.

⁵"And now what do I have here?" declares the LORD.

"For my people have been taken away for nothing, /and those who rule them mock,ᵃ" /declares the LORD. /"And all day long / my name is constantly blasphemed. / ⁶Therefore my people will know my name; /therefore in that day they will know /that it is I who foretold it. /Yes, it is I."

⁷How beautiful on the mountains /are the feet of those who bring good news, /who proclaim peace, /who bring good tidings, /who proclaim salvation, /who say to Zion, / "Your God reigns!" / ⁸Listen! Your watchmen lift up their voices; /together they shout for joy. / When the LORD returns to Zion, /they will see it with their own eyes. /⁹Burst into songs of joy together, /you ruins of Jerusalem, / for the LORD has comforted his people, / he has redeemed Jerusalem. / ¹⁰The LORD will lay bare his holy arm /in the sight of all the nations, /and all the ends of the earth will see /the salvation of our God.

ᵃ5 Dead Sea Scrolls and Vulgate; Masoretic Text *wail*

52:1-2 The second call to **Awake** supports the claims of the previous verses and extends the implications of those claims. Instead of seeing herself as one who is drunk and trampled by the boots of conquerors, **Zion** should see herself as one who is clothed with **strength** and **garments of splendor** which God provides. **Jerusalem** should accept God's claim of security and trade her **chains** for a throne.

52:3-6 Two factors account for the legitimacy of Zion's transformation. First, the nations have no claim on her. God has already rejected the notion that he has sold his people (50:1). Since they **were sold for nothing**, no payment is necessary for their redemption. God's rightful claim to Israel that guaranteed an end of the bondage to **Egypt** and to **Assyria** applies to Babylon as well. The second justification of this drastic transformation is the response of the nations to Zion's captivity. Since God's **name is constantly blasphemed** as a result of Zion's humiliation, he must take action to reverse and judge this serious offense. In the process, since he has **foretold** what he will do, God's **people will know [his] name**. They are being called to acknowledge him on the basis of his past faithfulness. If they fail to do so, at least they will recognize his true nature when he redeems them again.[1]

52:7-10 Verses 7-10 jump ahead from the promise to the time of fulfillment, viewing the joyful return from exile as an accomplished fact. This passage uses the imagery of a runner bringing back **good news**[2] to the **watchmen** of the city who eagerly await a report on the battle. The news of **peace** and **salvation** is so wonderful that even the **feet** of the messenger are deemed **beautiful**. The heart of the good news is the proclamation to the inhabitants of Jerusalem that **"Your God reigns!"** God resolves this issue that has seemed to be in doubt in the hearts of some when he **returns to Zion** and thus brings comfort to **his people**. He answers any questions about "the arm of the LORD" (51:9) when he "lays it bare" in redeeming Jerusalem.[3]

Once again, the promises here reach beyond the return from exile.[4] The **salvation of our God** that will become evident to **all the**

---

[1]Cf. "they will see it with their own eyes" in verse 8.

[2]מְבַשֵּׂר (*m^ebaśśēr*) is used twice in verse 7 ("who bring good news" and "who bring good tidings.")

[3]In verse 10 the NIV translates the first verb as a future ("will lay bare"), but it is a perfect tense like the verbs at the end of verse 9 ("has comforted," "has redeemed") and should be translated accordingly (cf. NASB, "has bared").

[4]Cf. the comments on 51:4-5. Paul's application of verse 7 to the proclamation of the gospel in Rom 10:15 indicates his recognition of the broader scope of this passage.

ends of the earth results not from the return alone, but from all that occurs because God did not abandon his people in exile. Only God's power could bring about this unlikely result (note how God's **arm** acting on behalf of **the nations** links verse 10 with 51:5).

Depart from the Place of Your Bondage (52:11-12)

[11]Depart, depart, go out from there! / Touch no unclean thing! / Come out from it and be pure, / you who carry the vessels of the LORD. / [12]But you will not leave in haste / or go in flight; / for the LORD will go before you, / the God of Israel will be your rear guard.

52:11-12 The final double imperative explicitly calls for action by those whom God has redeemed. These verses generally reflect the exodus from Egypt, with two exceptions. God prepares the way for departure, but his people must respond to his call to **go out from there!** They must acknowledge the holiness of their God (cf. Exod 19:10-13). They will enjoy God's protective presence all around them (cf. Exod 13:21; 14:19-20). Whereas they left Egypt with material goods given to them by the Egyptians (Exod 12:35-36), now they are commanded, "**Touch no unclean thing!**" The call to separation is thus even greater. Furthermore, while the Israelites prepared to leave Egypt hastily (Exod 12:11), they **will not leave in haste** on this occasion.[5] The circumstances of the return from exile will be much more favorable in light of the official support of Cyrus.

As with this entire section, verses 11-12 anticipate the return from Babylonian exile, but they also transcend that event. Perhaps the general call to depart **from there** rather than "from Babylon" reflects that intention.[6] Paul uses the exhortation to "Touch no unclean thing!" in his call for Christians to live in such a way that they constitute a dwelling place for God (2 Cor 6:17). John's call to "Come out of her, my people" as he announces the fall of the latter-day Babylon in Revelation 18:4 also signals the broader application of these words. "There is more to be left behind than Babylon; there is the whole ambience of worldliness and estrangement from God

---

[5]Motyer (*Prophecy*, p. 422) points out that the word for "haste" (חִפָּזוֹן, *ḥippāzôn*) appears outside of this verse only in Exod 12:11 and Deut 16:3, both of which refer to the urgent departure from Egypt.

[6]Webb, *Message*, p. 208. Motyer (*Prophecy*, p. 421) maintains that "*From there* is a really great difficulty for all who propose a Babylonian location for the prophet: how could he say *from there* if he meant 'from here'?"

that it represents. The physical 'leaving' of 48:20 is here overlaid and transcended by a notion of setting out and pilgrimage which is essentially moral and spiritual."[7]

[**Note:** Verses 13-15 appear with the following section in chapter 53.]

---

[7]Webb, *Message*, p. 208.

ISAIAH 53

4. The Servant Experiences Death, but God Exalts Him (52:13–53:12)

The fourth and climactic servant song explains why suffering has entered into the description of the servant of the LORD, but for the first generations of Isaiah's audience this song must have raised as many questions as it answered. The basic thrust of the passage is plain enough, but who could experience this level of suffering and rejection and still emerge victorious? How could anyone intercede for the sins of others by his death?

Each of the five three-verse stanzas of the song opens into the next as the portrait unfolds. The first serves as something of an overview of triumph and suffering, followed by an elaboration of the servant's unattractiveness, a surprising twist as to why the servant suffers, the apparent tragedy of his silent acceptance of his role, and finally God's transformation of this apparent tragedy. Throughout the song the hearer should feel the tension between the servant's experience of suffering and the accomplishment of God's powerful purpose through him.

An Overview of the Tension: Exaltation and Disfigurement (52:13-15)

¹³**See, my servant will act wisely**[a]; / he will be raised and lifted up and highly exalted. / ¹⁴Just as there were many who were appalled at him[b]— / his appearance was so disfigured / beyond that of any man / and his form marred beyond human likeness— / ¹⁵so will he sprinkle many nations,[c] / and kings will shut their mouths because of him. / For what they were not told, they will see, / and what they have not heard, they will understand.

[a]13 Or *will prosper*   [b]14 Hebrew *you*   [c]15 Hebrew; Septuagint *so will many nations marvel at him*

52:13 The final servant song introduces the servant (הִנֵּה...עַבְדִּי,

hinnēh...'abdî) in a way very similar to his introduction in the first servant song in 42:1 (עַבְדִּי הֵן, *hēn 'abdî*). As the portrait of the servant draws to a close, however, the opening stanza of this song brings together the seemingly dissonant elements of glorious success and horrible disfigurement. The emphasis at the outset is on the former, for the servant **will act wisely**[1] and consequently **he will be raised and lifted up and highly exalted**. The same words for "raised" and "lifted up" appear in Isaiah's vision of God on his throne in 6:1.[2]

52:14 The servant's exaltation will be preceded, however, by an experience so terrible that he will be **disfigured** beyond recognition. The third servant song also connects the servant's openness to God's instruction (the essence of wisdom) with the experience of abuse (50:4-6). True wisdom manifests itself in doing the will of God, and Israel's history has demonstrated that those who follow God in a time of unfaithfulness will suffer rejection and mistreatment (cf. Elijah and Ahab). Yet just as the third servant song promises divine vindication in the end (50:7-9), so here also God will cause the servant's work to prevail.

Several issues of translation impact the proper understanding of verses 14-15. In the first line of verse 14, the best manuscript evidence indicates that people **were appalled at** "*you*."[3] The pronoun is singular, but the NASB takes it collectively and supplies the explanatory words "*My people*." Also important is the construction formed by **just as** (כַּאֲשֶׁר, *ka'ăšer*) at the beginning of verse 14 and **so** (כֵּן, *kēn*) at the beginning of verse 15 (the word for "so" also appears before "his appearance was so disfigured . . ." in verse 14, although the NIV does not translate it). This construction sets up a correspondence between the reaction to the hardships of Israel — or more likely the faithful remnant or a representative individual like Isaiah — and the reaction to the servant. The servant's wisdom and ultimate exaltation, therefore, derive at least in part from his identification with those who suffer.

52:15 The proper translation of the word the NIV renders **sprinkle** is also at issue. The two main objections to this translation are:

---

[1]Some translations render this word (יַשְׂכִּיל, *yaśkîl*) as "prosper" (cf. NASB, NIV textual note). Both notions are associated with the word, but the prosperity is the result of acting wisely. In 53:10 God's will prospers in the servant's hand, although a different word (יִצְלָח, *yiṣlaḥ*) is used there.

[2]These words also describe God in 33:10.

[3]Cf. the NIV textual note.

1) when the word here (נזה, *nzh*) means "sprinkle" in its other appearances it refers to a liquid that is sprinkled "upon" something; and 2) "sprinkle" does not provide a proper parallelism to **and kings will shut their mouths because of him**.[4] The alternative is to trace the word to an Arabic root meaning "startle."[5] In this case verse 15a represents a continuation of the shocked reaction to the servant in verse 14b on the part of **many nations** and **kings** who **shut their mouths** because of the magnitude of his sufferings (cf. Job 21:5). Scripture also speaks of mouths being shut, however, in awareness of guilt (cf. Job 5:16; Ps 63:11; 107:42; Rom 3:19), a situation which appropriately parallels the ritual purity context of sprinkling (cf. Exod 29:21; Lev 5:9; 14:7,16,27,51; 16:14,19; Num 8:7).

Regardless of the way verse 15a should be understood, the latter part of verse 15 indicates that those who previously **were not told** about God's work through the servant will ultimately **see** and **understand**. They will come to terms with the remarkable way that God triumphs through one who has been brought so low. The question at this point is whether or not those to whom this message *is* revealed will accept it by faith.

A Heightening of the Tension: The Power of God and the Rejection of Men (53:1-3)

¹Who has believed our message / and to whom has the arm of the LORD been revealed? / ²He grew up before him like a tender shoot, / and like a root out of dry ground. / He had no beauty or majesty to attract us to him, / nothing in his appearance that we should desire him. / ³He was despised and rejected by men, / a man of sorrows, and familiar with suffering. / Like one from whom men hide their faces / he was despised, and we esteemed him not.

53:1 The second and third stanzas of the song shift from God's perspective ("my servant") to that of a group of human witnesses ("our message"). The second stanza intensifies the picture of the servant's lack of initial human appeal by tracing it to his beginnings. In the process serious questions emerge as to the appeal of the **message** to which Isaiah and his disciples bear witness (cf. 8:16-18). The call for God to reveal his **arm** in the passage preceding this servant song

---

[4]Oswalt, *Isaiah* 2, p. 374, n. 56.
[5]Cf. the NIV textual note.

(51:9) assumes a context of weakness in which the people cannot perceive God at work. Who, then, will see the power of God (cf. 52:10) **revealed** in one who appears so unattractive and unsuccessful?

53:2a Verse 2 compares the servant to a **tender shoot** and a **root out of dry ground** as he grows up before God. These images represent that which is small and fragile (cf. 37:27), yet they also link the servant to the hope for the future expressed earlier in Isaiah. In 4:4ff. Zion's future glory is expressed in terms of the beauty and glory of the "Branch of the LORD." In 6:13 Israel retains hope only because "the holy seed will be the stump in the land" (cf. Job 14:7-9). Most significantly, the Davidic Messiah is described as a "shoot" that "will come up from the stump of Jesse" (11:1,10). Not only does this passage link the servant with the messianic promise to David, therefore, but it also demonstrates that the notion of a Messiah with humble origins is not a new idea. David himself was an unlikely candidate as king and suffered greatly at the hands of Saul before God affirmed David's selection by establishing his rule over Israel.

53:2b-3 Genesis 29:17 uses the same words for the **beauty** (תֹּאַר, *tō'ar*) and **appearance** (מַרְאֶה, *mar'eh*) the servant lacks to describe Rachel.[6] This verse contrasts Rachel with her sister Leah and thus explains Rachel's greater appeal to Jacob. Even the witnesses must confess that they are initially as superficial as Jacob in the way they perceive the servant. The outer frame of verse 3 continues the same theme. The verse is bracketed by the word **despised** (נִבְזֶה, *nibzeh*). Oswalt points out that the Hebrew word does not carry the same connotation of contempt as the English word, but instead implies that the servant is "worthless, unworthy of attention."[7] The two qualifying phrases (**rejected by men** and **we esteemed him not**) support this understanding.

Whereas one might not be attracted to or pay no attention to someone who lacks physical attractiveness, something more must account for the extreme reaction in the middle of verse 3. The servant so obviously reflects **sorrows** and **suffering** that he becomes **one from whom men hide their faces**.[8] The literal rendering **a man**

---

[6]Motyer, *Prophecy*, p. 428.
[7]Oswalt, *Isaiah* 2, p. 383.
[8]The *Tanakh*, the translation of the Jewish Publication Society, renders this phrase, "As one who hid his face from us" and connects it to the requirements for lepers in Leviticus 13:45ff. This translation is possible but does not fit the parallelism as well as the NIV.

of sorrows reflects the Hebrew construct state ("man/woman of . . ." or "son/daughter of . . .") that describes a fundamental characteristic of a person. The word for "sorrows" (מַכְאֹבוֹת, *makōbôth*) refers primarily to the experience of pain. It describes the "suffering" God observed in the experience of the Israelite slaves in Egypt (Exod 3:7). "Suffering" (חֳלִי, *ḥŏlî*) refers to human weakness, normally as it manifests itself in sickness. This suffering is "known" (literally) to the servant in the sense that he has experienced it.

A Pivotal Moment for the Tension: Suffering and Substitution (53:4-6)

⁴Surely he took up our infirmities /and carried our sorrows, / yet we considered him stricken by God, / smitten by him, and afflicted. / ⁵But he was pierced for our transgressions, / he was crushed for our iniquities; / the punishment that brought us / peace was upon him, /and by his wounds we are healed. / ⁶We all, like sheep, have gone astray, /each of us has turned to his own way; /and the LORD has laid on him / the iniquity of us all.

53:4-5 The heart of the song provides a critical turn as the reason for the suffering of God's faithful servant comes to light, as does the tragic irony of his rejection by man. The striking feature of these verses is the juxtaposition of third person pronouns (he/his/him) and first person plural pronouns (we/our/us).[9] Also important are the verbal links between verse 4 and verse 3. The very **infirmities** (the same word as "suffering" in verse 3) and **sorrows** of the servant that led the witnesses to "hide their faces" from him prove to be their own! They **considered** (the same word as "esteemed" in verse 3) **him stricken by God**, but he was struck with the punishment they deserved!

This stanza multiplies the expressions for what the servant experiences (he is **smitten, afflicted, pierced, crushed**;[10] he receives **punishment** and **wounds**). Such a multiplication of terms represents typical Hebrew style in conveying the full range of pain and suffering. It also clarifies that these experiences are due to the **transgressions** and **iniquities** of others. Because of what the servant **took up** and **carried**, the guilty will enjoy **peace** with God and be **healed**.

---

[9]Several of these pronouns are in an emphatic position in the Hebrew text.

[10]Webb (*Message*, p. 211) points out that the words "pierced" (cf. 51:9; Job 26:13; Zech 12:10) and "crushed" (Ps 89:10; 143:3) "indicate a violent death."

53:6 The use of the passive voice in verses 4-5 might leave in doubt who is responsible for the servant's sufferings. The witnesses originally conclude that God has stricken him for his own sins. As with Job's friends, however, they only see part of the picture. The last line of verse 6 acknowledges that God is indeed responsible for these hardships, but he inflicts what "we all" deserve, not what the servant deserves. Verse 6 thus also makes it clear that the work of the servant has an extensive application (**We all, each of us, of us all**). Considering the universal need for cleansing and forgiveness, which applies even to Isaiah (6:5), the servant emerges more clearly as an individual (not the collective Israel or faithful remnant) who acts on behalf of the straying **sheep**.

The notion of the death of an innocent for the sins of others is not new to Israel. The clearest picture of "substitutionary atonement" appears in the ritual of the Day of Atonement in Leviticus 16. In an expansion of the symbolism of the typical sacrifices, the high priest slaughters one goat as a sin offering (v. 15). He places his hands on a second goat, confesses the sins of the people which are thus transferred to the goat's head, and has the goat led away from the camp (vv. 20-22). Yet even though Moses perhaps sought to offer himself on behalf of Israel after the golden calf (Exod 32:32), the Old Testament nowhere countenances human sacrifice (cf. the prohibition of child sacrifice in Lev 18:21; Deut 18:10).

A Resumption of the Tension: The Death of the Innocent Sufferer and the Future (53:7-9)

⁷He was oppressed and afflicted, / yet he did not open his mouth; / he was led like a lamb to the slaughter, / and as a sheep before her shearers is silent, / so he did not open his mouth. / ⁸By oppression[a] and judgment he was taken away. / And who can speak of his descendants? / For he was cut off from the land of the living; / for the transgression of my people he was stricken.[b] / ⁹He was assigned a grave with the wicked, / and with the rich in his death, / though he had done no violence, / nor was any deceit in his mouth.

[a]*8 Or From arrest*   [b]*8 Or away. / Yet who of his generation considered / that he was cut off from the land of the living / for the transgression of my people / to whom the blow was due?*

53:7-8 Now that the *cause* of the servant's suffering has emerged, the song turns to consider the implications for the servant's future that *result from* the role he is called to assume. In bearing the consequences of the straying of the sheep, he becomes **like a lamb** who is being led **to the slaughter**. Sheep are **silent** when taken away to their fate because they do not know what lies ahead. The servant, on the other hand, deliberately does **not open his mouth** even though he knows he is the victim of **oppression**.[11] The reminder that the servant **was stricken**[12] not for his own sins but **for the transgression of my people** (cf. v. 5) highlights his innocence, a point that verse 9b makes explicitly.

As a result of his silent acceptance of the injustice against him, the servant pays the ultimate price in being **cut off from the land of the living**. The notion of being "cut off" in the Old Testament indicates one who dies under God's judgment.[13] Although the particular form of the verb used here (נִגְזַר, *nigzar*) is not typical, it makes the same point (cf. the same verb in 2 Chr 26:21; Ps 88:5 [v. 6 in Hebrew]). For an Israelite, to die under such circumstances or to die prematurely or childless was considered a great disgrace. The question **"who can speak of his descendants?"** seems to reinforce the shameful plight of the servant. The word for "descendants" (דּוֹר, *dôr*) normally refers to a period of time or to those who live in that time (in both cases the English "generation" suffices). The servant's offspring are mentioned in verse 10, but the connection of that thought to verse 8 may be indirect if this verse points to a life too brief to produce descendants. If the intent instead is to reflect on the *people* of his generation, their complicity in the servant's mistreatment becomes the issue. Both understandings ("And who can speak of his lifetime/contemporaries?") parallel effectively with the first line of verse 8.

53:9 The servant's burial also reflects on the assessment of his life. An understanding of how verse 9 addresses this question hinges on the nature of the parallelism between **the wicked** and **the rich** in

---

[11]The word for "oppressed" in verse 7 (נָגַשׂ, *ngś*) is used to describe the "slave drivers" who treated the Israelites harshly in Egypt (cf. Exod 3:7), as well as their Babylonian captors (Isa 14:4). It is also applied to Israelites when they mistreat one another (Isa 3:5,12; 58:3). The word for "oppression" in verse 8 (עֹצֶר, *'ōṣer*) is different, and it implies restraint or confinement. The combination of nouns "oppression and judgment" could be taken to mean a "restraint of justice," i.e., injustice (Oswalt, *Isaiah* 2, p. 393).

[12]The word translated "stricken" (נֶגַע, *nega'*) typically refers to a mark or wound inflicted either by another person or by a disease.

[13]Cf. Exod 12:15; 31:14; Lev 7:20; 17:4,14; Num 9:13; 15:30-31; Job 4:7; Ps 37:22,28; Isa 11:13; 14:22; 29:20; 48:19.

the first two lines. On the surface the two terms appear basically synonymous. The NIV apparently understands them this way because it links the two lines together with **and** while contrasting the servant's humiliation with his innocence in the second half of the verse (introduced by **though**). In this case the "rich" would be the wicked who abuse their power by oppressing others (cf. Ps 49:5-6 [vv. 6-7 in Hebrew]).[14]

The NASB, on the other hand, translates verse 9:

> His grave was assigned with wicked men,
> Yet he was with a rich man in His death,
> Because he had done no violence,
> Nor was there any deceit in His mouth.

According to this translation, the wicked and the rich are contrasted, and the servant's final place with the rich is "because" of his innocence. The NASB also deals literally with the plural of "wicked" and the singular of "rich." As Motyer points out, the singular form of "rich" (עָשִׁיר, *'āšîr*) "is only a collective when it stands in contrast to another singular representing a different class of person (e.g., the poor); in every other case the singular represents a singular and the plural a plural."[15] According to this reading verse 9 begins to point to the servant's vindication even in the circumstances surrounding his death as he is spared from a burial with the wicked.

A Resolution of the Tension: The Will of God and the Triumph over Death (53:10-12)

[10]**Yet it was the LORD's will to crush him and cause him to suffer, / and though the LORD makes[a] his life a guilt offering, / he will see his offspring and prolong his days, / and the will of the LORD will prosper in his hand. /** [11]**After the suffering of his soul, / he will see the light ˻of life˼[b] and be satisfied[c]; / by his knowledge[d] my righteous servant will justify many, / and he will bear their iniquities. /** [12]**Therefore I will give him a portion among the great,[e] / and he will divide the spoils with the strong,[f] / because he poured out his life unto death, / and was numbered with the transgressors. / For he bore the sin of many, / and made intercession for the transgressors.**

---

[14]Cf. Oswalt, *Isaiah 2*, p. 398.
[15]Motyer, *Prophecy*, p. 435.

ᵃ*10* Hebrew *though you make*   ᵇ*11* Dead Sea Scrolls (see also Septuagint); Masoretic Text does not have *the light ⌊of life⌋.*   ᶜ*11* Or (with Masoretic Text) ¹¹*He will see the result of the suffering of his soul / and be satisfied*   ᵈ*11* Or *by knowledge of him*   ᵉ*12* Or *many*   ᶠ*12* Or *numerous*

53:10 The final stanza of the song begins with a striking assertion: no matter how much the servant is abused or treated unjustly by man, God assumes ultimate responsibility for what the servant experiences. In saying that the servant's crushing experience is the **will** (חָפֵץ, *ḥāpheṣ*) of God, Isaiah stresses that it pleases God by accomplishing his purpose (this word is often translated in terms of "delight" or "pleasure"). In contrast to the empty worship Isaiah describes at the opening of the book (cf. 1:11—"I have no *pleasure* in the blood of bulls and lambs and goats"), **the will [*ḥāpheṣ*] of the LORD will prosper** by the sacrifice of the servant.

The servant advances the will of God in his role as a **guilt offering** (אָשָׁם, *'āšām*). This designation makes the sacrificial language of verses 4-6 more explicit. The guilt offering (cf. Lev 5:14–6:7; 7:1-6) is one of Israel's primary atoning sacrifices. A unique aspect of this sacrifice is the inclusion of restitution along with the cleansing/atoning effect of the sacrificial victim's death. Perhaps the broader scope of the guilt offering accounts for its use in describing the significance of the servant's suffering and death.

The three positive elements mentioned in verse 10b occur as the *result* of the servant's role as a guilt offering, not *in spite of* it. The concessive word **though** (אִם, *'im*) would be better translated "if" or "when." The results are surprising, to be sure, given the death of the servant as an essential element of his role as a guilt offering (cf. vv. 8-9). By revealing God's hand in the servant's experience, however, a major purpose of the song's final stanza emerges: God can vindicate his faithful servants even in death. Whereas the preceding stanza presented the seemingly hopeless plight of one who dies unjustly, these verses present the servant's capacity by the power of God to **see his offspring and prolong his days**. In the larger context, the servant's work answers the question raised by the formerly barren Zion about the origin of all the children she will one day see (49:19ff.; cf. 54:1ff.).[16] The apparently tragic plight of the servant thus becomes pivotal for the accomplishment of God's purpose.

53:11 In verse 10 the servant sees his "offspring" (literally, "seed"). In verse 11 the Hebrew text leaves unstated what he sees

---

[16]Ibid., p. 440.

after [or "because of"] **the suffering of his soul**, although the NIV follows all the Qumran manuscripts of Isaiah and the Septuagint in adding the word **light**.[17] The phrase **by his knowledge** could either mean "by what he knows" or "by what [others] know about him." Both the emphasis on the servant and the parallelism favor the former and thus connect his knowledge with his "satisfaction" rather than his justification of others as in the NIV. The first two lines would therefore read:

> Because of his suffering he will see;
> He will be satisfied by his knowledge.

These words, along with the rest of the verse, indicate the servant's recognition in the end that what he has done has not been in vain. His sacrifice not only pleases God but it also satisfies the servant.

The parallelism of the last two lines of verse 11 indicates both what satisfies the servant (he **will justify many**) and the basis of that justification (**he will bear their iniquities**). The description of the servant as **righteous** represents a significant word play on "justify."[18] The servant's innocence has already been declared. In order to justify (= declare or make righteous) those who have gone astray, the servant must, as with the animal sacrifices, be "without defect" (Lev 1:3). The irony of the extreme suffering and death of a righteous individual proves to be an essential element to his accomplishment of God's purpose for him.

The two references to the **many** whom the servant justifies by bearing their sins in verses 11-12 correspond to the two uses of the same word in 52:14-15 for those who are initially turned away by the servant's disfigurement. Motyer defines the term as "a precise company, numerous but not all-inclusive."[19] It is a reference at first to the faithful remnant, to those "who pursue righteousness and who seek the LORD" (51:1). Through these God will work to extend the ministry of the servant so that the "many" will encompass all who "believe the message" (cf. 53:1).

53:12 Therefore at the beginning of verse 12 introduces the reward God bestows upon the servant for his incredible self-giving

---

[17]The words "of life" are purely an explanatory addition, as indicated by the brackets in the text.

[18]The two words are placed together (צַדִּיק יַצְדִּיק, *yaṣdîq ṣadîq*) at the beginning of the second line of verse 11.

[19]Motyer, *Prophecy*, p. 442.

work, and **because** in the middle of the verse reiterates the nature and effects of his work. The first half of the verse contains greater difficulties, so it might be helpful to begin with the basis of the servant's reward. The parallelism between **poured out his life unto death** and **was numbered with the transgressors** resembles that of verse 8, where "he was cut off from the land of the living" parallels "for the transgression of my people he was stricken." In both cases the servant's death identifies him with sinners. The reference in verse 12 particularly emphasizes that identification, with the last two lines of the verse clarifying the reason for the servant's close association with the transgressors (to bear their sins and in so doing to make **intercession** for them).

The biggest question for the first two lines of verse 12 involves a translation in which God allots the servant a **portion** *along with* the **great** ("many")[20] and the servant will **divide the spoils with the strong**.[21] Motyer considers the results of such a translation to be anticlimactic and suggests an alternative such as: "I will apportion to him the many, and the strong he will apportion as spoil."[22] This translation is possible and might appear to honor the servant more by placing him above rather than among those for whom he dies. In light of the emphasis on the servant's identification with sinners at the end of the verse, however, the context favors the more customary reading. The servant moves from being one from whom people turn away to one with whom and through whom they joyfully receive the covenant blessings God intends for his people.[23]

ISAIAH'S PORTRAYAL OF THE SERVANT OF THE LORD: SUMMARY AND CONCLUSIONS

The "suffering servant" song is clearly one of the most significant and hotly debated passages in Isaiah, if not the entire Bible. Because Christians understandably see Jesus throughout this passage, every

---

[20]The word (רַבִּים, *rabbîm*) is translated "many" in 52:14-15 and 53:11 and should be translated the same here.

[21]Cf. the NIV, NASB, ESV, NRSV, etc.

[22]Motyer, *Prophecy,* pp. 442-443.

[23]The same verb (חלק, *ḥlq*) lies behind "I will give him a portion" and "he will divide." It is the word used for dividing the land after the conquest in fulfillment of God's covenant promise (cf. Josh 13:7).

effort has been made in the commentary to this point to consider all of the servant songs solely within the context of Isaiah.[24] The time has come, however, to consider the servant songs in the larger context of Scripture, including the New Testament identification of the servant with Jesus.

In the first 39 chapters of the book of Isaiah, God applies the designation "servant" to Isaiah himself (20:3), to Eliakim (22:20), and to David (37:35). In chapters 40–48 the label is applied to Israel in a collective sense, frequently in parallel with terms such as "chosen" or "witnesses" (cf. 41:8-9; 43:10; 44:1,21,26; 45:4; 48:20). Unlike Isaiah, Eliakim, and David, however, Israel collectively has miserably failed in its role as God's servant. Isaiah has pointed out Israel's failure from the beginning of the book, and in 42:19 this failure is explicitly connected to the servant image:

> Who is blind but my servant,
> and deaf like the messenger I send?
> Who is blind like the one committed to me,
> blind like the servant of the LORD?

Isaiah 42 also introduces the first of the "servant songs" (vv. 1-7) that present the ideal servant, the one who faithfully and effectively accomplishes God's will. In the first song he appears as one who is gentle and compassionate, yet empowered by God so that he "establishes justice on earth" and functions as "a light to the Gentiles." Chapters 40–48 emphasize the sovereignty of God and the way he delivers Israel from Babylonian exile through Cyrus. Since the servant theme in these chapters highlights Israel's failed servanthood, 42:1-7 might be initially understood to anticipate a time when Israel will more faithfully fulfill its role as God's servant-witness.

The focus shifts significantly in Isaiah 49–57. These chapters say nothing about Cyrus, but instead move the servant to center stage. In fact, after the final servant song (52:13–53:12), Isaiah does not mention the servant again although God's people are designated by the plural "servants" several times in the rest of the book (cf. 54:17; 56:6; 63:17; 65:9,13-15; 66:14).

Isaiah 49 opens this section of the book with the second servant song. In verse 3 Israel is paralleled with the servant for the last time. This point is significant because here the servant songs begin to dis-

---

[24]It is for this reason that the commentary has avoided capitalizing the word "servant."

tinguish between Israel and the servant. In verse 5 the servant functions "to bring Jacob back" to God, and in verse 6 "to bring back the preserved of Israel." The one who restores Israel also assumes the role assigned to servant-Israel in the first song as "a light for the Gentiles" in order to bring "salvation to the ends of the earth."

The third servant song (50:4-9) implicitly contrasts the servant with Israel by portraying him as one who is receptive to God and thus obedient and thoroughly instructed. In what might appear to be a strange combination, this song also introduces the servant as one who receives abuse. In spite of this abuse, the servant is determined to remain faithful, confident that God will vindicate him no matter what man attempts to do against him. Although the notion of the ideal servant's suffering might be surprising, many other faithful servants of God, including the prophets, have also experienced violent rejection.

The final servant song (52:13–53:12) brings together the distinction between the servant and Israel and the theme of suffering, taking each to a higher level. The servant suffers *because of* Israel's failures and *on behalf of* Israel's failures. Isaiah has made it clear from the outset that the reason for Israel's failure to enjoy the covenant blessings and to fulfill God's purpose toward the nations is sin. The downward spiral of Israel's rebellion has descended so far that prophetic messages and acts of discipline will not suffice. The earlier chapters of Isaiah juxtapose analyses of Israel's seemingly hopeless spiritual condition with scenes of a glorious future (cf. 1:2-9 with 2:1-4; 3:8-9 with 4:2-6; and 5:1-7,25-30; 6:11-13; 8:21-22 with 9:1-7). Although Isaiah accounts for this transformation by saying, "The zeal of the LORD Almighty will accomplish this" (9:7), he never explains how God will overcome the problem of sin. The final servant song roots the explanation in the person of the servant.

The servant will suffer, even to the point of death. Yet because he is innocent and righteous, his death can bring peace and healing to the guilty ones for whom he suffers. In 1:5-6, Israel is portrayed as a person beaten and wounded from head to toe as a result of sin. Much of the language from that passage reappears in 53:4-5 as the blows and wounds are laid upon the servant. By taking Israel's sins upon himself, the servant makes it possible for Israel's relationship with God to be restored and through Israel for God's saving power to be revealed to the nations. God thus begins his work of restoration by returning his people from exile through a powerful pagan king, but he accomplishes a greater work of restoration through a suffering servant. Because in his death the servant accomplishes God's will, God also vindicates him and gives him an exalted future.

Who, then, is this servant? As noted above, Israel would seem at first to be the obvious answer. As Isaiah's portrait of the servant unfolds, however, Israel becomes an object of the servant's ministry, along with the nations who need to "see the light" that sinful Israel has actually obscured. Isaiah clearly seeks both to identify the servant with Israel and to distinguish the two at the same time. This point favors identifying the servant as a group or individual *within* Israel through whom God restores his people and accomplishes his outreach to the nations. The faithful remnant certainly suffered as a result of the sins of the nation as a whole. Their very existence can be considered redemptive in that God spared the nation for their sake (cf. 65:8; the results of the failure to find such a "remnant" in Sodom and Gomorrah). On an individual level, righteous persons like Jeremiah suffered at the hands of — and in a sense on behalf of — the nation (cf. Jer 11:18-20).

There is no doubt some measure of appropriateness in identifying faithful individuals with the ideal servant. In Isaiah 65:8, however, God says he will not destroy the entire nation because of his *servants*. As noted above, the exclusive use of the plural after the final servant song appears deliberate. In every age faithful believers serve God as they bear witness to him. The New Testament repeatedly labels Christians "servants/slaves" (δοῦλοι). When Jesus appears to Paul on the road to Damascus, he says, "I have appeared to you to appoint you as a servant[25] and as a witness of what you have seen of me and what I will show you." The opening verses of Revelation describe John as a "servant . . . who testifies to everything he saw." Both of these individuals suffer greatly in fulfilling their calling.

Attempts to identify the servant of Isaiah's servant songs with such individuals fall short, however, because of the climactic elements in the final song. The servant's suffering occurs not merely because of his *association with* the covenant people (cf. righteous individuals like Daniel in the exile), or *on behalf of* the covenant people (serving as a preservative element), or because of *the hostility of* the covenant people (cf. Jeremiah). The serious problem of Israel's sin requires a suffering with a greater meaning than any of these

---

[25]The word here is ὑπερέτης (*hyperetēs*).

possibilities, as does the sacrificial language of Isaiah 52:13–53:12. Sin is the obstacle that lies between Israel as God's covenant people and Israel as God's witness/light to the nations. The servant must be able to remove that obstacle if the will of the LORD is to prosper in his hand (53:10).

The New Testament identifies Jesus with the servant in numerous passages. Jesus' healing ministry is cast as the fulfillment of the first servant song (Matt 12:15-21). Jesus exhorts his disciples to recognize that the greatest among them must be their servant (Matt 20:26), even as he has come to them "not to be served but to serve, and to give his life as a ransom for many" (Matt 20:28).[26] It is in this role as "ransom" that Jesus is most closely linked to the final servant song. He is "the Lamb of God, who takes away the sin of the world" (John 1:29). The Ethiopian eunuch is reading about the suffering servant when God sends Philip to him to explain that the prophet is speaking about Jesus, leading to the eunuch's conversion (Acts 8:26ff.). Peter calls Christians who suffer for their faith to look to the example of Jesus who, though sinless, silently accepted mistreatment and in the process "bore our sins in his body on the tree" (1 Pet 2:21-25).

Jesus' nature, the New Testament claims, uniquely qualifies him to bear the sins of others. Hebrews stresses his special relationship to the Father as the foundation for his fulfillment of the ideals of sacrifice and priesthood. In him alone the righteousness of God has been revealed so that, even though all have sinned, God can remain just and still justify those who turn to Jesus (Rom 3:21-26).

The New Testament also presents Jesus as the messiah, raising the issue of the relationship between the servant and the messiah. Parallels between the servant songs and the messianic texts in the earlier chapters of Isaiah have already been pointed out.[27] In 55:3 God speaks of an "everlasting covenant" based on his "faithful love promised to David, and in the next verse refers to David as a "witness to the peoples." It is inappropriate, therefore, to draw a complete line of separation between the messiah and the servant. It is more accurate to speak of a shift of emphasis from the more customary Davidic messiah in the earlier portions of Isaiah to the servant in the later portions of the book while retaining lines of continuity between the two.

---

[26]Notice the use of the word "many" as in Isa 53:11-12.
[27]Cf. the comments on 42:1-4; 49:22.

The historical bridge in Isaiah 36–39 points to a significant reason for this shift of emphasis. Although messianic texts such as 9:1ff. and 11:1ff. have implications beyond Israel's immediate future, God does deliver Israel from the Assyrian threat (chapters 1–35) through one from the line of David (Hezekiah). Isaiah 40–66, on the other hand, considers Israel's future in light of the Babylonian exile. The line of David survives, but never resumes its place on an earthly throne with political and military power. Isaiah's servant songs mark another step in the progress of God's revelation. Through them God makes known (and history confirms) that a better future and the inclusion of the nations in the covenant relationship will not come about through political power but through redemptive suffering.

If it was God's intention to prepare his people for a redemptive sufferer, centuries of Jewish bondage to a succession of conquerors seem to have undermined that intention. When Peter first publicly confesses Jesus as the messiah and Jesus responds by speaking of the necessity of his suffering and death, Peter cannot harmonize the two ideas (Matt 16:16ff.). If Jesus' closest disciples struggle to grasp this concept, how much more would the crowds who longed to be free of foreign rule?

Little if any evidence exists for a Jewish expectation of a suffering messiah by the first century, especially one whose death provides atonement. Some have detected such an expectation among the Dead Sea Scrolls, but the case is tenuous at best.[28] An interesting response to a suffering messiah appears in the Targum[29] Jonathan on Isaiah 52:13–53:12. The date of this Targum is debated, so it is not clear if it is written in response to Christian teaching. The Targum interprets this passage from Isaiah messianically, but it attributes only the triumphant elements to the messiah. The suffering it applies either to the Jewish people or to the Gentiles who are punished by the messiah.[30] For whatever reason, this interpretation obviously resists associating suffering and death with the messiah.

---

[28]Cf. the refutation in John J. Collins, *The Scepter and the Star: The Messiahs of the Dead Sea Scrolls and Other Ancient Literature* (New York: Doubleday, 1995), pp. 123-126.

[29]A "Targum" is an Aramaic translation of the Hebrew Scriptures. In some cases these translations are literal and straightforward, but in others they can be highly interpretive.

[30]Cf. the discussion in Hyam Maccoby, *Early Rabbinic Writings* (Cambridge: Cambridge, 1988), pp. 198-203.

In time Judaism did come to embrace the notion of a suffering messiah. The failure of the Bar Kokhba revolt (A.D. 125-135), which had raised hopes of a messianic overthrow of Rome, may have opened the door to consideration of this concept.[31] Once again, no atoning significance is attached to the death of this messianic figure. Since the Middle Ages, however, at least partly in response to Christian teachings, "the prevailing exegesis among the Jews [has] regarded the Suffering Servant as being the Jewish people itself, whose sufferings were regarded as atoning for the sins of the world."[32]

Given the atmosphere of the hunger for political freedom in the first century, how culpable were the first disciples of Jesus for failing to recognize a place for the suffering and death of the messiah according to Scripture? Jesus' words to the disciples on the road to Emmaus (Luke 24:25-27) are pointed:

> He said to them, "How foolish you are, and how slow of heart to believe all that the prophets have spoken! Did not the Christ have to suffer these things and then enter his glory?" And beginning with Moses and all the Prophets, he explained to them what was said in all the Scriptures concerning himself.

Apart from the servant passages, the evidence appears to be meager for such an understanding.[33] The language Luke uses to describe Jesus' instruction to the disciples, however, obviously consists of more than the listing of a number of proof texts. Perhaps he draws their attention to the consistent way God has worked through that which is weak and insignificant by human standards. Perhaps he points to the initial decision by David's family not even to bring him before Samuel as one who might be God's anointed, or to David's many hardships before he is vindicated as king. Perhaps he leads them to consider the many laments in the psalms. The classic lament, Psalm 22, demonstrates how God is glorified when he vindicates the righteous sufferer. Given the significant passages in Isaiah and the larger context of the Old Testament, a messiah who triumphs through suffering and death should not have been such a surprise.

---

[31]Cf. Sukkah 52; Sanhedrin 98 in the Babylonian Talmud.
[32]Maccoby, *Early*, p. 202.
[33]Cf. Zech 9:9, where Zion's king is "gentle and riding on a donkey" as he comes.

The major argument against identifying the servant ultimately with Israel or the faithful remnant or righteous individuals is that these identifications fail to do justice to the atonement language of 52:13–53:12. The system of atonement through animal sacrifices revealed most fully in Leviticus affirms God's holiness, the disastrous effects of alienation from God because of sin, and the death penalty for sin that the animal substitutes pay. This system communicates powerfully, yet is fundamentally flawed because of the limitations of the human priests and the animal sacrifices.[34] The New Testament claims that the suffering and death of Jesus as the Son of God provide atonement for sin once and for all. Any alternative that denies the need for atonement or holds that sinful human beings by their own righteousness can provide this atonement fails to do justice to the very foundations of the Old Testament, not just to a single passage in Isaiah.

---

[34]The animal sacrifices offered by the Levitical priesthood were, by God's grace and in anticipation of the work of Christ, effective in atoning for sin. Their inherent limitations, however, mark them as "prophetic" and therefore they continually point forward to their fulfillment.

ISAIAH 54

B. THE CONSEQUENCES OF THE SERVANT'S WORK (54:1–57:21)

1. God Renews the Covenant with his People (54:1-17)

The first servant song prompts the response of a "new song" of praise to God (42:10 ff.). It also presents a time of decision since the frustrated pangs of childbirth (42:14) are replaced by the preparation of a way of blessing (42:15-16) for all except those who continue to pursue idols (42:17). The second servant song also calls for praise for God's compassion to his people (49:13). God reassures them that he loves them and that their period of bereavement will be followed by a multitude of "children" whose existence can only be explained as the work of God (49:14-23). Following the third servant song another call to decision appears (50:10-11). God also reminds his people of their roots in Abraham and Sarah, an old, barren couple (51:1-2). The God who blessed and multiplied them can do the same for those coming out of exile, prompting joyful singing (51:3).

Isaiah continues this pattern in the chapters that follow the fourth servant song.[1] The redemptive work of the suffering servant

---

[1] The joyful circumstances in Isa 54:1–56:8 are deliberately placed immediately after the revelation of the suffering servant. In fact, the servant's work proves to be pivotal for everything Isaiah promises for the future. What, therefore, are the implications of the Christian identification of the suffering servant with Jesus for Isaiah's message? Does everything await the servant's arrival? No, Isaiah continues to address Israel's relationship with God. While his message speaks to the restoration and maintenance of God's covenant with Israel in anticipation of the coming of Jesus, it also transcends that aspect of God's work. Incorporated within Isaiah's message to Israel are elements that involve the church age with its inclusion of the nations, and even the culmination of God's redemption of his fallen creation. Knowledge of those details, however, emerges only through God's

makes clearer how God can be so gracious to his rebellious people. Chapter 54 opens with a call to sing God's praises for his faithfulness as he restores his marriage relationship with Zion after her desolation. In the latter portion of the chapter Isaiah uses the imagery of the rebuilding of the physical city. In both cases the ultimate point is the resumption of a line of descendants who will experience the blessings of God and serve God's purpose in light of the peace made available by the work of the servant.

The Restored Marriage (54:1-10)

¹"Sing, O barren woman, / you who never bore a child; / burst into song, shout for joy, / you who were never in labor; / because more are the children of the desolate woman / than of her who has a husband," / says the LORD. / ²"Enlarge the place of your tent, / stretch your tent curtains wide, / do not hold back; / lengthen your cords, / strengthen your stakes. / ³For you will spread out to the right and to the left; / your descendants will dispossess nations / and settle in their desolate cities. / ⁴"Do not be afraid; you will not suffer shame. / Do not fear disgrace; you will not be humiliated. / You will forget the shame of your youth / and remember no more the reproach of your widowhood. / ⁵For your Maker is your husband— / the LORD Almighty is his name— / the Holy One of Israel is your Redeemer; / he is called the God of all the earth. / ⁶The LORD will call you back / as if you were a wife deserted and distressed in spirit— / a wife who married young, / only to be rejected," says your God. / ⁷"For a brief moment I abandoned you, / but with deep compassion I will bring you back. / ⁸In a surge of anger / I hid my face from you for a moment, / but with everlasting kindness / I will have compassion on you," / says the LORD your Redeemer.

⁹"To me this is like the days of Noah, / when I swore that the waters of Noah would never again cover the earth. / So now I have sworn not to be angry with you, / never to rebuke you again. /

---

later revelation and would thus not be available to Isaiah's initial audience. The commentary will thus continue to apply the text initially to the future of Israel/Zion, but with the understanding that these entities look beyond the physical descendants of Abraham and the city of Jerusalem to the larger covenant realities they embody in Isaiah's day (cf. the way the cities of Babylon and Jerusalem represent the two possible responses to God in Revelation). Oswalt discusses this point as well (*Isaiah* 2, p. 418, n. 30).

¹⁰**Though the mountains be shaken /and the hills be removed, /yet my unfailing love for you will not be shaken /nor my covenant of peace be removed," /says the** LORD, **who has compassion on you.**

54:1-3 As mentioned above, following the second servant song, Isaiah personifies Zion the ruined city as a "bereaved and barren" woman who suddenly finds herself surrounded by a multitude of children (49:14 ff.). God has routinely worked through barren women and reversed their circumstances to reveal his power (cf. Sarah, Rebekah, Rachel, Hannah[2]). Since children represent one of the covenant blessings (cf. Deut 28:11), barrenness can also indicate that one is under God's judgment. After the promise of "offspring" to the servant (53:10), chapter 54 opens with a **barren woman** who will **shout for joy** because of the abundance of her children.[3] In 33:20 Zion is compared to a tent that will not have to be moved because of the security God provides. Here God increases Zion's descendants so much that the **tent** must be enlarged.

54:4-6 In verses 4-8 the image shifts from a woman in distress because she is barren to one who suffers because she has been **deserted** and **rejected**. As with barrenness, rejection can bring **shame** and **disgrace**. Israel will be able to **forget** the parallel experiences of bondage in Egypt (**the shame of your youth**) and the exile in Babylon (**the reproach of your widowhood**)[4] due to the identity of her **husband**.[5] Because of who he is and the investment he has made in the covenant relationship, God **will call** [Israel] **back**.

54: 7-8 These two verses stress God's compassionate nature as the foundation for Israel's restoration. The language of verse 6 ("deserted"[6] and "rejected") might imply that this wife has been wronged by her husband. She is not innocent, however, but experiences a righteous **anger**. Her hope lies in the fact that God's **compassion** (רַחֲמִים,

---

[2]Hannah's song (1 Sam 2:1-10) particularly emphasizes the theme of God's reversal of the plight of the humble.

[3]Paul brings together the servant's work and the covenant promises tied to Jerusalem as he applies Isa 54:1 to "the Jerusalem that is above" in Gal 4:26-27. The "children of promise" receive their covenant blessings through the death of the servant.

[4]Alternatively, the references to youth and widowhood could be a general way of describing the woman's entire life (cf. Oswalt, *Isaiah* 2, p. 418).

[5]Cf. the use of "for" at the beginning of verse 5. The NIV omits three uses of the word "for" (כִּי, *ki*) in verse 4 (before "you will not suffer shame," "you will not be humiliated," and "you will forget the shame of your youth").

[6]The word (עָזַב, *'zg*) is translated "abandoned" in verse 7.

raḥămîm) and **kindness** (חֶסֶד, *ḥesed*) prevail over his anger in that he gives fresh opportunities to those who sin (cf. Exod 34:6-7). His anger is momentary, but his kindness is **everlasting** (cf. Ps 30:5).

54:9-10 God compares his grace to Israel in the present context to the circumstances surrounding **Noah** and the flood.[7] How can the flood or the Babylonian exile attest to God's compassion? Both represent devastating times of judgment. Yet both also reflect a divine response that falls short of the total destruction the sins in each case deserve (Gen 6:5-7; Isa 1:9).[8] Just as God took a covenant oath not to destroy the earth as he did in the waters of the flood (Gen 9:8-17), he takes a similar oath in verse 9 regarding the exile. The words **never** and **again** at the end of this verse probably reflect an attempt by the NIV translators to employ variety in the language of the parallelism, but in the process make the point sound stronger than Isaiah intended. More literally, God swears "not to be angry with you or to rebuke you."

Concerning the promise in verse 9, Oswalt asks, "Is he swearing never to allow his anger to flow in an unrestrained manner, or not to allow a foreign power to hold his people as captives again? Or is he saying that he will not allow biblical faith to be brought so near to dissolution again?"[9] Oswalt favors the latter, which comes closer to the point of the promise after the flood as well. God is gracious and compassionate when his judgments or acts of discipline — no matter how extreme — protect humanity as a whole or his covenant people from self-destruction.

The fact that the flood and the exile represent times when God withholds total destruction demonstrates his commitment to the covenant relationship. His **unfailing love** (*ḥesed*) is more stable and immovable than the powerful **mountains**. The possibility that the mountains could be **shaken** or even **removed** exists, but not the shaking or removal of God's **covenant of peace**.[10] Only God's **compassion** could account for this stability, given the frail and fickle nature of his covenant partners.

---

[7]The NIV's "To me this is like the *days* of Noah" is more literally "To me this is the *waters* of Noah," although the word for "days" (יְמֵי, *yᵉmê*) is very close to the word for "waters" (מֵי, *mê*).

[8]The same is true of the golden calf incident that preceded the revelation of God's nature in Exod 34:6-7 quoted above.

[9]Oswalt, *Isaiah* 2, p. 422.

[10]For more on this "covenant of peace," see the comments on 55:3.

The Rebuilt City (54:11-17)

¹¹"O afflicted city, lashed by storms and not comforted, / I will build you with stones of turquoise,ᵃ / your foundations with sapphires.ᵇ / ¹²I will make your battlements of rubies, / your gates of sparkling jewels, / and all your walls of precious stones. / ¹³All your sons will be taught by the LORD, / and great will be your children's peace. / ¹⁴In righteousness you will be established: / Tyranny will be far from you; / you will have nothing to fear. / Terror will be far removed; / it will not come near you. / ¹⁵If anyone does attack you, it will not be my doing; / whoever attacks you will surrender to you.

¹⁶"See, it is I who created the blacksmith / who fans the coals into flame / and forges a weapon fit for its work. / And it is I who have created the destroyer to work havoc; / ¹⁷no weapon forged against you will prevail, / and you will refute every tongue that accuses you. / This is the heritage of the servants of the LORD, / and this is their vindication from me," / declares the LORD.

ᵃ*11* The meaning of the Hebrew for this word is uncertain.   ᵇ*11* Or *lapis lazuli*

54:11-12 The description of Israel at the opening of verse 11 bears no relation to the strength offered by God in the previous verse. Although the **city** imagery emerges in the following lines, the NIV adds the word in the translation of the first line of verse 11. At first, however, the people are **afflicted**, **lashed by storms** and **not comforted**. They face this plight as a result of their rejection of God, but God gives them a glimpse of a better future. He will construct that future as he promises to **build**¹¹ them into a strong and beautiful city with precious stones (cf. Rev 21:10-21).

54:13-17 The focus of God's building efforts is not physical, however, but personal. In numerous ways he will make them like the servant. They will be **taught by the LORD** (50:4-5); they will experience God's **vindication** when opposed by their enemies (50:7-9); and as they are built by God, they will be called his **servants**. Because they are "taught by the LORD," they will experience **peace**. Because God establishes them in **righteousness**, any cause of **fear** will be **far removed** from them. Because God is the sovereign creator, **no weapon forged against** his children has any chance to **prevail**.

---

¹¹The form of the word translated "build" (מַרְבִּיץ, *marbîṣ*) typically refers to causing sheep to lie down (cf. Ps 23:2; Isa 13:20; Jer 33:12; Ezek 34:15).

True servants of God enjoy a rich inheritance (**heritage**, נַחֲלָה, *naḥălāh*). When someone's life is battered and chaotic, the primary desire is for stability. The work of the servant provides hope for the fulfillment of that desire, whether communicated through the picture of a reconciled marriage or a fortified city that gives its inhabitants peace and safety. All other blessings depend on that solid foundation.

ISAIAH 55

2. God Freely Pardons His People (55:1-13)

Isaiah's figurative description of Zion in 54:11-12 provides part of the background for John's vision of "the Holy City, the new Jerusalem, coming down out of heaven from God" (Rev 21:2). After this vision John extends an invitation (Rev 22:17): "The Spirit and the bride say, 'Come!' And let him who hears say, 'Come!' Whoever is thirsty, let him come; and whoever wishes, let him take the free gift of the water of life." Isaiah 55 also contains an extended invitation to participate in the blessings of the renewed Zion. Both invitations are equally gracious and equally urgent.

The Gracious Banquet (55:1-2)

¹"Come, all you who are thirsty, / come to the waters; / and you who have no money, / come, buy and eat! / Come, buy wine and milk / without money and without cost. / ²Why spend money on what is not bread, / and your labor on what does not satisfy? / Listen, listen to me, and eat what is good, / and your soul will delight in the richest of fare.

Food and water are two of man's most critical needs. A person would be willing to pay an extreme price or consume almost anything that could potentially satisfy these needs. In Isaiah 36:2, Sennacherib's representatives had attempted to intimidate the people of Jerusalem by warning them that under siege they would "have to eat their own filth and drink their own urine." In an earlier siege against Samaria, "a donkey's head sold for eighty shekels of silver, and a fourth of a cab of seed pods [or dove's dung] for five shekels" (2 Kgs 6:25). That same siege exposed the most drastic illustration of this principle, when parents resorted to cannibalizing their own children (2 Kgs 6:26 ff.).[1]

---

[1] The covenant curses warn of this extreme consequence of unfaithfulness (cf. Lev 26:29; Deut 28:53,57).

55:1-2 In this passage God invites those **who have no money** to **come, buy and eat!** Such an invitation would be cruel except that God offers an unusual transaction, one which requires no payment for the food that is offered. What could better capture the notion of grace than the offer of what a person needs the most **without money and without cost?** In spite of God's graciousness, people regularly spurn his grace. This tendency prompts the questions at the opening of verse 2. Food and drink usually require a person either to **spend money** or to **labor** for it. To acquire good food in this fashion rather than to receive it as a gift is ridiculous enough. To pursue **what is not bread** and thus **what does not satisfy** rather than to receive good food as a gift is patently absurd. The person who would make such a foolish choice recalls the deluded idolater in 44:20 who "feeds on ashes, a deluded heart misleads him; he cannot save himself, or say, 'Is not this thing in my right hand a lie?'"

It is difficult to imagine that someone would choose expensive, unsatisfying food over free, nutritious food. This passage is not ultimately about food, however, but what satisfies on an even deeper level. Unfortunately, recognizing what satisfies spiritually is more difficult than recognizing what satisfies physically. This lack of spiritual perception has been central to Isaiah's analysis of Israel's condition throughout the book. For this reason Israel is emphatically exhorted to **listen**[2] in order to **eat what is good**. Early on God established the priority of his word over bread. In Deuteronomy 8:3 Moses explains that God had allowed the people to experience hunger and then had fed them in order to teach them "that man does not live on bread alone but on every word that comes from the mouth of the LORD."

The Everlasting Covenant (55:3-5)

³Give ear and come to me; /hear me, that your soul may live. /I will make an everlasting covenant with you, / my faithful love promised to David. /⁴See, I have made him a witness to the peoples, /a leader and commander of the peoples. / ⁵Surely you will summon nations you know not, /and nations that do not know you will hasten to you, /because of the LORD your God, /the Holy One of Israel, /for he has endowed you with splendor."

---

[2]The combination of the imperative and the infinitive absolute (שִׁמְעוּ שָׁמוֹעַ, *šim'û šāmôa'*) draws special attention to the call to listen.

55:3 In these verses God brings his people closer to the true meaning of the rich blessings he freely offers them. The key remains to **hear** (שְׁמַע, *šm'*) what God says, but instead of exhorting them to "come [לְכוּ, *lᵉkû*] to the waters" or to "come [*lᵉkû*], buy and eat," God says **come** [*lᵉkû*] **to me**. God himself is the sustenance that truly satisfies (cf. John 6:25ff.). If the failure to respond to God is rooted in a lack of trust, he reminds them of his **everlasting covenant** with them that is equated with his **faithful love promised to David**. God's covenant promise to David (2 Sam 7:11b-16) that his kingdom and throne will stand forever overwhelms David (2 Sam 7:18-21). David recognizes the conditional element in this promise, which he makes explicit in his exhortation to Solomon (1 Kgs 2:1-4). God proves his faithfulness to his covenant with David throughout the period of the monarchy in Israel. Although the Babylonian exile seems to end the reign of Davidic kings, the survival of a descendant of David in the exile (2 Kgs 25:27-30) and beyond the exile (Zerubbabel; cf. Matt 1:12) keeps the covenant promise alive.

When Isaiah attempts to persuade Ahaz to trust in God, he does so in part by referring to the king as "house of David" (Isa 7:13). God's faithfulness to David and his descendants extends to the people as a whole since the king represents and thus in a sense embodies his people. In 54:10 God speaks of "my unfailing love for you" (חַסְדִּי מֵאִתֵּךְ, *ḥasdî mē'ittēk*) and parallels it with "my covenant of peace" (בְּרִית שְׁלוֹמִי, *bᵉrîth šᵉlômî*). In 55:3 God's **everlasting covenant** (בְּרִית עוֹלָם, *bᵉrîth 'ôlām*) parallels his **faithful love promised to David** (חַסְדֵי דָוִד הַנֶּאֱמָנִים, *ḥasdî dāwid hanne'ĕmānîm*).[3]

55:4-5 The goal of the Davidic messiah to reach out to the **nations** in verses 4-5 explains why God remains faithful to his covenant promise to David, but it also demonstrates how this anointed one embodies Israel's calling to the nations (Gen 12:2-3; Exod 19:5-6) and it connects him to the servant (Isa 42:6-7; 49:6; 52:15). God's faithfulness to his covenant with David and the implications of that covenant for reaching the nations also appear prominently in Psalms 18 and 89, for example.[4] The point of all these connections is to establish that

---

[3]Ezekiel 34:25 and 37:26 both speak of a "covenant of peace" (in the latter passage it is also described as an "everlasting covenant"). Both contexts deal with the restoration of David as king/shepherd over Israel (cf. 34:23-24; 37:24-25).

[4]Note the close relationship between verse 5a and Ps 18:43 (44 in Hebrew). Cf. Motyer, *Prophecy*, pp. 454-455.

God's offer is reliable even if it sounds too good to be true and even if the Davidic covenant appears to be in jeopardy.

The Effective Word (55:6-13)

⁶Seek the LORD while he may be found; /call on him while he is near. / ⁷Let the wicked forsake his way / and the evil man his thoughts. / Let him turn to the LORD, and he will have mercy on him, /and to our God, for he will freely pardon.

⁸"For my thoughts are not your thoughts, / neither are your ways my ways," /declares the LORD. / ⁹"As the heavens are higher than the earth, /so are my ways higher than your ways /and my thoughts than your thoughts. / ¹⁰As the rain and the snow /come down from heaven, /and do not return to it /without watering the earth /and making it bud and flourish, /so that it yields seed for the sower /and bread for the eater, / ¹¹so is my word that goes out from my mouth: /It will not return to me empty, /but will accomplish what I desire /and achieve the purpose for which I sent it. / ¹²You will go out in joy /and be led forth in peace; /the mountains and hills /will burst into song before you, /and all the trees of the field /will clap their hands. / ¹³Instead of the thornbush will grow the pine tree, /and instead of briers the myrtle will grow. / This will be for the LORD's renown, /for an everlasting sign, /which will not be destroyed."

55:6 God reveals his graciousness to those he has created for a relationship with him before he invites them to "come to me" (v. 3). Given human sinfulness and the consequent tendency to disregard God, the exhortation to **seek the LORD** and to **call on him** would be meaningless apart from God's active pursuit of his rebellious creatures. The inclusion of the qualifying element **while he may be found/while he is near**, however, lends a sense of urgency to the call to seek God. "There are decisions to be made. There is a banquet spread, but the guests must come."⁵ God extends grace not only by self-revelation and his willingness to forgive, but also by his patience and long-suffering (cf. Exod 34:6-7). Yet the opportunity to respond to God's self-revelation does not last forever. God's removal of his protective presence from Jerusalem before the Babylonian destruction (Ezekiel 10) illustrates this danger. In addi-

---

⁵Webb, *Message*, p. 218.

tion, a refusal to respond to God tends to debilitate the person through a hardening of the heart.

55:7 Verse 7 helps to define what it means to seek God and begins the process of explaining why one should do so. To **turn to the LORD** inevitably means to turn *away from* that which is contrary to him and his will.[6] The use of the strong word **forsake** (עזב, *'zb*) calls attention to the exclusive covenantal nature of the relationship God seeks because it is the same word used in the call of a man to "leave" his father and mother in order to cling to his wife (Gen 2:24). Seeking God also demands a true commitment, not just a superficial change, because it requires abandoning a prior **way** of life as well as former **thoughts**. The initial reason for making such a radical turnaround is that God **will have mercy on/will freely pardon** one who sincerely responds to God's gracious initiative.

55:8-9 God's offer of pardon should provide sufficient motivation for seeking him, but the remaining verses in the chapter further substantiate the call to partake of his grace. Verses 8, 10, and 12 each open with the word "for" (כי, *kî*), although the NIV only translates the first occurrence.[7] In verse 7 sinners are called to forsake their "ways" and "thoughts." In verse 8 the same words are used as God distinguishes his **thoughts** (מחשבות, *maḥšᵉbôth*) and his **ways** (דרכים, *dᵉrākîm*) from those of his people. God's nature is so much more elevated, in fact, that it can be compared to the way **the heavens are higher than the earth** (cf. 40:22). God's holiness, in essence, refers to his "otherness." In 57:15 God will reveal the ironic truth that the high and holy one dwells with the lowly.

> For this is what the high and lofty One says—
> he who lives forever, whose name is holy:
> "I live in a high and holy place,
> but also with him who is contrite and lowly in spirit,
> to revive the spirit of the lowly
> and to revive the heart of the contrite.

This reality affirms the importance of repentance for drawing near to God. Yet God also exhorts his people to "be holy, because I am holy" (Lev 11:44; cf. Heb 12:14; 1 Pet 1:15-16). The very nature of

---

[6]The word for "turn" (שוב, *šûb*) frequently refers to repentance (cf. Isa 1:27; 6:10; 59:20).

[7]Cf. the analysis of the structure of these verses in Motyer, *Prophecy*, p. 456.

God demands that those in relationship with him seek to conform to his ways. God is willing to pardon the failures of sinful human beings,[8] but he will not and cannot disregard the apathy of those who callously disregard his holiness.

55:10-11 The reason given in verses 10-11 for seeking God moves from the nature of God to the nature of his word. The opening of God's message of comfort to those facing exile contrasts the permanent validity of the word of God with the fading glory of man (40:6-8). The emphasis here is on the power of the word as God claims that **it will not return to me empty, but will accomplish what I desire and achieve the purpose for which I sent it**. Once again God refers to the relationship between heaven and earth, but in this case he uses the analogy of **the rain and the snow** that **come down from heaven and do not return to it without watering the earth**. God's word promises and delivers life as surely as the renewing waters from heaven.

Like any analogy, however, the one in verses 10-11 is imperfect. The relationship between rain and life for plants is essentially automatic: if the rains come, the plants will spring to life. The relationship between the word of God and life for God's people depends on whether or not they will receive it. This concept underlies the entire chapter, as the exhortation at the beginning of the chapter to eat and drink what God freely provides indicates. Whereas the plants gladly drink the life-giving waters, people frequently resist God's gracious provisions. God does not say, however, that his word satisfies everyone's thirst, but that it accomplishes the purpose for which he sends it. The warning God gives Isaiah about the lack of reception his message will receive (6:9ff.) does not, therefore, negate this promise. God sends his word both to give life and to expose those who stubbornly resist it and grow ever harder in heart (cf. John 12:47-48).

55:12-13 The final reason for seeking God in verses 12-13 in a sense maintains the context of heaven and earth as it anticipates the "new heavens and new earth" of 65:17ff. The redemption that awaits those who turn to God results in a renewal of creation that far surpasses what happens as a result of the rain. The physical creation is personified as it celebrates with the redeemed the removal of the

---

[8]At this point it is helpful to remember the connection between this passage and the work of the servant.

curse of sin that plagues every aspect of creation until that day (Gen 3:17-19; Rom 8:19-22). The **thornbush** and **briers** will be replaced by beautiful and productive trees.

It is only fitting that the **everlasting sign** of the renewed creation will stand **for the LORD's renown**. He is the one who provides redemption through the servant. He is the one who reveals himself as a gracious and generous God. He is the one who proves that he can be trusted and that he has the power to back up what he promises. How foolish and self-condemning to refuse the invitation of such a God!

ISAIAH 56

3. God Clarifies the Definition of His People (56:1-8)

In the previous chapter Isaiah has stressed God's graciousness and the proper response to it by seeking God and pursuing his ways. While these verses continue to emphasize how to respond to the grace of God, an even more striking element emerges in regard to the *scope* of God's grace. Israel's call to maintain purity by separating from the pagan nations and even sources of defilement within Israel has always stood in tension with the call to be a light and a blessing to the nations. Here God offers full inclusion and blessing to foreigners and eunuchs, categories of individuals who formerly have enjoyed limited opportunities at best. In light of the work of the servant, God is preparing a vision of a people who are defined by their response to him rather than by their descent from Abraham or their physical wholeness.

The Basis of Blessing and Inclusion (56:1-2)

¹This is what the LORD says:
"Maintain justice / and do what is right, / for my salvation is close at hand / and my righteousness will soon be revealed. / ²Blessed is the man who does this, / the man who holds it fast, / who keeps the Sabbath without desecrating it, / and keeps his hand from doing any evil."

56:1 The passage begins with a straightforward declaration. God's desire for **justice** (מִשְׁפָּט, *mišpāṭ*) and **right**eousness (צְדָקָה, *ṣᵉdāqāh*) is nothing new (cf. 1:17). He calls his people to reflect his nature. This exhortation, in fact, derives from the fact that the appearance of God's **salvation/righteousness** is **close at hand**. This causal (**for**) connection continues Isaiah's perspective that God's deliverance, though from a human perspective seems delayed, from

God's perspective is imminent.[1] It also demonstrates that the human pursuit of justice and righteousness results from God's salvation. "In other words, obedience is to be lived out as a response to salvation."[2]

56:2 The two designations for **man** at the beginning of verse 2 (אֱנוֹשׁ, *'ĕnôš* and בֶּן אָדָם, *ben 'ādām*) frequently highlight human frailty and mortality. In anticipation of the following verses, Motyer sees them here as emphasizing "the common humanity of all" and removing "the old boundaries of descent and privilege."[3] **Blessed** (אַשְׁרֵי, *'ašrê*; cf. Ps 1:1) is everyone, therefore, who embraces the salvation of God that flows from his very nature and **holds it fast** (i.e., clings to it, does not let it go).

As in Psalm 1, God summarizes the response that yields blessing under two headings which address what should be avoided and what should be pursued. Negatively, this refers to one who **keeps his hand from doing any evil**. Positively, it refers to one **who keeps the Sabbath**. To "desecrate" (חלל, *ḥll*) the Sabbath is to disregard it by working (Exod 31:14). When Ezekiel surveys Israel's history of unfaithfulness, he repeatedly mentions the desecration of the Sabbath (Ezek 20:13,16,21,24). Christians frequently view the Sabbath only through the maze of regulations the Pharisees attached to it and fail to appreciate how significant it is in the larger scope of God's relationship with Israel. This significance includes its association as here with justice.

> For the Sabbath had to do with rest; not just for masters, but for servants as well, and even for working animals and resident foreigners. To keep the Sabbath meant, among other things, that you served the God who created the world and cared for everyone and everything in it. It also had to do with perfection or completeness. It recalled the completeness of God's original work of creation, and looked forward to the time when his work of re-creation would also be complete. The Sabbath rest was a sign of the final rest which all God's people will enjoy in the new heavens and new earth (66:22-23). So there is no petty legalism here. The Sabbath is viewed not as an end in itself, but

---

[1]Cf. 13:6,22; 46:13 ("righteousness" and "salvation" are paralleled in this verse as well).

[2]Oswalt, *Isaiah*, p. 455.

[3]Motyer, *Prophecy*, p. 464.

as a sign that the whole of life was to be lived in submission to God, and that meant sharing his concern for justice.[4]

The Object of Blessing and Inclusion (56:3-8)

³Let no foreigner who has bound himself to the LORD say, / "The LORD will surely exclude me from his people." / And let not any eunuch complain, / "I am only a dry tree."
⁴For this is what the LORD says:
"To the eunuchs who keep my Sabbaths, / who choose what pleases me / and hold fast to my covenant— / ⁵to them I will give within my temple and its walls / a memorial and a name / better than sons and daughters; / I will give them an everlasting name / that will not be cut off. / ⁶And foreigners who bind themselves to the LORD / to serve him, / to love the name of the LORD, / and to worship him, / all who keep the Sabbath without desecrating it / and who hold fast to my covenant— / ⁷these I will bring to my holy mountain / and give them joy in my house of prayer. / Their burnt offerings and sacrifices / will be accepted on my altar; / for my house will be called / a house of prayer for all nations." / ⁸The Sovereign LORD declares— / he who gathers the exiles of Israel: / "I will gather still others to them / besides those already gathered."

56:3 The first two verses introduce nothing particularly controversial. Verse 3, however, surprises the listener. Most Israelite hearers of this message from Isaiah would likely assume that verses 1-2 address what it means to be a faithful Israelite. Even though God has presented a vision of a future when the nations will join Israel in receiving God's blessings ever since his initial promise to Abraham (Gen 12:2-3; cf. Isa 2:2-4), the exact nature of that union has not been specified. The language used in these verses of the **foreigner** and the **eunuch**, therefore, might be considered shocking. For centuries, Israel's practice has been governed by passages such as Deuteronomy 23:1-8 that prohibit or restrict anyone "who has been emasculated by crushing or cutting," as well as those descended from pagan nations, from entering "the assembly of the LORD."

The foreigner under discussion in verse 3 **has bound himself to the LORD**, an expression that calls to mind the way the Levites came to be elevated to their special role. The word for "bound" (לוה, *lwh*)

---
[4]Webb, *Message*, p. 221.

provides a wordplay for the name of Levi at birth (Gen 29:34) as Leah rejoices that "Now at last my husband will become *attached* to me." A similar wordplay appears in Numbers 18:2,4 as God tells Aaron to have the Levites "join" the priests and assist them in their work. The Levites had earlier come to the aid of Moses in the aftermath of the golden calf incident (Exod 32:26-29; cf. also Esth 9:27; Isa 14:1; Zech 2:11). The implication of this expression is that this passage anticipates those outside of Israel who will bind themselves to God.

The foreigner and the eunuch under consideration here, though committed to God (cf. vv. 4,6), both experience understandable insecurities about their future status. The foreigner's fear that **the LORD will surely exclude me from his people** may reflect Israel's ritual purity regulations, including those in Deuteronomy 23:1-8. The emphatic verb "will surely exclude" (הַבְדֵּל יַבְדִּיל, *habdēl yabdîl*) refers to making a separation/distinction. God used the same verb when he told Aaron to instruct his sons to "*distinguish* between the holy and the common, between the unclean and the clean" (Lev 10:10). In Ezekiel 22:26 God charges the priests with a failure to make this distinction, leading at least in part to the destruction and exile at the hands of the Babylonians. It may seem somewhat ironic, therefore, that God is about to describe a future, in light of the work of the servant, in which the divisions between Israelite and Gentile will be broken down. The eunuch's concern for being **only a dry tree** points to his obvious inability to perpetuate his line through descendants.

56:4-5 God first speaks to the **eunuchs** whose lives conform to the description of faithfulness in verses 1-2. He promises them something **better than sons and daughters**. Even though they cannot produce children, they will receive from God **an everlasting name that will not be cut off.** This name is associated with a **memorial** inside God's **temple** (literally, "house"). The reference is not intended literally,[5] but the notion of such an honor for a eunuch in the very presence of God is both shocking to the outsider and affirming to the eunuch. The situation stands in stark contrast to the pitiable construction by the childless Absalom of a "monument to himself" to cause his name to be remembered (2 Sam 18:18). Absalom is remembered for his shameful rebellion against his

---

[5]Cf. the promise to make each overcomer in the church at Philadelphia "a pillar in the temple of my God" (Rev 3:12).

father, but the faithful eunuchs will share in the praise that belongs to God's name ("renown," 55:13).

56:6-7a The meaning of the **foreigners who bind themselves to the LORD** is elaborated and includes **to serve him, to love the name of the LORD, and to worship him**. The irony of the foreigners' heart for worship should not be lost on the Israelites for whom pleasing worship has proven such a challenge. Whereas the sins of the inhabitants of Jerusalem ultimately drive God from the temple and result in destruction and exile, God promises to **bring** faithful non-Israelites to his **holy mountain** and accept their worship (contrast 1:13-15). They will experience the **joy** that God gives to those who sincerely seek him.

56:7b-8 God reaffirms his universal purpose by designating his **house** as **a house of prayer for all nations**[6] (cf. 1 Kgs 8:41-43) and by proclaiming his intention to **gather still others** in addition to **the exiles of Israel**.[7] He has already tied the goal of extending his mission beyond the repentance and restoration of Israel to the work of the servant (42:6; 49:6; 52:15).

The conversion of the Ethiopian eunuch in Acts 8:26ff. illustrates perfectly the joyful hope this passage presents. He is both a foreigner and a eunuch, yet is obviously a sincere seeker of God. The fact that he is reading about the suffering servant in Isaiah makes his experience an even more fitting fulfillment of the way God intends to universalize his work of redemption. The inclusion of individuals such as the Ethiopian eunuch was far from painless, but Isaiah leaves no doubt that God intends to create one people from those of any nation or background who commit themselves to him.

4. God Gives Peace to His People (56:9–57:21)

As with chapters 40-48, chapters 49-57 contain tremendous promises for a hopeful future but conclude with a solemn reminder of painful present conditions. The concluding note of each section, "There is no peace," says my God, "for the wicked," exhorts the pres-

---

[6]Jesus cites these words in condemning the inappropriate and distracting business practices in the Court of the Gentiles in the temple precincts (Matt 21:13; Mark 11:17; Luke 19:46).

[7]These words are very similar to those of Jesus in John 10:16 as he speaks of "other sheep that are not of the sheep pen" that he must gather.

ent generation to turn from a way of life that offers no hope of peace and to pursue God who alone can give peace. Even in the condemnation of this passage, however, God reminds his people of his determination to give them peace and of the way they can find that peace in him.

Failed Leadership Jeopardizes Peace (56:9-12)

⁹**Come, all you beasts of the field, /come and devour, all you beasts of the forest! /** ¹⁰**Israel's watchmen are blind, /they all lack knowledge; /they are all mute dogs, /they cannot bark; /they lie around and dream, /they love to sleep. /** ¹¹**They are dogs with mighty appetites; /they never have enough. /They are shepherds who lack understanding; /they all turn to their own way, /each seeks his own gain. /** ¹²**"Come," each one cries, "let me get wine! /Let us drink our fill of beer! /And tomorrow will be like today, /or even far better."**

56:9,12 These verses contain numerous connections with both the immediate and the larger context of Isaiah. Verses 9 and 12 bracket the passage with the cry to **Come**. In verse 12 Israel's corrupt leaders call one another to drink **wine** and **beer** and in their intoxicated state delude themselves into thinking that **tomorrow will be like today, or even far better**. They sound very much like the drunken leaders Isaiah describes in earlier chapters (cf. 5:11ff.; 28:7ff.) who arrogantly reject God's warnings and shore up their defenses through vain dependence upon idolatry and foreign alliances.

The failure of Israel's leadership results in a call for the **beasts of the field** to come and feast upon the rebels, signaling the enactment of the covenant curses for disobedience (cf. Lev 26:22; Deut 28:26; 32:24). This tragic turn of events stands in stark contrast to God's gracious call to "come, buy wine and milk without money and without cost" at the opening of chapter 55.[8]

56:10-11 Israel's leaders are first described as **watchmen**, people who occupy a position of great responsibility (cf. Ezek 3:17-21; 33:1-9). Because they prefer to **lie around and dream**, however, they are about as useful as **blind** watchmen or **mute dogs** who **cannot bark**.

---

[8]John juxtaposes "the wedding supper of the Lamb" (Rev 19:9) with "the great supper of God" (Rev 19:17-18) in which the birds feast upon those slain by God's judgment.

These absurd metaphors reveal how defenseless a group is without vigilant leadership. Whereas the analogy of the watchmen points out the carelessness or incompetence of Israel's leaders, the analogy of the **shepherds** hints at their abuse of those for whom they should be caring. Because of their **mighty appetites**, these leaders **never have enough**, and thus each one continually **seeks his own gain** rather than the welfare of the flock. The fact that these shepherds **all turn to their own way** helps to explain why, according to 53:6, "we all, like sheep, have gone astray, each of us has turned to his own way." How can a people rise above their leadership? Ezekiel 34 makes clear the way Israel's shepherds have abused and taken advantage of the flock.

One thread that ties the two analogies together is the ignorance of the leaders. In verse 10 the blind watchmen (literally) "do not know." The shepherds "do not know fullness/satisfaction" and "they do not know understanding."[9] A lack of knowledge in the Old Testament typically indicates a deficit in *relationship* more than in *information*. Godly leadership comes from knowing God, and the fundamental problem of Israel's leaders derives from this lack of knowledge. Ultimately it is for this reason that those who should help to secure peace are instead contributing to its absence.

---

[9]Cf. Motyer, *Prophecy*, p. 468.

ISAIAH 57

Idolatry Jeopardizes Peace (57:1-13)

¹The righteous perish, / and no one ponders it in his heart; / devout men are taken away, / and no one understands / that the righteous are taken away / to be spared from evil. / ²Those who walk uprightly / enter into peace; / they find rest as they lie in death.

³"But you—come here, you sons of a sorceress, / you offspring of adulterers and prostitutes! / ⁴Whom are you mocking? / At whom do you sneer / and stick out your tongue? / Are you not a brood of rebels, / the offspring of liars? / ⁵You burn with lust among the oaks / and under every spreading tree; / you sacrifice your children in the ravines / and under the overhanging crags. / ⁶⌊The idols⌋ among the smooth stones of the ravines are your portion; / they, they are your lot. / Yes, to them you have poured out drink offerings / and offered grain offerings. / In the light of these things, should I relent? / ⁷You have made your bed on a high and lofty hill; / there you went up to offer your sacrifices. / ⁸Behind your doors and your doorposts / you have put your pagan symbols. / Forsaking me, you uncovered your bed, / you climbed into it and opened it wide; / you made a pact with those whose beds you love, / and you looked on their nakedness. / ⁹You went to Molech[a] with olive oil / and increased your perfumes. / You sent your ambassadors[b] far away; / you descended to the grave[c] itself! / ¹⁰You were wearied by all your ways, / but you would not say, 'It is hopeless.' / You found renewal of your strength, / and so you did not faint.

¹¹"Whom have you so dreaded and feared / that you have been false to me, / and have neither remembered me / nor pondered this in your hearts? / Is it not because I have long been silent / that you do not fear me? / ¹²I will expose your righteousness and your works, / and they will not benefit you. / ¹³When you cry out for help, let your collection ⌊of idols⌋ save you! / The wind will carry all of them off, /

a mere breath will blow them away. / But the man who makes me his refuge / will inherit the land / and possess my holy mountain."

ᵃ9 Or *to the king*   ᵇ9 Or *idols*   ᶜ9 Hebrew *Sheol*

57:1-2 Isaiah includes a brief, almost parenthetical, note about the suffering of the **righteous** between his rebuke of corrupt leadership and his condemnation of idolatry. In times characterized by such circumstances, faithful individuals will inevitably face hardships and perhaps even **perish**.[1] To make matters worse, no one seems to care. The expression **no one ponders it** *in his heart* [עַל לֵב, *'al lēb*] might be contrasted with God's promise in 40:2 to "Speak *tenderly* [*'al lēb*] to Jerusalem." Although people in general are oblivious to the plight of the righteous, God cares for them because in their death they **are taken away to be spared from evil**. While those who remain will reap the bitter consequences of their rebellion, the faithful departed will **enter into peace** and **find rest**. The message of the prophetess Huldah to Josiah about his death illustrates this principle (2 Kgs 22:19-20). This message of comfort contains at least a hint that something meaningful lies beyond this life (cf. 25:7-8).

57:3-4 But you (וְאַתֶּם, *wəʾattem*) in verse 3 marks a strong contrast with what Isaiah has just said regarding the righteous. The description in the following verses again brings Isaiah's message back to the present condition of his generation. This generation is the product (גֶּרַע, *geraʿ*) of bad parenting. The children rebel against the covenant because they are **offspring of adulterers and prostitutes** (cf. 1:21). They treat those who speak the truth with contempt (cf. 28:9-18) because they are **the offspring of liars**.

57:5-10 Not surprisingly, these people who have a "family history" of unfaithfulness to God continue in those ways. They **burn with lust** and establish **a pact with those whose beds [they] love**. Literally, they pursue idolatry to such an extent that they even practice child sacrifice.[2] Their **pagan symbols** (זִכָּרוֹן, *zikkārôn*) are actually a "remembrance/memorial." Placing them on their **doorposts**

---

[1]Cf. the treatment of the true prophets (1 Kgs 18:4) and Naboth (1 Kgs 21) during the reign of Ahab and Jezebel.

[2]"Molech" in verse 9 is literally "king" (מֶלֶךְ, *melek*), but the association of this Ammonite god with child sacrifice likely accounts for the shift. "King," however, serves as a better parallel to "ambassadors" in the second half of the verse. In either case, Israel's descent to the "grave" (שְׁאוֹל, *šəʾôl*) reflects the same type of blind, foolish decision as the one reflected in the sarcastic language of 28:14-15.

(מְזוּזָה, *mᵉzûzāh*) is an affront to God since the doorposts are to remind his people of his faithfulness and their covenant with him (cf. Exod 12:21ff.; Deut 6:9). The fact that they are **wearied** by their **ways** but refuse to give up and find **renewal of [their] strength** represents a faint parody of God's great promise in 40:29-31.

In light of the blatant and determined nature of Israel's rebellion, God is justified in asking (v. 6), **should I relent?** The word for "relent" (נחם, *nḥm*) can also be translated "repent" and on numerous occasions refers to God's decision to change his course of action in light of humans' changing response to him (Jer 18:7-10; cf. Gen 6:6; Exod 32:14; 1 Sam 15:11; Jonah 3:10; 4:2).[3] The ominous tone of God's question in this instance, however, stems from the people's failure to see a need for their repentance.

57:11-13 God traces Israel's unfaithfulness and lack of repentance in verse 11 to the fear of another. The "fear of the LORD" constitutes an exclusive relationship (Deut 10:12,20; Josh 24:14; 2 Kgs 17:35). In 8:11ff. Isaiah was warned not to fall into the trap of fearing what many of his countrymen fear, leading them to "consult the dead on behalf of the living." Here God traces Israel's failure to remember him or ponder their circumstances in their hearts[4] to his long period of silence. Motyer points out that the word for **silent** (חשה, *ḥšh*) refers more to inactivity than lack of speech and suggests that this period refers to "Isaiah's preaching during the long dark days of Manasseh."[5] As in chapter 8, however, God's refusal to bless his people during a time of rebellion does not provide them with an excuse because they have "the law" and "the testimony" (8:20). God will not remain inactive, but in his time will **expose** the counterfeit nature of the **righteousness** and **works**[6] of those who fear others rather than God. A **collection of idols**[7] provides such an insubstantial

---

[3]Translators sometimes obscure the use of this strong but potentially confusing language for God by using alternative renderings such as "was grieved" or "changed his mind." Scripture seeks to avoid the notion that God is fickle or that he has sinned or erred by denying that he "repents" as humans do (Num 23:19; 1 Sam 15:29).

[4]Cf. the parallel expression in verse 1.

[5]Motyer, *Prophecy*, p. 474.

[6]One way of capturing the sense of verse 12 would be to put these words in quotation marks to indicate the contrast between the way the sinners see themselves and the way God sees them.

[7]Note that "of idols" is an insertion into the text, but a necessary and appropriate one in context.

fortress that **a mere breath will blow them away** (cf. Ps 1:4), but those who trust in God will receive the substantial inheritance of **the land**. The parallel reference to **my holy mountain**, in light of 2:2-3 and 56:7 (cf. 65:9-11), looks beyond a simple inheritance of physical property to the realization of the ultimate blessings of God's covenant promises.

Penitence Prepares the Way for Peace (57:14-21)

[14]And it will be said:
"Build up, build up, prepare the road! / Remove the obstacles out of the way of my people." / [15]For this is what the high and lofty One says— /he who lives forever, whose name is holy: / "I live in a high and holy place, /but also with him who is contrite and lowly in spirit, / to revive the spirit of the lowly /and to revive the heart of the contrite. / [16]I will not accuse forever, /nor will I always be angry, /for then the spirit of man would grow faint before me— /the breath of man that I have created. / [17]I was enraged by his sinful greed; /I punished him, and hid my face in anger, /yet he kept on in his willful ways. / [18]I have seen his ways, but I will heal him; /I will guide him and restore comfort to him, /[19]creating praise on the lips of the mourners in Israel. / Peace, peace, to those far and near," /says the LORD. "And I will heal them." / [20]But the wicked are like the tossing sea, /which cannot rest, /whose waves cast up mire and mud. / [21]"There is no peace," says my God, "for the wicked."

The transition at the end of verse 13 introduces the hopeful conclusion of chapters 49–57. The bleak prospects in Isaiah's day for a righteous and trusting Israel will not stop God from accomplishing his purpose. The existence of a faithful remnant, no matter how small, holds out the prospect for a better future because of God's ability to work through that which is weak by human standards. The focal point of this section, the final servant song, demonstrates how God can transform what appears to be an abject defeat into glorious triumph.

57:14-15 In language reminiscent of the opening of chapter 40, God promises to **remove the obstacles out of the way of my people**. As the previous verses have made clear, the biggest obstacle is a lack of faith in God that results in a failure to repent and turn from unrighteous ways. If Israel is going to resume its journey on the **road** that God has chosen, the preparatory work must be directed to their hearts. Ironically, the exalted God (cf. 6:1-4) who dwells[8] **in a high and holy place** will only reside with a person **who is contrite and lowly in spirit**. The servant himself, who will ultimately "be raised and lifted up and highly exalted" (52:13) is first "crushed for our iniquities" (53:5).[9] God's goal is to give new life ("revive," לְהַחֲיוֹת, *lᵉhaḥăyôth*; cf. Ps 34:18; 51:17; 147:3), but first people must realize their need for that life.

57:16-17 Since God is the one who brings about the awareness of need by his acts of discipline, he must be conscious of the limits of his mortal creatures. He will not contend[10] with them **forever**, lest they **grow faint**. The challenge for him is great, however, because he has previously taken severe measures against his rebellious child Israel, **yet he kept on in his willful ways**.[11] Singling out **greed** may focus attention on Israel's leaders (cf. 56:11).[12] Greed also highlights the internal dimension of the problem (cf. the tenth commandment's prohibition against coveting).

57:18-21 Given the discouraging tone of verse 17 and God's full awareness of Israel's situation (**I have seen his ways**) at the opening of verse 18, the promise to **heal** and **guide** and **restore comfort** comes as a surprise. Yet God has demonstrated his power by bringing about dramatic turnarounds before (cf. the transition from 8:5-8 and 8:9-10). In this case he steps in not to defeat a foreign invader, but to renew his own people. God's power is evidenced here by the act of **creating** [ברא, *br'*] **praise on the lips** of his people. The willing praise that God deserves from his redeemed people is not possible until sinners realize their condition and recognize God as the one who can save them. This change, in turn, is not possible unless God reaches out to humanity to make his righteousness and his love known.

The NIV moves **the mourners** from the end of verse 18 to the first line of verse 19. In its proper location God promises to "restore

---

[8]The word for "live" (שׁכן, *škn*) is related to the word for God's dwelling place, or tabernacle (מִשְׁכָּן, *miškān*) in the midst of his people.

[9]"Crushed" (מְדֻכָּא, *mᵉdukkā'*) and "contrite" (נִדְכָּא/דַּכָּא, *dakkā'/nidkāh*) are from the same root.

[10]The word translated "accuse" (רִיב, *ryb*) is used in the sense of a legal proceeding (cf. 3:13), but it refers in a broader sense to what God does to turn his people back to him.

[11]Literally, "in the way of his heart."

[12]The same word for "greed" (בֶּצַע, *beṣa'*) is rendered "gain" in 56:11.

comfort to him and to his mourners." The conjunction "and" in Hebrew can sometimes function in an explanatory fashion. In this case the words "to his mourners" describe who receives the healing and guidance and comfort from God (cf. 30:19-21). Although many in Israel might continue in their sinful ways, those who respond to God's overtures with penitence will enjoy the **peace** that will be made everywhere available (**far and near**). The **wicked**, on the other hand, are those who refuse to respond to God and thus inevitably deprive themselves of peace. For them all that remains is the restless turbulence of the **tossing sea**. As at the end of the previous section of Isaiah (cf. v. 21 and 48:22), God's manifestations of sovereignty (Cyrus) and grace (the suffering servant) confront humanity with a decision carrying far-reaching consequences. The final section of Isaiah elaborates upon the nature of both the decision and its consequences.

ISAIAH 58

III. THE FAITHFULNESS OF GOD AND THE FUTURE OF HIS SERVANTS (58:1–66:24)

A. GOD'S COMMITMENT TO RENEW HIS RELATIONSHIP WITH HIS PEOPLE (58:1–59:21)

1. Israel's Misguided Religion (58:1-14)

The final section of Isaiah begins the same way the book as a whole does, by highlighting a serious flaw in Israel's approach to the worship of God. As in the first case, one could argue whether this problem is a cause or a result of Israel's overall spiritual decline. In all likelihood it is probably a cause *and* a result, since meaningful worship both flows from and enhances a proper relationship with God. What really matters is that Israel hears this message and overcomes the impasse to receiving God's blessings.

Numerous parallels exist between this chapter and 1:10-20. In both passages God rejects worship that does not result in positively transformed human relationships. Neither text indicates that the outward practices being described are improper (contrast 57:5-9). The problems reside in the hearts of the worshipers and their decidedly pagan view of the nature of God. The passages differ in two significant ways. The focus on fasting in chapter 58 implies a greater sense of urgency on the part of the worshipers, in contrast to the more routine practices such as sacrifices, prayers, and festivals in chapter 1. In addition, whereas the first passage heavily stresses ethical reform, chapter 58 also highlights the importance of finding delight in worshiping God.

Religion That Fails to Connect (58:1-5)

¹"Shout it aloud, do not hold back. / Raise your voice like a

trumpet. / Declare to my people their rebellion / and to the house of Jacob their sins. / ²For day after day they seek me out; / they seem eager to know my ways, / as if they were a nation that does what is right / and has not forsaken the commands of its God. / They ask me for just decisions / and seem eager for God to come near them. / ³'Why have we fasted,' they say, / 'and you have not seen it? / Why have we humbled ourselves, / and you have not noticed?'

"Yet on the day of your fasting, you do as you please / and exploit all your workers. / ⁴Your fasting ends in quarreling and strife, / and in striking each other with wicked fists. / You cannot fast as you do today / and expect your voice to be heard on high. / ⁵Is this the kind of fast I have chosen, / only a day for a man to humble himself? / Is it only for bowing one's head like a reed / and for lying on sackcloth and ashes? / Is that what you call a fast, / a day acceptable to the LORD?

58:1 The emphatic opening call to proclaim this message marks its importance (cf. 1:2,10; 40:2,3,6,9). Comparing the prophetic voice to a **trumpet** (שׁוֹפָר, *šôphār*) recalls the solemn occasion at Mt. Sinai before God spoke to Moses (Exod 19:16-19). God's message since chapter 40 has largely been one of comfort, but here, as in chapter 1, he proclaims the sins of Israel as manifested in their worship. The parallel between **my people** and **the house of Jacob** indicates a pervasive problem and shifts the reader from a consideration of the faithful remnant in 57:14ff. to the people as a whole.[1]

58:2 The beginning of the description of Israel's relationship with God in verse 2 provides no indication of a problem. The people daily **seek** God.[2] They "delight"[3] in the knowledge of his **ways**. The NIV twice adds the word "seem" in this verse in an attempt to remove the tension the text will resolve shortly. The problem with this intervention is its implication of Israel's blatant hypocrisy. While

---

[1] Cf. Webb, *Message*, p. 225, n. 34.

[2] The pronoun "me" in "they seek me out" is placed in an emphatic position at the beginning of the verse.

[3] This word (חָפֵץ, *ḥps*), translated "eager" here, brackets chapter 58. It appears again at the end of this verse ("eager"), as well as in verse 3 ("as you please") and twice in verse 13 ("as you please"). The root is typically used in a positive sense, indicating the pleasure or delight experienced by God or man. In this chapter, however, it represents Israel's selfish pursuit of pleasure that disregards God and thus misses the true object of delight.

hypocrisy is a possible explanation, it is more likely that Israel has grown so ignorant of the truth about God and his ways that they believe they are approaching him properly. The only clear indication of a problem in verse 2 is in the beginning of the words: **as if they were a nation** [כְּגוֹי, *kᵉgôy*; literally, "like a nation"] **that does what is right and has not forsaken the commands of its God**. The issue is not that they are pretending to be something they are not, but that they are not what they think they are. This situation is more difficult to expose than hypocrisy. It is also more dangerous because in their naive desire for **just decisions** and for **God to come near** they do not realize what the consequences will be.

The people reveal their flawed theology (to God, though not to themselves) in their frustration with how unproductive their fasting has been. Fasting accompanies mourning, including penitence for sin, the kind of humbling which was revealed as a key trait of the faithful remnant (cf. 57:15; Joel 2:12-14). Scripture commands fasting only on the Day of Atonement,[4] but individuals and the community as a whole fasted on a number of important occasions and several set times of fasting emerged after the exile (cf. Zech 7:1-7). Like any ritual, however, the act of fasting fails to produce positive results when it is misdirected.

58:3-4a God thus calls Israel's attention[5] to the defects in their fasts. Verse 3b sums up these defects under two headings, both of which contradict the true meaning of fasting. First, how can a fast be legitimate if it is also a time when **you do as you please** (literally, "you find pleasure")? This charge confirms that their fasting does not reflect a humbling experience but is instead a self-seeking endeavor. Further, how can God be pleased with a religious act that results in exploiting one's **workers**? The point here may be that a wealthier individual who fasts expects his workers to make up what he leaves undone during his "religious holiday." Verse 4a elaborates on this second charge, perhaps reflecting an irritable and combative spirit as a result of hunger.

---

[4]The command to "deny yourselves" in Lev 16:29,31 is interpreted as a command to fast. The same expression (נֶפֶשׁ + עִנָּה, *'innāh + nepheš*) appears in 58:3,5 and is translated by the NIV as "humbled ourselves/humble himself."

[5]Verses 3b and 4a are introduced by הֵן (*hēn*, "Look/Behold"). The NIV opens verse 3b with the weaker "Yet" and uses no introductory word in verse 4.

58:4b-5 God denies that the kind of fasting he has witnessed will cause his people's **voice to be heard on high**. It is not **the kind of fast** he has **chosen**. In other words, God does not respond favorably to acts of worship — even if they are outwardly correct — unless they are approached with the spirit and intent for which he has designed them. Since Israel's fasting is motivated by selfish desire and results in violence and oppression, it obviously fails to meet God's standards. The two occurrences of **only** in verse 5 are words again supplied by the NIV, but in this case the context more obviously warrants them. There is nothing inappropriate in humbling oneself or in **bowing one's head** or in **lying on sackcloth and ashes** in connection with a fast. The problem occurs when these activities represent the *only* legitimate indicators of fasting. Absent the qualities God will describe in the following verses, these outward demonstrations are meaningless.

Religion That Results in Blessing (58:6-14)

⁶"Is not this the kind of fasting I have chosen: / to loose the chains of injustice / and untie the cords of the yoke, / to set the oppressed free / and break every yoke? / ⁷Is it not to share your food with the hungry / and to provide the poor wanderer with shelter— / when you see the naked, to clothe him, / and not to turn away from your own flesh and blood? / ⁸Then your light will break forth like the dawn, / and your healing will quickly appear; / then your righteousness[a] will go before you, / and the glory of the LORD will be your rear guard. / ⁹Then you will call, and the LORD will answer; / you will cry for help, and he will say: Here am I.

"If you do away with the yoke of oppression, / with the pointing finger and malicious talk, / ¹⁰and if you spend yourselves in behalf of the hungry / and satisfy the needs of the oppressed, / then your light will rise in the darkness, / and your night will become like the noonday. / ¹¹The LORD will guide you always; / he will satisfy your needs in a sun-scorched land / and will strengthen your frame. / You will be like a well-watered garden, / like a spring whose waters never fail. / ¹²Your people will rebuild the ancient ruins / and will raise up the age-old foundations; / you will be called Repairer of Broken Walls, / Restorer of Streets with Dwellings. / ¹³"If you keep your feet from breaking the Sabbath / and from doing as you please on my holy day, / if you call the Sabbath a delight / and the LORD's holy day honorable, / and if you honor it by not going your own way

/ and not doing as you please or speaking idle words, / ¹⁴then you will find your joy in the LORD, / and I will cause you to ride on the heights of the land / and to feast on the inheritance of your father Jacob." / The mouth of the LORD has spoken.

ᵃ8 Or *your righteous One*

58:6 In contrast to the oppression and violence that have resulted from Israel's fasting, verses 6-12 present the righteous counterpart, as well as the divine blessings that flow from a proper fast. As God describes **the kind of fasting I have chosen**, he does not speak of the fasting itself but of the *result* of this fasting. When people truly humble themselves before God, they come to desire what God desires. Rather than complaining about God's failure to respond to their virtuous acts of piety, they act to relieve the suffering of those for whom God cares. They seek to **satisfy the needs of the oppressed** (v. 10) rather than their own.

58:7 Perhaps verse 7 best illustrates how misguided Israel's fasting has been. They fast and wonder why God does not give them more as a result of their sacrifice. God's desire is instead that this voluntary abstinence from food will demonstrate that they are able to share their abundant resources with those who have even less. In addition, going without food allows them to focus on what is most important. God caused Israel to experience hunger in the wilderness so that they could learn that "man does not live on bread alone but on every word that comes from the mouth of the LORD" (Deut 8:3). This lesson apparently needs to be taught again.

58:8-12 God desires to bless and is abundantly able to do so, but not in a way that reinforces unhealthy beliefs or practices. To seek blessings to the neglect or harm of others is selfish, and to attempt to use God and the religious practices he has instituted as means to our selfish ends dishonors him and deprives us of fellowship with him. True blessings come indirectly as we seek God and his will (cf. Matt 6:33). Verses 8-9a promise **light** (in the sense of a new day dawning), **healing**, and God's protective presence to those whose fasting produces the proper fruit. Verses 10b-12 also promise **light** (in the sense of a clear understanding of God's purposes?),⁶ the satisfaction of **needs**, strength, **waters** that **never fail**,⁷ and the rebuild-

---

⁶Motyer, *Prophecy*, pp. 481-482.
⁷The word for fail (כזב, *kzb*) is the same word used for Israel proving "false" in 57:11. God proves to be reliable even though Israel does not.

ing of **the ancient ruins**. These blessings transcend anything the people had originally imagined, but they come only to those who seek God's honor rather than their own (cf. Eph 3:20-21).

58:13-14 The final two verses of the chapter return to the first failure of Israel's fasting as pointed out in verse 3: "on the day of your fasting, you do as you please." The end of verse 13 speaks of **not doing as you please**, and yet the alternative is not a self-denial that robs life of all pleasure. Instead God calls his people to a path of **delight** and **joy**. Before turning to consider how this alternative comes about, a significant shift in verse 13 should be noted. Why has the subject changed from fasting to the **Sabbath**? Like fasting, Sabbath observance could be viewed as an inconvenient obligation that thus becomes counterproductive. The most blatant example of this thinking occurs in Amos 8:4-6, wherein certain individuals cannot wait for the Sabbath to be over so that they can get back to cheating the poor. Faithful observance of the Sabbath has already appeared as a litmus test for those God blesses, including foreigners and eunuchs, in 56:1-8.

Perhaps the subtle shift from fasting to the Sabbath also points to God's intent to bless through what he commands. Deuteronomy stresses that God gives his commandments for the good of his people (cf. 6:24; 10:13; 30:15). Although the purpose of the Sabbath can be distorted or missed altogether, this **holy day** provides a clearer opportunity to see the positive intent of God's commandments than fasting. A significant new word enters the vocabulary of "delight" in this chapter that clarifies the changed perspective he wants his people to experience. God does not merely desire his worshipers to avoid **breaking the Sabbath** by pursuing their own pleasures. He wants them to consider the Sabbath a **delight** (עֹנֶג, *'ōneg*), a day they recognize as **holy** and desire to honor. The ultimate goal is not to honor a day, however, but to experience God by the proper observance of that day. The first line of verse 14, therefore, uses the same root behind the noun "delight" in calling the worshiper to "find delight" (תִּתְעַנַּג, *tith'annag*) **in the LORD**.

The same verb form in verse 14 appears in Psalm 37:4: "Delight yourself (*tith'annag*) in the LORD and he will give you the desires of your heart." This verse might appear on the surface to contradict the call of Isaiah 58 not to seek selfish pleasures but in reality affirms the prophet's message. The psalmists no more encourage paganizing Yahweh by viewing him as one capable of manipulation for human ends than do the prophets (cf. Psalm 50). The point of Psalm 37:4 is not to give God lip-service in order to get from him what you want. It is rather to find your ultimate delight in God so that your desires will conform to that which is within his will. Similarly, Isaiah contrasts "doing as you please" with finding delight in God. Religious rituals become burdensome when they represent requirements to be met in order to win God's favor. They become delightful when they serve as opportunities to know and enjoy a relationship with God more fully. Only when one seeks God as an end and not as a means to an end may the full measure of covenant blessings (**the inheritance of your father Jacob**) be enjoyed.

ISAIAH 59

2. Israel's Separation from God (59:1-21)

Whether Israel's confusion over why their fasting has not prompted God's blessings stems from ignorance or hypocrisy, the people have proven to be blind to their own sinfulness. The implication at the beginning of this chapter is that Israel considers God to be unaware of their situation or unable to help, a false impression that Isaiah moves quickly to dispel. The blinding effect of sin obscures Israel's ability to see that their sin is the problem. Escape from this vicious cycle remains hopeless unless God steps in to intervene.

God Accuses Israel of Sin (59:1-8)

¹Surely the arm of the LORD is not too short to save, / nor his ear too dull to hear. / ²But your iniquities have separated / you from your God; / your sins have hidden his face from you, / so that he will not hear. / ³For your hands are stained with blood, / your fingers with guilt. / Your lips have spoken lies, / and your tongue mutters wicked things. / ⁴No one calls for justice; / no one pleads his case with integrity. / They rely on empty arguments and speak lies; / they conceive trouble and give birth to evil. / ⁵They hatch the eggs of vipers / and spin a spider's web. / Whoever eats their eggs will die, / and when one is broken, an adder is hatched. / ⁶Their cobwebs are useless for clothing; / they cannot cover themselves with what they make. / Their deeds are evil deeds, / and acts of violence are in their hands. / ⁷Their feet rush into sin; / they are swift to shed innocent blood. / Their thoughts are evil thoughts; / ruin and destruction mark their ways. / ⁸The way of peace they do not know; / there is no justice in their paths. / They have turned them into crooked roads; / no one who walks in them will know peace.

59:1-2 Impatience with the **arm** [i.e., power] **of the LORD** has appeared before in Isaiah (cf. 51:9-10). God has also previously denied that his arm is **too short** to reach them in their distress (50:2).¹ The insinuation that God's **ear is too dull to hear** is ironic in light of Israel's almost total failure to listen to God (cf. 6:9-10). The great prayers in Nehemiah 9 and Daniel 9 reveal that righteous individuals in the exile vindicate God and recognize that Israel's sins have created the separation between God and his people. The word for **separated** (מַבְדִּילִים, *mabdîlîm*) describes the distinction (לְהַבְדִּיל, *lăhabdîl*) the priests were to teach Israel "between the holy and the common, between the unclean and the clean" (Lev 10:10). Now Israel is in the category of the unclean from which God must separate himself (cf. Ezekiel 8–10). This state explains the sense in which their **sins have hidden his face . . . so that he will not hear**.

59:3-4 Isaiah exonerates God from guilt in verse 1 by affirming the present capacity of his "arm" and "ear," but Israel's guilt extends to their **hands, fingers, lips,** and **tongue**. The charges of violence (cf. 1:15,21), deception (9:15; 28:15; 30:9), and injustice (cf. 1:17) that have characterized Israel from the beginning of the book manifest themselves in deeds and words that betray their professed devotion to God. Because they **rely on empty arguments**² **and speak lies**, it should not be surprising that they will **conceive trouble and give birth to evil**. Israel's frustration with her inability to give birth to anything more substantive than "wind" (cf. 26:17-18) tells only half the story. In addition to failing to bear the fruit that God desires, Israel reaps a bitter fruit as a result of rebellion.

59:5-8 Isaiah illustrates the "trouble"³ and "evil"⁴ to which Israel has given birth by a pair of unflattering images. To **hatch the eggs of vipers** is to produce that which endangers by its poison. In other words, they bring destruction rather than deliverance into the world. To **spin a spider's web** is to construct something that is useless as **clothing** by which they might **cover themselves** (cf. 28:20).⁵ Just as Adam and Eve could cover their nakedness with fig leaves but

---

¹In Isa 50:2 God's "arm" is parallel to his "strength."

²The word for "empty arguments" (תֹּהוּ, *tōhû*) refers to chaos, emptiness, confusion. It describes the "formless" state of the world (Gen 1:2), but also the "ruined" city (Isa 24:10), the "confusion" of pagan images (Isa 41:29), and the "worthless" nature of that in which idol makers trust (Isa 44:9).

³עָמָל (*'āmāl*) implies labor, toil.

⁴אָוֶן (*'āwen*) refers more to the trouble or sorrow that results from sin.

⁵Job 8:14-15 uses a spider's web to portray that which is fragile and fails to give support.

could not conceal their shame before God, Israel's efforts to clothe themselves adequately prove futile. The Israelites' failure to clothe the naked in their midst (58:7) ultimately exposes their own nakedness. Before the chapter is finished, God will clothe himself as a warrior against his people's enemies (v. 17) and will ultimately clothe his people with "garments of salvation" (61:10). Until that day, however, Israel's **crooked roads** mean that **no one who walks in them will know peace** (cf. 48:22; 57:21).

Israel Suffers Because of Sin (59:9-15a)

⁹So justice is far from us, / and righteousness does not reach us. / We look for light, but all is darkness; / for brightness, but we walk in deep shadows. / ¹⁰Like the blind we grope along the wall, / feeling our way like men without eyes. / At midday we stumble as if it were twilight; / among the strong, we are like the dead. / ¹¹We all growl like bears; / we moan mournfully like doves. / We look for justice, but find none; / for deliverance, but it is far away.

¹²For our offenses are many in your sight, / and our sins testify against us. / Our offenses are ever with us, / and we acknowledge our iniquities: / ¹³rebellion and treachery against the LORD, / turning our backs on our God, / fomenting oppression and revolt, / uttering lies our hearts have conceived. / ¹⁴So justice is driven back, / and righteousness stands at a distance; / truth has stumbled in the streets, / honesty cannot enter. / ¹⁵Truth is nowhere to be found, / and whoever shuns evil becomes a prey.

59:9-14 The perspective shifts in verse 9 as a frustrated Israelite — perhaps Isaiah himself — leads the people in a lament for their circumstances.[6] Unlike many of the laments in Psalms, in which a righteous sufferer cries out to God for vindication, here the cry is for deliverance from circumstances a sinful people have brought upon themselves (vv. 12-13). The primary casualties within Israelite society as a result of these sins are **justice**, **righteousness**, and **truth**. Isaiah parallels justice and righteousness in verses 9 and 14, but he substitutes **deliverance** for righteousness in verse 11. Motyer sees this variation as a clue for understanding the meaning of these flex-

---

[6]The use of the first person plural pronouns incorporate either the people as a whole as Isaiah identifies himself with them (cf. 6:5; 53:6), or a smaller group that shares in Isaiah's mourning over Israel's plight (cf. 57:19).

ible terms. "*Justice* is not 'the just society' as such but the rule of God which will set everything to rights; *righteousness* has the same meaning as in 56:1, the coming act of God in which he will vindicate and display his righteousness and fulfil all his righteous purposes."[7]

Since neither God's deliverance nor the light of truth have a home in Israel, the people dwell in perpetual **darkness**. God's face cannot shine upon them (v. 2; Num 6:24-26) in their present condition, one that constitutes a fulfillment of the covenant curses (Deut 28:28-29). Their isolation leaves them groping about for direction even in the glaring sun of **midday**. Their blindness, of course, is spiritual rather than physical (cf. 6:10). The one glimmer of hope lies in the fact that at least some recognize their blindness. At present, however, all they can do is **growl** and **moan** like animals in distress.

59:15a At the end of these verses, justice, righteousness, and truth are personified as unwelcome guests who are driven away and denied entrance to Zion. If these qualities are rejected in the larger society, the person who **shuns evil** will not be welcome either (cf. Amos 5:10,13). Such a person will likely be targeted as **prey** (מִשְׁתּוֹלֵל, *mištôlēl*; literally, "one to be plundered"). If the faithful, penitent remnant represents the best hope for Israel's future and they are threatened from within, how will God's purpose prevail? As usual, God himself will give the victory.

God Intercedes for Israel's Sin (59:15b-21)

The LORD looked and was displeased / that there was no justice. / ¹⁶He saw that there was no one, / he was appalled that there was no one to intervene; / so his own arm worked salvation for him, / and his own righteousness sustained him. / ¹⁷He put on righteousness as his breastplate, / and the helmet of salvation on his head; / he put on the garments of vengeance / and wrapped himself in zeal as in a cloak. / ¹⁸According to what they have done, / so will he repay / wrath to his enemies / and retribution to his foes; / he will repay the islands their due. / ¹⁹From the west, men will fear the name of the LORD, / and from the rising of the sun, they will revere his glory. / For he will come like a pent-up flood / that the breath of the LORD drives along.ᵃ

²⁰"The Redeemer will come to Zion, / to those in Jacob who repent of their sins," / declares the LORD.

---

[7]Motyer, *Prophecy*, p. 486.

²¹"As for me, this is my covenant with them," says the LORD. "My Spirit, who is on you, and my words that I have put in your mouth will not depart from your mouth, or from the mouths of your children, or from the mouths of their descendants from this time on and forever," says the LORD.

ᵃ*19* Or *When the enemy comes in like a flood, / the spirit of the LORD will put him to flight*

59:15b-16 Although God on the one hand has hidden his face from his people because of their sins, he remains aware of their circumstances and passionate about his purpose through them. What God sees (or rather, does not see) displeases him (literally, "is evil in his eyes") and appalls him.[8] His response to the absence of **justice** with a promise of **salvation** supports Motyer's observation on the meaning of righteousness and justice in the previous section (cf. 45:8; 46:13).[9] The lack of **one to intervene** leads God to step in and act on behalf of his people. The same word for "intervene" (מַפְגִּיעַ, *maphgiaʿ*) applies to the suffering servant in 53:12. Like the suffering servant passage, this chapter acknowledges humanity's guilt and helplessness before God. In neither case is there any hope on the basis of human merit. Only the character of God provides hope, and thankfully in both contexts God works **salvation for him**[self] on the basis of **his own righteousness**.

59:17-19a In this context, however, God does not save in the garb of a suffering servant. Instead he clothes himself as a warrior. His garments consist of his character and corresponding actions. Once again, his **righteousness** is parallel to his **salvation** and his **vengeance** to his **zeal**. God's zeal refers to his passion for his people (קִנְאָה, *qinʾāh*, can also be translated "jealousy") that leads him to act on their behalf and against their enemies because those who are opposed to God's people are also opposed to him. God will thus **repay wrath to his enemies** from the **west** to the **rising of the sun** so that **they will revere his glory**.

---

[8]The word for "appalled" (שָׁמֵם, *šmm*) is a strong one, used for the sense of shock, horror, or desolation resulting from a great disaster. It describes the reaction to the servant in 52:14. Perhaps it was these associations that led the Septuagint translators to substitute "he observed" and the Targum to substitute "it was known before him." Cf. Oswalt, *Isaiah* 2, p. 525, n. 62.

[9]The word for "deliverance" in verse 11 and "salvation" in verse 16 is from the same Hebrew root (יָשַׁע, *yšʿ*).

59:19b-20 Isaiah compares God's extensive judgment to a **pent-up flood** (literally, "river"). This picture recalls the "mighty floodwaters" of the Euphrates with which God threatened Judah in the days of Ahaz for rejecting "the gently flowing waters of Shiloah" in the alliance with Assyria (8:6-8). Those waters would reach "to the neck," indicating Sennacherib's assault against Judah that ended with his forces encircling Jerusalem. This time the waters will come against the hostile nations. The whole tenor of verses 15b-19 is somewhat surprising since the focus of the chapter has been on Israel's sins. In verse 20, however, God the **Redeemer** comes to **Zion**. As redeemer he comes only **to those in Jacob who repent of their sins**. Just as the penitence led by Hezekiah resulted in deliverance from the Assyrians around Jerusalem, so penitence alone will save those in Zion from God. This point is important for understanding Paul's reference to verses 20-21 in Romans 11:26-27 to explain how "all Israel will be saved." Only those who repent of their sins are legitimate citizens of Zion.

59:21 The covenant faithfulness that God affirms in the closing verse of the chapter refers to those described in the previous verse. God seeks to turn the impenitent back to him, but in the end only those who respond to his gracious overtures are heirs to the covenant promises. God's **Spirit** and his **words** are his gifts to those who will receive them and abide from generation to generation. Without the life and power that come from God's Spirit, and without his words to guide, his people are lost. God has committed himself to this covenant,[10] and he will ensure that there will always be humble, penitent individuals who will accept God's gracious provisions and fulfill his sacred purpose. In a subtle way, this final verse anticipates the great new covenant promises in Jeremiah 31:31ff. and Ezekiel 36:22ff. which Isaiah roots in the work of the servant (42:6; 49:8).[11]

---

[10]Cf. the emphatic pronoun וַאֲנִי (wa'ănî, "As for me") at the beginning of the verse.

[11]Cf. Wolf, *Interpreting Isaiah*, p. 235.

ISAIAH 60

B. GOD'S COMMITMENT TO REVEAL HIS GLORY THROUGH HIS PEOPLE (60:1–61:11)

1. God's Light in a World of Darkness (60:1-22)

Israel's sin, as detailed in the previous two chapters, has created a situation like that described at the end of chapter eight, in which the people will "see only distress and darkness and fearful gloom, and they will be thrust into utter darkness" (8:22). Yet just as Isaiah 9 opens with an unexpected promise of light in the darkness through the one who "will reign on David's throne" (9:7), Isaiah 60 also begins with a promise of light that is mediated by God's anointed (61:1 ff.).

The promises of this chapter connect closely not only to the rest of Isaiah's message,[1] but also to other prominent texts. The priestly blessing invokes God's "face to shine upon" his people (Num 6:25). Sin has hindered God's ability to "shine" on Israel, but God has already expressed his determination to overcome this sin (59:15b-21). Isaiah 60 describes both the transforming effects of God's glorious presence among his people (vv. 1-11) and the protection his presence will provide (vv. 12-22). In so doing this chapter anticipates the later vision of Zechariah, who is told of the futility of physically measuring the walls around Jerusalem because God himself "will be a wall of fire around it" and "its glory within" (Zech 2:5). The fact that the nations will either be drawn to the light God manifests among his people for blessing or oppose God's work and be destroyed reflects God's original covenant with Abraham (Gen 12:3).

Isaiah 60 is framed by the appearance of God's glory among his people as light (vv. 1,19) and the ramifications of that reality. Once

---

[1] Motyer (*Prophecy*, p. 494) points out that Isaiah uses the metaphor of light more than the other prophets (cf. 2:5; 5:20; 9:2; 10:17; 42:6; 49:6; 51:4).

again God is the initiator in his relationship with his people; without his gracious self-revelation his purpose will not be accomplished. Only as God manifests himself to his people and they receive and are transformed by him can true progress occur. Apart from this divine initiative, humanity continues to grope hopelessly in the dark for meaningful solutions to the problems of a fallen world.

The Light of God's Presence Attracts Those Who See His Glory in His People (60:1-10)

¹"Arise, shine, for your light has come, / and the glory of the LORD rises upon you. / ²See, darkness covers the earth / and thick darkness is over the peoples, / but the LORD rises upon you / and his glory appears over you. / ³Nations will come to your light, / and kings to the brightness of your dawn.

⁴"Lift up your eyes and look about you: / All assemble and come to you; / your sons come from afar, / and your daughters are carried on the arm. / ⁵Then you will look and be radiant, / your heart will throb and swell with joy; / the wealth on the seas will be brought to you, / to you the riches of the nations will come. / ⁶Herds of camels will cover your land, / young camels of Midian and Ephah. / And all from Sheba will come, / bearing gold and incense / and proclaiming the praise of the LORD. / ⁷All Kedar's flocks will be gathered to you, / the rams of Nebaioth will serve you; / they will be accepted as offerings on my altar, / and I will adorn my glorious temple.

⁸"Who are these that fly along like clouds, / like doves to their nests? / ⁹Surely the islands look to me; / in the lead are the ships of Tarshish,ᵃ / bringing your sons from afar, / with their silver and gold, / to the honor of the LORD your God, / the Holy One of Israel, / for he has endowed you with splendor.

¹⁰"Foreigners will rebuild your walls, / and their kings will serve you. / Though in anger I struck you, / in favor I will show you compassion.

ᵃ9 Or *the trading ships*

60:1-2 The call for Israel to **Arise** (cf. 52:2) and **shine** because her **light has come** and **the glory of the LORD** has risen upon her reveals a critical sequence of events. The manifestation of God's presence by the parallel concepts of "light" and "glory" (cf. 58:8) precedes[2] and

---

[2]The verbs "has come" and "rises" are both in the perfect tense, indicating a completed action, even though the NIV translation of the latter verb does not reflect that fact.

makes possible (**for**, כִּי, *kî*) Israel's capacity to fulfill the imperatives to arise and shine. In the beginning the world was cloaked in darkness, a situation which was not "good" until God introduced light (Gen 1:1-5). As a result of sin, **darkness covers the earth** in a different sense, an even more disastrous situation which cries out for God's intervention.

60:3 God illuminated the original physical darkness by creating the heavenly lights; he seeks to illuminate the spiritual darkness by creating a people who reflect his light. In both cases God is the source of light and without him nothing but darkness remains. To dispel spiritual darkness, however, requires that his people respond to him in a way that truly reflects his glory to the world and that those in the darkness recognize and receive the light. The call in this passage is for Israel to respond to God in such a way that **nations will come to your light** (cf. 2:2-4). Israel's failure to fulfill this calling will be overcome by the servant's role as "a light to the Gentiles" (42:6; 49:6). Simeon, to whom the Spirit reveals that he will not die before seeing the Messiah, takes the infant Jesus in his arms and proclaims him "a light for revelation to the Gentiles and for glory to your people Israel" (Luke 2:32; cf. Acts 13:47; 26:23). The servant's ultimate revelation of God does not, however, negate the importance of Israel's role (or the church's) to reflect God's light/glory.

60:4-5 The latter half of this chapter, along with many other passages in Scripture, makes it clear that just as God's people frequently fail to reflect his light to a darkened world, so the darkened world frequently fails to accept God's light when it is revealed. In the tenth plague, God made a distinction between Israel and Egypt by casting the Egyptians into total darkness while giving light to the Israelites. The distinction failed, however, to soften Pharaoh's hardened heart. The prologue to John's Gospel compares Jesus to the light that shone into the darkness of the original creation, except that the light of Jesus' "glory of the One and Only, who came from the Father" was not "recognized" by many (John 1:1-14). In 2 Corinthians 4:6 Paul affirms that "God, who said, 'Let light shine out of darkness,' made his light shine in our hearts to give us the light of the knowledge of the glory of God in the face of Christ." In verse 4, however, he also acknowledges that "[t]he god of this age has blinded the minds of unbelievers, so that they cannot see the light of the gospel of the glory of Christ, who is the image of God."

The first part of Isaiah 60, however, focuses on the positive picture in which God's people reflect his light and the nations are drawn to it. Just as the attractive power of God's law in Zion results in a great peace in which "[n]ation will not take up sword against nation" (2:4), so God's light will effect peace with the nations. After the description of the servant as "a light for the Gentiles" in 49:6, Isaiah says these new believers will bring Israel's children home, with kings serving as their "foster fathers" and queens as their "nursing mothers" (49:22-23).[3] The present passage parallels and expands that picture.

60:6-9 The geographical details of verses 6-9 illustrate the impact of God's light in Israel, which will extend in all directions.[4] The mention of **Sheba** and **Tarshish** recalls the glory days of Solomon.[5] The nature and effects of this glory, however, far exceed that of Solomon's wealth. The **young camels of Midian** reflect an ancient adversary (Judges 6) that now joins in honoring God.

The details, however, merely fill out the image and are not the primary focus. They embody the picture of God's triumph that expands the notion of the covenant people beyond a single nation. All alike join in **proclaiming the praise of the LORD**.[6] All of the nations' sacrifices **will serve** God[7] and **will be accepted as offerings** by him. Even the most distant peoples (**the islands**) **look to** God.[8] Isaiah reminds his hearers that this new situation attests **to the honor of the LORD your God** because he is the one who **has endowed you with splendor**.[9] In other words, since the beauty that

---

[3]Cf. the close relationship of 60:4 to 49:18,22.

[4]"*Midian* is in the far south, *Ephah* to the east of the Persian Gulf, *Sheba* in the deep south, *Kedar* and *Nebaioth* to the east in the northern reaches of the Arabian desert." (Motyer, *Prophecy*, p. 495).

[5]The queen of Sheba praised God for what she saw in Solomon's kingdom and gave the king valuable gifts (1 Kgs 10:2,9-10). The NIV textual note on 1 Kings 10:22 indicates that the Hebrew for the "trading ships" by which gold and other precious items were delivered to Solomon literally means "ships of Tarshish."

[6]The word for "proclaiming the praise" (בשׂר, *bśr*) is the Hebrew equivalent of "preaching the gospel/good news" (cf. 40:9; 41:27; 52:7; 61:1).

[7]The word for "serve" (שׁרת, *šrt*) typically refers to priestly or other religious forms of ministry. Cf. also verse 10.

[8]The word for "look to" (קוה, *qwh*) means to "wait for" or to "look for eagerly/expectantly." Cf. the parallelism of the last two lines of 51:5; also 8:17; 25:9; 33:2.

[9]"Endowed you with splendor" (פארך, *pē'ărāk*) is literally, "he has made you beautiful." This root is prominent in this passage. It is translated "adorn" in verses 7 and 13, "glory" in verse 19, and "for the display of my

God bestows upon his people draws others to him, all praise should be directed to the one who is the source of this beauty.

60:10 Why is there a causal relationship[10] between the first half of verse 10, in which **Foreigners will rebuild your walls, and their kings will serve you**, and the move from God's striking his people to showing them **compassion** in the second half of the verse?[11] For one thing, God has used the nations as agents of his anger against Israel, so it is fitting that he also express his **favor** by the religious service[12] of these nations on behalf of his people. In addition, the nations should feel gratitude for those by whom they come to know God (cf. 61:5-6,9; Rom 11:13 ff.). This image of once-hostile nations who rebuild Israel's walls sets the stage for a consideration of the security of God's people in regard to those who do not submit to God's redeeming work through them.

The Light of God's Presence Protects from Those Who Oppose His Glory in His People (60:11-22)

¹¹**Your gates will always stand open, / they will never be shut, day or night, / so that men may bring you the wealth of the nations— / their kings led in triumphal procession. / ¹²For the nation or kingdom that will not serve you will perish; / it will be utterly ruined.**

¹³**"The glory of Lebanon will come to you, / the pine, the fir and the cypress together, / to adorn the place of my sanctuary; / and I will glorify the place of my feet. / ¹⁴The sons of your oppressors will come bowing before you; / all who despise you will bow down at your feet / and will call you the City of the LORD, / Zion of the Holy One of Israel.**

¹⁵**"Although you have been forsaken and hated, / with no one traveling through, / I will make you the everlasting pride / and the joy of all generations. / ¹⁶You will drink the milk of nations / and**

---

splendor" in verse 21. In addition, "my glorious temple" in verse 7 is literally, "the house of my beauty" (בֵּית תִּפְאַרְתִּי, *bêth tiph'artî*).

[10]The word for "Though" in the middle of verse 10 (כִּי, *kî*) would be better translated "for/because."

[11]The translation "I will show you compassion" perhaps takes the verb (רִחַמְתִּיךְ, *riḥamtîk*) as a prophetic perfect, but a rendering such as "I have shown you compassion" (cf. NASB, ESV) more accurately captures the intent of anticipating a time when God has already acted on behalf of his people (cf. the comments on v. 1).

[12]Cf. the comments on the word "serve" in verse 7.

be nursed at royal breasts. / Then you will know that I, the LORD, am your Savior, / your Redeemer, the Mighty One of Jacob. / ¹⁷Instead of bronze I will bring you gold, / and silver in place of iron. / Instead of wood I will bring you bronze, / and iron in place of stones. / I will make peace your governor / and righteousness your ruler. / ¹⁸No longer will violence be heard in your land, / nor ruin or destruction within your borders, / but you will call your walls Salvation / and your gates Praise. / ¹⁹The sun will no more be your light by day, / nor will the brightness of the moon shine on you, / for the LORD will be your everlasting light, / and your God will be your glory. / ²⁰Your sun will never set again, / and your moon will wane no more; / the LORD will be your everlasting light, / and your days of sorrow will end. / ²¹Then will all your people be righteous / and they will possess the land forever. / They are the shoot I have planted, / the work of my hands, / for the display of my splendor. / ²²The least of you will become a thousand, / the smallest a mighty nation. / I am the LORD; / in its time I will do this swiftly."

60:11-12 The symbolic nature of the walls described in verse 10 should be obvious from the fact that their **gates will always stand open**. A wall with open gates provides no real security, but the open gates allow the free flow of **the wealth of the nations**. The same situation characterizes the even more obviously symbolic walls of the New Jerusalem (Rev 21:25). The security of God's people derives from God himself, not from walls (cf. Zech 2:4-5). The word for **led in triumphal procession** (נהג, *nhg*) can be used either in a hostile sense (cf. 20:4) or in a nurturing sense (cf. 49:10). Since the tone of verse 12 is obviously hostile and it bases its perspective on verse 11 (**For**, כי, *kî*), these verses convey a different perspective on the nations. God gives his people a total victory, whether it is through the "conversion" of the receptive among the nations or through the destruction of those who oppose his people. Significantly, the word for **serve** used to describe the appropriate response of the nations to Israel in verse 12 (עבד, *'bd*), does not carry the same connotation of "ministry" as the word used in verses 7 and 10.

60:13-14 In verses 13-14 the proud nations will be humbled before tiny Israel whom they **despise**. **The glory of Lebanon** has appeared previously in 35:2 to describe God's transformation of "the desert created by human pride (ch. 34)."[13] The cedars of

---

[13]Oswalt, *Isaiah* 2, p. 549.

Lebanon represent the arrogant assertion of human wealth or power before God that must eventually fall (cf. 2:13; 37:24). When God brings about this great reversal, those who have sought to be **oppressors** of Israel will be compelled to acknowledge **the City of the LORD**. The ultimate goal of this work is neither the humiliation of the former aggressors nor the enrichment of Israel. Rather, the goal is to vindicate God, against whom any opposition to the covenant people is ultimately directed. At the end of verse 13, the dual images of beauty (**adorn**, פְּאֵר, *p'r*) and glory (**glorify**, כבד, *kbd*) are directed to the **sanctuary** that affirms God's redeeming presence in the midst of his people. Parallel to **my sanctuary** is **the place of my feet**, an allusion to David's reference to the ark of the covenant as God's "footstool" (1 Chr 28:2; cf. Ps 99:5; 132:7).

60:15 Since, in fulfillment of the covenant with Abraham, the nations will either favor the covenant people and be blessed or oppose them and be cursed by God, Isaiah presents a radically different picture of the future from the one the prophet or his hearers have known. They have known what it is like to feel **forsaken and hated** (cf. 62:4), but that temporary experience will be replaced by God's establishment of them as **the everlasting pride and the joy of all generations**. Oswalt points out that the words for "pride" (גָּאוֹן, *gā'ôn*) and "joy" (מָשׂוֹשׂ, *māśôś*) appear numerous times in the preceding chapters, but typically in regard to vain attempts to exalt oneself or find joy through wine or song rather than through God.[14] Only God can bestow these qualities legitimately, and only to those who seek him.

60:16 The future also marks a transition from fearing and suffering at the hands of the nations to being sustained by them. The references to drinking **the milk of nations** and being **nursed at royal breasts** (literally, "the breasts of kings!") reminds the reader again of the figurative nature of these promises. The end of verse 16 also reinforces the goal of the text as a whole: to honor God and stress the importance of relationship with him. The chapter begins with God's causing his glory to rise upon Israel. His actions seek a recognition that he alone is the **Savior**, the **Redeemer**, the **Mighty One** of his people. The nature and quantity of all attendant blessings are secondary to this recognition of the greatest blessing of all.

60:17-19 In a further set of contrasts, God promises to furnish

---

[14]Ibid., p. 552.

his people's rebuilding efforts with the strongest and most precious materials. Once again, however, these elements simply point to what is even stronger and more precious in relationship with God. The true blessing is being ruled by **peace** and **righteousness**, in being guarded by **Salvation** and **Praise**, and in being perpetually illuminated by the constant presence of **the LORD** himself. The latter point both returns to the theme with which the chapter begins and provides additional backdrop (cf. v. 11) to John's vision of the New Jerusalem (Rev 21:22-23; 22:5).

60:20-22 The closing notes of the chapter reaffirm God's commitment to his people and the goal of his investment in them. "He has not only put them where they are (*planted*) but has made them what they are (*work of my hands*)."[15] God nurtures and shapes his people that they might reveal his beauty (**for the display of my splendor**, לְהִתְפָּאֵר, *lᵉhithpā'ēr*) to a world that desperately needs to see it. All that he has promised he will bring to pass. The words **in its time I will do this swiftly** both affirm God's sovereignty and caution against predicting the timing of his promises. Similarly, many of the parables and parts of the book of Revelation promote a perspective of urgency and imminence for Jesus' disciples, yet those same sources also enjoin the virtue of patient endurance. These seemingly contradictory stances recognize that God can and will act swiftly, but only when in his wisdom the time is right.

> Although it may take a long time for all things to be ready, nevertheless, when they are ready, God will suddenly bring it to pass. This is the way it was with the first coming. It seemed that the Messiah would never come; but when the time was right, he was suddenly present, and those who were not prepared had no time to get prepared. So it will be in the consummation of all things. Suddenly the sun will leap over the horizon, and God's everlasting day will be here.[16]

What constitutes the fulfillment of the glorious promises of Isaiah 60? The support Israel received in the return from exile and the rebuilding of Jerusalem represents a measure of the fulfillment, but certainly does not exhaust the picture presented here. The extensive inclusion of Gentiles into the church also falls under the

---

[15]Motyer, *Prophecy*, p. 499.
[16]Oswalt, *Isaiah* 2, p. 561.

umbrella of this text. The incorporation of elements from this chapter in the closing visions of Revelation, however, indicates that the full enjoyment of the hopes of Isaiah 60 await the time when God's dwelling with redeemed humanity finds its culmination in the eternal state. In the meantime God's people continue to receive the challenging call of reflecting the light of God's glory into a world with much remaining darkness.

ISAIAH 61

2. God's Light in Zion (61:1-11)

This chapter contains numerous links to chapter 60, which will be detailed below. What chapter 61 adds is an elaboration upon the agent by whom God's light shines in the world and the resulting transformation of his people that allows them to minister to the nations. The most striking portions of the chapter in this regard are the two first-person sections in verses 1-3 and verses 10-11.

The Agent of God's Light (61:1-3)

¹**The Spirit of the Sovereign LORD is on me,** /because the LORD has anointed me /to preach good news to the poor. /He has sent me to bind up the brokenhearted, /to proclaim freedom for the captives /and release from darkness for the prisoners,[a] / ²to proclaim the year of the LORD's favor /and the day of vengeance of our God, /to comfort all who mourn, /³and provide for those who grieve in Zion— /to bestow on them a crown of beauty instead of ashes, /the oil of gladness /instead of mourning, /and a garment of praise /instead of a spirit of despair. /They will be called oaks of righteousness, /a planting of the LORD /for the display of his splendor.

[a]*1* Hebrew; Septuagint *the blind*

61:1a References to the **Sovereign LORD** (אֲדֹנָי יהוה, *'ădōnāy YHWH*) frame this chapter (vv. 1,11). The designation accords well with God's supervision of events in the previous chapter. But who is the one who speaks in the first person in these opening verses, the one God has **anointed** with his **Spirit** to carry out his will? The Spirit is said to rest upon both the messianic king (11:2) and the servant (42:1). The liberating work described here parallels the work of the servant (cf. 42:7; 49:9), as well as the establishment of righteous and peaceful rule by the royal anointed (cf. 9:7; 11:4-9). The shining of

God's light into the darkened Gentile regions (9:1-2) and the raising of a banner for the nations (11:10-12) are additional themes from the messianic texts that are closely tied to the context of these verses. Oswalt goes so far as to claim that in passages like this one Isaiah seeks to bring about a "synthesis of the Servant and the Messiah."[1] The work of the person who speaks at the opening of Isaiah 61 is the kind of work Isaiah has revealed to be beyond the capabilities of the ordinary people with whom God enters into covenant. Only the one God has singled out as his anointed servant can accomplish the transformation these verses describe.

61:1b-3a God's designated agent will **preach good news** [לְבַשֵּׂר, *lᵊbaśśēr*] **to the poor**. The "poor" are those who suffer deprivation or distress of any kind. In Deuteronomy 15:4 God tells Israel that "there should be no poor among you." Poverty existed in Israel, however, due to human sinfulness. The "good news" is of great interest to the poor because it attacks the root cause of poverty.[2] The poor, like the **brokenhearted** (נִשְׁבְּרֵי־לֵב, *nišbᵊrê-lēb*), are typically open to the good news because they have been humbled. Psalm 34:18 proclaims that God "is close to the brokenhearted and saves those who are crushed in spirit." The end of verse 2 promises **comfort** for **all who mourn**, and the beginning of verse 3 offers provision **for those who grieve in Zion**. The faithful remnant has already been designated as "the mourners in Israel" in 57:19. Similarly, Jesus affirms the blessedness of "the poor in spirit" and "those who mourn" (Matt 5:3-4). The point here is not to bestow inherent virtue on poverty or grief, but to acknowledge that a message is good news only to those who recognize it as such. A major theme of Isaiah has been the disastrous consequences of a lack of spiritual perception.

The proclamation of **freedom for the captives** in **the year of the LORD's favor** is an allusion to the Year of Jubilee (Lev 25:8 ff.). The word for "freedom" (דְּרוֹר, *dᵊrôr*) is a technical term for the release that was to occur in this fiftieth year (Lev 25:10). The Year of Jubilee represents a provision of God to restore the inevitable imbalances that occur in the course of human societies that leave people no recourse but to sell their property or themselves in order to pay

---

[1] Oswalt, *Isaiah* 2, p. 563.

[2] Acts 4:34 provides something of a counterpart to Deuteronomy 15:4. The gospel created a community that shared its possessions so that "[t]here were no needy persons among them."

their debts. This occasion thus provides a fitting motif for the good news of God's greater redemption of a fallen world.

The expression **release from darkness for the prisoners** contains an interesting mixture of metaphors. "Prisoners" refers literally to those who are bound. The word for "release" (פְּקַח, *p^eqaḥ*), however, refers almost exclusively to the opening of the eyes. Perhaps 42:7, in the context of describing the servant's role as "a light for the Gentiles," most clearly spells out the meaning of this combination of images. In that verse God will empower his servant "to open eyes that are blind, to free captives from prison and to release from the dungeon those who sit in darkness." Presumably on this basis the NIV adds the words "from darkness" in 61:1. The connection to the servant song strengthens the identification of the speaker here with the servant, and the allusion to dispelling the darkness ties the work of God's anointed in chapter 61 to God's own work in chapter 60.

Parallel to "the year of the LORD's favor" is **the day of vengeance of our God**. The close association of divine favor and vengeance should not surprise, for salvation and judgment have been presented as inseparable before (cf. 51:5; 59:17). Comfort cannot come to those who grieve unless God defeats the individuals and circumstances that cause the grief. The transformation from **ashes** and **mourning** and **a spirit of despair** to that which would accompany joyful celebration also requires the overthrow of all that stands in the way of that transformation.

61:3b Not only do the reversals in verse 3 recall the previous chapter (60:17), but so does the emphasis on beautification. The words for **crown of beauty** (פְּאֵר, *p^e'ēr*) and **for the display of his splendor** (לְהִתְפָּאֵר, *l^ehithpa'ēr*) derive from the same root used prominently in chapter 60. The latter expression also retains the focus on properly reflecting the glory/beauty of God. An additional link between the two chapters is the notion of a **planting** of God that bears fruit in **righteousness** (cf. 60:21). In 60:21, however, God's planting is described as a **shoot** (נֵצֶר, *nēṣer*, cf. 11:1), whereas in 61:3 the result is **oaks of righteousness**.

Jesus uses the opening words of Isaiah 61 to define his calling in his hometown synagogue of Nazareth (Luke 4:16-21). He cuts the quotation short, however, leaving out the reference to "the day of vengeance of our God." As closely linked as salvation and judgment are, Jesus faces a major challenge in forging a chronological distinction between them in the minds of his disciples. Jesus comes both to save and to judge, and his work will not be complete until his salvation and his judgment both are complete. The disciples learn that the way of the cross is not only the way of messianic success, but that it is the path they must follow as well. Victory by means of weakness and apparent loss is not the final chapter in the story. In the end the gospel message will prevail and all enemies will be defeated and removed from any and all power. In the meantime, however, Jesus' selective application of Isaiah 61:1-2 to himself teaches a vital lesson in the distinction between the purpose of his first coming and that of his second coming.

The Effects of God's Light (61:4-9)

⁴**They will rebuild the ancient ruins / and restore the places long devastated; / they will renew the ruined cities / that have been devastated for generations. / ⁵Aliens will shepherd your flocks; / foreigners will work your fields and vineyards. / ⁶And you will be called priests of the LORD, / you will be named ministers of our God. / You will feed on the wealth of nations, / and in their riches you will boast.**

⁷**Instead of their shame / my people will receive a double portion, / and instead of disgrace / they will rejoice in their inheritance; / and so they will inherit a double portion in their land, / and everlasting joy will be theirs.**

⁸**"For I, the LORD, love justice; / I hate robbery and iniquity. / In my faithfulness I will reward them / and make an everlasting covenant with them. / ⁹Their descendants will be known among the nations / and their offspring among the peoples. / All who see them will acknowledge / that they are a people the LORD has blessed."**

61:4-6 These verses closely parallel the themes of chapter 60, but the emphasis in the two chapters lies in a different place. Whereas chapter 60 stresses what the nations will contribute to and how they will serve the covenant people, chapter 61 highlights the reason for such willing subservience. From Israel's beginning as a people, God's goal has been the formation of "a kingdom of priests and a holy nation" (Exod 19:6). To the degree that this ideal is realized, to that same degree the mediatorial role of God's people is fulfilled in attracting others to God. Sandwiched between the assistance given by **aliens** and **foreigners** in verse 5 and the **wealth** they bestow on

Israel in verse 6b is the recognition of the role of the covenant people as **priests** and **ministers**.[3]

61:7-9 In addition to recognizing the priestly role of God's people, the nations will see that they are a people **blessed** by God (v. 9). Priestly status and outward blessing both derive from the hand of God and come only as God manifests the light of his presence so that his people open themselves to him. This openness to God results in a **double portion** as an **inheritance**,[4] **everlasting joy**, and an **everlasting covenant**. The enduring nature of God's covenant with his people is based on past promises as well as future ones that flow from those ancient sources (cf. 55:3; Jer 31:31-37). The reliability of these promises, in turn, is based on the nature of God. Because[5] he loves **justice**, he will prove himself a faithful covenant partner.

The Response to God's Light (61:10-11)

¹⁰**I delight greatly in the LORD; /my soul rejoices in my God. / For he has clothed me with garments of salvation /and arrayed me in a robe of righteousness, /as a bridegroom adorns his head like a priest, /and as a bride adorns herself with her jewels. /** ¹¹**For as the soil makes the sprout come up /and a garden causes seeds to grow, /so the Sovereign LORD will make righteousness and praise /spring up before all nations.**

These verses parallel 61:1-3 in more ways than in their first-person form of address. The imagery of clothing and the associated idea of beautification,[6] as well as the sprouting of righteousness, link these verses to 61:3. Rather than identifying the speaker as the servant/messiah, however, here the words represent a response to God's promises extending back to the beginning of chapter 60. In that case the speaker is probably either Isaiah or Zion (cf. 52:1). This understanding still retains a type of symmetry in the chapter, but it brackets vers-

---

[3]The opening of verse 6 (וְאַתֶּם, *wᵉʾattem*) sets up a strong contrast between the nations and the covenant people.

[4]The word "portion" has been added by the NIV, but is perhaps implied in the context of inheritance (cf. Deut 21:17; 1 Sam 1:5; 2 Kgs 2:9). This reference could be intended as a counterpart to the "double" Israel received for all of her sins in exile (40:2; cf. Job 42:10; Zech 9:12).

[5]"For" (כִּי, *kî*) at the beginning of verse 8 indicates that God's love of justice is the basis of his faithfulness to the covenant.

[6]The word for "adorns his head" in verse 10 is פְּאֵר (*pᵉʾēr*).

es 4-9 with the one through whom God's light shines and the one(s) who enjoy the benefits of that light. Motyer's objection that the transformation of the covenant people has not yet occurred[7] overlooks the anticipatory nature of the closing celebration.

61:10-11 Clothing frequently symbolizes a person's status. Here that status is the **salvation** and **righteousness** that God graciously bestows upon his people. Through another unusual but insightful mixture of images (cf. the comments on verse 1), this new status is compared to that symbolized by the special garments worn by a **priest** or a **bride** and **bridegroom**. Just as God provides the adornment, so he causes life to spring forth from the ground. The occasion of harvest also elicits **praise**, but even that response is the work of God (cf. 57:19). The closing note, **before the nations**, reminds the covenant people that they are blessed not only for their own enjoyment, but also for the consequent blessing to others who need to see God's light.

---

[7]Motyer, *Prophecy*, p. 504.

ISAIAH 62

C. GOD'S COMMITMENT TO DEFEND THE CAUSE OF HIS PEOPLE (62:1–64:12)

1. God's Faithfulness to Zion (62:1–63:6)

This passage shares a number of elements with chapters 60–61: Zion's beauty shining before the nations; the comparison of God's relationship with Israel to a marriage. Whereas chapters 60–61 emphasize God's initiative and God's power to transform his people's situation, the present passage focuses on God's promises to remain faithful to what he has said he will do. Both aspects of God's nature should inspire confidence. His promises call not only for faith, but also for the kind of persistent intercessory prayer that is based on such promises. The first-person portions of chapter 62 (vv. 1,6a,8-9) convey God's promises and are followed by (Isaiah's?) anticipation of and call for the fulfillment of those promises.

God Promises to Glorify Zion (62:1-7)

¹For Zion's sake I will not keep silent, / for Jerusalem's sake I will not remain quiet, / till her righteousness shines out like the dawn, / her salvation like a blazing torch. / ²The nations will see your righteousness, / and all kings your glory; / you will be called by a new name / that the mouth of the LORD will bestow. / ³You will be a crown of splendor in the LORD's hand, / a royal diadem in the hand of your God. / ⁴No longer will they call you Deserted, / or name your land Desolate. / But you will be called Hephzibah,ᵃ / and your land Beulahᵇ; / for the LORD will take delight in you, / and your land will be married. / ⁵As a young man marries a maiden, / so will your sonsᶜ marry you; / as a bridegroom rejoices over his bride, / so will your God rejoice over you.

⁶I have posted watchmen on your walls, O Jerusalem; / they will

never be silent day or night. / You who call on the LORD, / give yourselves no rest, / ⁷and give him no rest till he establishes Jerusalem / and makes her the praise of the earth.

ᵃ*4 Hephzibah means* my delight is in her.   ᵇ*4 Beulah means* married.
ᶜ*5 Or* Builder

62:1-2 The parallel words **silent/quiet** in verse 1 imply inactivity as much as lack of sound.[1] God's refusal to stand idly by while the **righteousness** of Zion remains hidden from the **nations** is rooted in his commitment to reveal himself there. The rest of the passage makes clear, however, that the focus of God's work is not the *place* as much as its *people*. The counterpart to righteousness in verse 1 is **salvation**, while in verse 2 it is **glory**. Both derive from God, who reveals his glory **like a blazing torch** by saving his people. The transformation God will effect is so great that it calls for a **new name** for his people.[2] This new name, which only God has the authority to **bestow**, may be revealed in verses 4,12.[3]

62:3 Portraying Zion as a **crown of splendor** (עֲטֶרֶת תִּפְאֶרֶת, *'ăṭereth tiph'ereth*) returns to the image of derived beauty. This beauty comes only by residing **in the LORD's hand**. In 28:1-5 God rebukes Samaria as a proud "wreath" (*'ăṭereth*) whose fading "beauty" (*tiph'ereth*) contrasts with a future in which God "will be a glorious crown, a beautiful wreath for the remnant of his people." "What the Samarias of this world wish to be in themselves and never can be, God will give in his free grace to the city of his choice, whose inhabitants dare to trust him and believe in his promises."[4] As a **royal diadem** God's people both reflect God's rule and share in it.

62:4-5 In 50:1ff. God denies that he has divorced or sold his people, realizing that an experience such as exile could understandably lead them to that false conclusion. Under such circumstances they might accept the permanent legitimacy of names such as **Deserted** or **Desolate**. In response, God here promises that he will act on Zion's behalf so powerfully that the appropriateness of her true names, **Hephzibah** ("my delight is in her") and **Beulah** ("married"),

---

[1]For השׁה, *ḥšh*, cf. 65:6, in which the contrast to keeping silent is "pay back in full." For שׁקט, *šqṭ*, cf. 18:4, in which God's remaining quiet is parallel to his looking on from his dwelling place. Cf. Motyer, *Prophecy*, p. 505.

[2]Cf. the significance of giving new names to Abram and Sarai (Gen 17:3-8,15-16), Jacob (Gen 32:22-28).

[3]The faithful receive a similar promise in Revelation 2:17; 3:12.

[4]Oswalt, *Isaiah* 2, p. 580.

will be obvious (cf. 54:5-8).[5] In contrast to the separation of exile, Zion's **sons** will resume their "marriage" to the **land**. This marriage, however, simply reflects, as a covenant promise, the more fundamental union with God himself. The encouragement provided by God's covenant faithfulness reflects not a grudging acceptance of a past commitment but an eager anticipation of the time when God can again **rejoice** over his bride.

62:6 The glad cry of the **watchmen** who observe God's return to Zion has already been anticipated in 52:8. As God's servants (**I have posted**) they can no more be **silent** than God himself (v. 1). Their continuous activity as they anticipate God's return is largely a ministry of intercessory prayer. Verse 6a conveys God's desire, whereas verses 6b-7 exhort God's servants to carry out his will. Within a context that has strongly emphasized God's initiative and sovereign power, this call highlights the importance of prayer in bringing about God's will. The fact that God posts the watchmen and gives them their orders makes it clear that the role of intercessors is not to coerce God's activity. To **call on the LORD** is literally to "cause [him] to remember" (מַזְכִּיר, *mazkîr*), but the purpose of prayer is not to make sure God does not forget. The very point of this passage is to assure that God is faithful to his promises.

62:7 The role of prayer in the completion of God's will does not call into question God's memory or his faithfulness or his power. He works in conjunction with the faithful remnant (that he creates), however, in a way that ennobles his servants without compromising his nature or the accomplishment of his purpose. The prophetess Anna (Luke 2:36-38) is one who continually fasts and prays, "looking forward to the redemption of Jerusalem." In Revelation 8:3-5 the prayers of the saints go up before God and the consequences of those prayers fall to the earth. Since God has committed to carry out his will in conjunction with his servants, it stands to reason that his actions coincide with the call for them by his people. The believer can be boldest in prayers for God to do what he has promised he will do. In this case God promises to make his people **the praise of the earth** in order to draw the nations to him.

---

[5]Cf. God's promise that the names of the symbolic children of Hosea and Gomer, Lo-Ruhamah ("unloved") and Lo-Ammi ("not my people"), will give way to "My people" and "My loved one" (Hos 1:6–2:1).

God Promises to Restore Zion (62:8-12)

⁸The LORD has sworn by his right hand / and by his mighty arm: / "Never again will I give your grain / as food for your enemies, / and never again will foreigners drink the new wine / for which you have toiled; / ⁹but those who harvest it will eat it / and praise the LORD, / and those who gather the grapes will drink it / in the courts of my sanctuary."
¹⁰Pass through, pass through the gates! / Prepare the way for the people. / Build up, build up the highway! / Remove the stones. / Raise a banner for the nations.
¹¹The LORD has made proclamation / to the ends of the earth: / "Say to the Daughter of Zion, / 'See, your Savior comes! / See, his reward is with him, / and his recompense accompanies him.'" / ¹²They will be called the Holy People, / the Redeemed of the LORD; / and you will be called Sought After, / the City No Longer Deserted.

These verses reflect the themes of 40:1-11 and 52:1-12 in their focus on the return from exile and reversal of the covenant curses. While the promises here transcend that historical event, the hopes and prayers of 62:1-7 hinge on the time when the good news resounds that those who were in Babylon are coming home (40:9-10; 52:7ff.) by the power of God's arm (49:10; 52:10).

62:8-9 God's promises find their strongest confirmation in an oath that roots them in his very nature. He swears by himself in 45:23 (cf. Heb 6:13), but here he swears **by his right hand/mighty arm**, emphasizing his power to protect his people from their enemies and grant them peace. Such peace will allow them to enjoy the fullness of the covenant blessings. Deuteronomy 28:30ff. describes the covenant curse in which the gifts of God are forfeited to one's **enemies**. God promises a time of security when this tragic situation will no longer prevail. The true measure of the blessings God promises is not the preservation of the **harvest** but the opportunity to **praise the LORD** and to enjoy the fruit of the harvest **in the courts of my sanctuary**. Eating in the presence of God is an occasion for rejoicing (cf. Deut 12:7; 14:26) because it indicates a climate of peace and fellowship with the one who is the source of all blessings. "In a word, *the courts of my sanctuary* have ceased to be local and limited and have become a symbol of all life as lived in the presence of the Holy One and of every meal as sacred fellowship."[6]

---

[6]Motyer, *Prophecy*, p. 508.

62:10-11a The closing verses of chapter 62 move from promise to an anticipation of the fulfillment of those promises. The **gates** through which the people pass presumably envision the first phase of fulfillment in the departure from Babylon. The sounding of the words **prepare the way** (cf. 40:3-5; 57:14) and **raise a banner for the nations** (cf. 5:26; 11:10,12; 49:22) excites believers with the assurance that a day will arrive when these previously expressed hopes will come to fruition. In keeping with God's universal purpose, when the time arrives for Zion's salvation[7] (in the fullest sense), God will make sure it becomes known **to the ends of the earth**.

62:11b The last line of verse 11 is identical to the last line of 40:10. To what do the **reward** (שָׂכָר, śākār) and **recompense** (פְּעֻלָּה, pᵉ'ullāh) that God brings with him refer? The two words are synonyms, typically referring to a worker's wages.[8] In 61:8, God's faithfulness in granting a "reward" (pᵉ'ullāh) to the remnant is parallel to "make an everlasting covenant with them." The preceding verse speaks of the "double portion" of the "inheritance" the remnant will receive. Isaiah does not use the word "covenant" frequently, but his faithfulness to the covenant underlies his promises of restoration.[9] What God brings with him in 62:11, therefore, is not wages that he owes the faithful, but the fulfillment of the covenant to which he has committed himself. This understanding fits well with the purpose of this section to root the certainty of God's promises in his nature, especially his reliability.

62:12 In addition to the new names promised in verse 4, the last verse of the chapter adds to the collection of appropriate labels that will apply when God reveals his glory through his people. **Holy people** anticipates the fulfillment of God's original intention for Israel in Exodus 19:6. **Redeemed of the LORD** reaffirms that God is the powerful one who rescues them from their plight, although God insists that he does not pay money for them because no one has ever truly purchased them from him (cf. 50:1; 52:3). **City No Longer**

---

[7]The word the NIV translates "Savior" in verse 11 (יֵשַׁע, yēša') is actually "salvation." The masculine singular pronouns in the following lines probably account for the NIV translation (in an attempt to provide the antecedent for the pronouns). Oswalt (*Isaiah 2*, p. 589) understands the word as a title for God ("he is *Salvation* itself").

[8]Cf. Lev 19:13; Deut 24:15, in which each of the words is used in the prohibition against withholding a poor person's wages.

[9]See the comments on 62:8-9.

Deserted overturns the fears that the exile represents God's complete and permanent rejection of his people (cf. v. 4).

The name **Sought After** (דְּרוּשָׁה, *dᵊrûšāh*) is more distinctive within this list and deserves special mention. It is proper to exhort people to seek God (cf. 55:1), but one of the distinctive traits of the God of the Bible is his determination to seek even those who refuse to seek him. In fact, as has been indicated in this commentary previously, without God's pursuit of mankind there would be no possibility of seeking him. The story of Israel in the Old Testament reveals this transforming truth in a powerful way. Isaiah speaks originally to those who are tempted to interpret the exile as the end of God's pursuit of Israel. As understandable as that conclusion is from a human perspective, God promises to make his people aware that they will always be his "Sought After."

ISAIAH 63

God Promises to Avenge Zion (63:1-6)

¹Who is this coming from Edom, / from Bozrah, with his garments stained crimson? / Who is this, robed in splendor, / striding forward in the greatness of his strength?

"It is I, speaking in righteousness, / mighty to save."

²Why are your garments red, / like those of one treading the winepress?

³"I have trodden the winepress alone; / from the nations no one was with me. / I trampled them in my anger / and trod them down in my wrath; / their blood spattered my garments, / and I stained all my clothing. / ⁴For the day of vengeance was in my heart, / and the year of my redemption has come. / ⁵I looked, but there was no one to help, / I was appalled that no one gave support; / so my own arm worked salvation for me, / and my own wrath sustained me. / ⁶I trampled the nations in my anger; / in my wrath I made them drunk / and poured their blood on the ground."

Once again Isaiah ties redemption closely to judgment. God's salvation extends to all who will accept it, but his saving work cannot come to completion without the judgment of those who reject him and threaten the security of the faithful. The closest parallel to this passage is 59:15b-20, but the inseparable nature of salvation and judgment also appears in 34:8; 35:4; 61:1-2. This subject, therefore, is as important among God's promises as that which is detailed in the two preceding sections.

63:1 Edom typifies the enemies of God's people in 34:5, and the Edomite city of **Bozrah** is singled out in 34:6. Here their significance is also tied to their use in a pair of wordplays. Edom is related to the word **red** (אדם, *'ādōm*). The significance of **garments** (cf. 61:3,10) shifts here to a robe stained with the blood of slain enemies (cf. Rev 19:13, where the image applies to Jesus in the final judgment). Bozrah comes from a root that is used for the cutting off of grape clusters, which ties in to the image of the **winepress** in which the juice of the grapes symbolizes the blood that is spilled in judgment (cf. Lam 1:15; Joel 3:13; Rev 14:17-20; 19:15). To make the nations "drunk" (v. 6) also uses the wine imagery in reference to drinking the cup of wrath (cf. 51:17).

63:3-6 This passage stresses even more than 59:16 the fact that God acts alone in bringing about this judgment. The picture of God looking around and finding **no one to help** raises the level of tension and highlights the absolute necessity of God's actions on behalf of his people. God stands alone in his **vengeance** not only because no one would join him, but also because he alone has the authority and moral purity to do so (Deut 32:35; cf. Rom 12:19; Heb 10:30). The concept of vengeance implies acting on behalf of oneself or a closely related party.[1] Human beings find it difficult to carry out such actions without hatred and excess, but God in his holiness seeks only to maintain his commitment to the "redeemed"[2] and to his larger redemptive purpose through them.

2. The Proper Response to God's Promises (63:7–64:12)

Motyer speaks of Isaiah's tendency to bring the reader frequently to a point where it seems everything has been fulfilled, only to pick up with another theme.[3] This approach results in a layering effect, sometimes referred to as recapitulation, that highlights the complex, multidimensional nature of God's activity.[4] Motyer's point is illustrated by the apparent finality of 63:1-6, followed by more that God's people need to hear.

Whatever God reveals about the future aims not to satisfy human curiosity but to point out the way one should live in the present. In this case the call for intercessory prayer in 62:6-7 is instrumental in bringing about the judgment scene in 63:1-6. God's call finds a

---

[1]Webb, *Message*, pp. 239-240.
[2]The word גְּאוּלַי (gᵊ'ûlay) is better rendered "my redeemed" than "my redemption."
[3]Motyer, *Prophecy*, p. 512.
[4]Many interpreters see a similar approach in Revelation. This similarity should not be surprising considering the overall influence of Isaiah on the language and concepts in Revelation (cf. the new heavens and new earth Isaiah is about to introduce in 65:17).

response in Isaiah's petition in the present section, elaborating upon what that prayer should look like. Webb ranks this prayer among the finest intercessory prayers in Scripture.[5] As such it has much to say not only about the circumstances of Isaiah's day, but also about the nature of prayer in general. Prayer lays claim to God's promises and in the process boldly confronts the apparent failure of those promises to come to fruition.

Praise God for Past Mercies (63:7-10)

⁷I will tell of the kindnesses of the LORD, / the deeds for which he is to be praised, / according to all the LORD has done for us— / yes, the many good things he has done / for the house of Israel, / according to his compassion and many kindnesses. / ⁸He said, "Surely they are my people, / sons who will not be false to me"; / and so he became their Savior. / ⁹In all their distress he too was distressed, / and the angel of his presence saved them. / In his love and mercy he redeemed them; / he lifted them up and carried them / all the days of old. / ¹⁰Yet they rebelled and grieved his Holy Spirit. / So he turned and became their enemy / and he himself fought against them.

63:7 Generally speaking, any good prayer should include, and probably begin with, praise to God. A hallmark of an exemplary intercessory prayer is its recognition that hope lies in the nature of God, not in anything the person praying has to offer. Recounting God's goodness, love, power, and faithfulness serves both to encourage those involved in the prayer and to remind them of the proper basis of appeal. In the Hebrew text, verse 7 begins and ends with the word **kindnesses** (plural of חֶסֶד, *ḥesed*). The word denotes God's covenant loyalty, but his relationship with his people consists of more than fulfilling a legal requirement, as indicated by his **compassion**.

63:8-10 The parallelism between God's **sons** and his **people** recalls his redemption of Israel in the exodus from Egypt (Exod 4:22; 6:7).[6] God is justified in expecting that those he has saved **will not be false** to him, although he will be quickly disappointed. This presentation of the way God enters into relationship with Israel

---

[5]Webb, *Message*, p. 241 (cf. Motyer, *Prophecy*, p. 512).
[6]Motyer, *Prophecy*, p. 513.

seems to raise questions about his foreknowledge. Isaiah may be using this language for rhetorical effect, however, and one should not read too much into it in terms of the divine nature. Yet the following verses reveal a God who could perhaps be described as "vulnerable." Because of Israel's rebellion they **grieved his Holy Spirit**.[7] Again, the attribution of traits such as grief to God reflects a necessary concession to human categories of experience, but a measure of truth remains in the imperfect analogy.[8] The point is that God knowingly enters into a relationship with a people whose disloyalty would cause us great pain if we were in God's place. In some manner beyond our comprehension, God experiences this pain as well.

God's identification with his people, even in their struggles, is seen in the words **In all their distresses he too was distressed**.[9] He is not some distant, impersonal force but a God who enters into the messy world of human relationships. God's people do not move first to tap into his power; he initiates the relationship as his **love and mercy** lead him to redeem them. When they were in Egyptian bondage, like a loving parent **he lifted them up and carried them** to safety (cf. Exod 19:4). This relationship reveals the pain God must have felt when, in response to Israel's blatant and persistent rebellion, **he turned and became their enemy and he himself fought against them**. In 28:21 God speaks of his "strange work" when he must fight *against* his people as he had formerly fought *for* them. Even in such strange circumstances, however, God is manifesting his "kindnesses" by working to restore his relationship with his people. He desires to bring them to the point that they will pray a prayer such as the one in the following verses, a prayer in which they acknowledge their sins and look to God to forgive them.

---

[7]The expressions "Spirit of God" and "Spirit of the LORD" are fairly common in the Old Testament, but "Holy Spirit" is not (cf. Ps 51:11). While caution should be exercised in reading the New Testament back into the Old, Oswalt notes that the Holy Spirit in verses 10 and 11 "is close to the fully developed NT concept of the third person of the Trinity" (*Isaiah* 2, pp. 607-608). Cf. the reference to grieving the Holy Spirit in Eph 4:30.

[8]Cf. references to God's jealousy, wrath, and even repentance.

[9]An alternate reading is "In all their distresses he did not distress," indicating that Israel, not God, was responsible for these problems. For the textual evidence, cf. Oswalt, *Isaiah 2*, pp. 600-601, n. 34.

Pray to God to Deliver As in the Past (63:11-64:3)

¹¹Then his people recalled[a] the days of old, / the days of Moses and his people— / where is he who brought them through the sea, / with the shepherd of his flock? / Where is he who set / his Holy Spirit among them, / ¹²who sent his glorious arm of power / to be at Moses' right hand, / who divided the waters before them, / to gain for himself everlasting renown, / ¹³who led them through the depths? / Like a horse in open country, / they did not stumble; / ¹⁴like cattle that go down to the plain, / they were given rest by the Spirit of the LORD. / This is how you guided your people / to make for yourself a glorious name.

¹⁵Look down from heaven and see / from your lofty throne, holy and glorious. / Where are your zeal and your might? / Your tenderness and compassion are withheld from us. / ¹⁶But you are our Father, / though Abraham does not know us / or Israel acknowledge us; / you, O LORD, are our Father, / our Redeemer from of old is your name. / ¹⁷Why, O LORD, do you make us wander from your ways / and harden our hearts so we do not revere you? / Return for the sake of your servants, / the tribes that are your inheritance. / ¹⁸For a little while your people possessed your holy place, / but now our enemies have trampled down your sanctuary. / ¹⁹We are yours from of old; / but you have not ruled over them, / they have not been called by your name.[b]

⁶⁴:¹Oh, that you would rend the heavens and come down, / that the mountains would tremble before you! / ²As when fire sets twigs ablaze / and causes water to boil, / come down to make your name known to your enemies / and cause the nations to quake before you! / ³For when you did awesome things that we did not expect, / you came down, and the mountains trembled before you.

[a]*11 Or But may he recall*   [b]*19 Or We are like those you have never ruled, / like those never called by your name*

Isaiah moves from a recollection of God's kindnesses to his powerful acts of deliverance, such as dividing the waters of the Red Sea before the pursuing Egyptian army. His point is to question how long God will fight against his people and when he will restore their fractured relationship. In fact, questions dominate the rest of Isaiah's prayer, giving it the quality of a lament (cf. Ps 22:1). Where is the powerful, compassionate God Israel has known in the past (63:11, 15)? Why does God allow his people to continue to wander from him

(63:17)? How can his people, in their present state, be saved (64:5)? The questions in a proper lament arise not so much from doubt as from a determined belief that faces frustration in the delay of the fulfillment of God's promises. An air of expectancy permeates Isaiah's prayer even as he acknowledges Israel's sins and their present plight because he knows the nature of God and his capacity to overcome all obstacles to the completion of his purposes.

63:11-14 In Psalm 51:11 God's Holy Spirit is parallel to his "presence." God's presence implies the full range of his attributes, and his **Holy Spirit** in Isaiah 63:11 is manifested in **his glorious arm of power** (v. 12). Isaiah longs for God to establish his **everlasting renown** (שֵׁם עוֹלָם, *šēm 'ôlām*) by delivering his people as he has before. The fact that God's **glorious name** (שֵׁם תִּפְאֶרֶת, *šēm tiph'āreth*) is so closely tied to the status of his people establishes the legitimacy of this prayer. Isaiah's intercession thus builds on the dual foundation of divine precedent and divine reputation. Not only does the exodus event provide an excellent backdrop for this foundation, but the emphasis on **Moses** as the **shepherd of** [God's] **flock** implicitly anticipates the messiah/servant through whom God will accomplish an even greater redemption (cf. Deut 18:15).

63:15-16 In 57:15 Isaiah describes God as one who lives "in a high and holy place, but also with him who is contrite and lowly in spirit." Isaiah's appeal in 63:15 indicates his perception that God is completely isolated from his people as he sits on his **lofty throne**. The question might be raised, however, as to how many in Israel are contrite and lowly in spirit in Isaiah's day. As a result, no outward evidence exists for God's **zeal**,[10] his **might** on behalf of his people, his **tenderness**, or his **compassion**. The word for **withheld** (הִתְאַפָּק, *hith'apaq*),[11] however, implies that hope remains. The same verb appears in Genesis 45:1 when Joseph finally breaks down and can no longer withhold his identity from his brothers.[12] The word seems to imply that something is held back only with difficulty. Perhaps this language explains why Isaiah turns immediately to God's relationship with his people as a **Father** in a truer and more meaningful sense than **Abraham** or **Israel**, who are no longer present to care for

---

[10]The word for "zeal" (קִנְאָה, *qin'āh*) also refers to God's "jealousy," that is, his passionate commitment to his people.

[11]Cf. 42:14 ("held myself back"); 64:12 ("hold yourself back").

[12]Wolf, *Interpreting*, p. 245.

or to help them. God, on the other hand, has been the **Redeemer from of old**. Isaiah is confident that God's relationship with his people is stable and enduring enough that he will not remain in apparent isolation.

63:17a Isaiah's questions for God at the beginning of verse 17 clearly do not represent an attempt to blame God for Israel's sinfulness and absolve Israel of responsibility. Such an approach would be an unwise approach in interceding with God and would contradict so much of what Isaiah has previously said. Isaiah has applied the word for **make us wander** (תַּתְעֵנוּ, *tath'ēnû*) to Israel's corrupt leaders,[13] but also to God's judgment on the hostile nations.[14] Although the word for **harden our hearts** (תַּקְשִׁיחַ לִבֵּנוּ, *taqšîaḥ libbēnû*) is not used either for the hardening of Pharaoh's heart in Exodus or for Israel's hardening in response to Isaiah's preaching (6:10), the point is the same. In making God the agent of Israel's aimlessness and unresponsiveness, Isaiah sees them as God's judgment on a people who have sinned so long and so deeply that they are incapable of turning back on their own. Rather than blaming God, Isaiah acknowledges that, unless God "returns" his people, they are without hope. By pointing out how hardened in sin Israel is, therefore, the prophet both maintains the desire for God to intervene and sets the stage for the need for forgiveness in the final segment of his prayer.

63:17b-19 Before closing this section, however, Isaiah accumulates more reasons for God to restore Israel's historic special relationship with him in what Oswalt calls "a storming of the gates of heaven with every tool [he] can use."[15] As God's **servants** Israel is to carry out God's purpose on earth, a task that cannot be completed without God's intervention. As God's **inheritance** (cf. Deut 4:20) Israel is his "treasured possession" called to be "a kingdom of priests and a holy nation" (Exod 19:5-6). How can this nation of priests function, however, when their **enemies have trampled down [their] sanctuary**? How can God be glorified in a people when, in the eyes of outside observers, it appears that he has **not ruled over them** and that **they have not been called by [his] name**?

---

[13]Cf. 3:12 ("lead you astray"); 9:16 [15 in Hebrew] ("mislead them").

[14]Cf. 19:14 ("make Egypt stagger"); 30:28 ("he places in the jaws of the peoples a bit that leads them astray").

[15]Oswalt, *Isaiah* 2, p. 614.

ISAIAH 64

Pray to God to Deliver As in the Past (63:11–64:3) (continued)

64:1-3 The shortcomings Isaiah has pointed out climax in a cry of frustration. Instead of the NIV's **Oh, that you would . . .**, the Hebrew construction requires a past tense: "Oh, that you *had* . . . ."[1] The situation would be far different, Isaiah says, if you had already intervened. The **heavens** are pictured as a curtain obscuring God's presence. If God had only torn away that obstacle, his power would have been manifested as powerfully as an earthquake or a **fire**. Psalm 18 is attributed to David in celebration of his deliverance from Saul and his other enemies. He sees God's answer to his prayers in terms of earthquakes and fire when God "parted the heavens and came down" (v. 9). Isaiah is aware that God has acted on behalf of his people in unexpected times and ways in the past and can only pray that he will do so again. "We too who are so often baffled by the way the Lord runs the world can identify with the spirit which wonders why he has acted in some other way — why he has not done something to check evil, change circumstances and people, rescue his own — rather than, as it appears, done nothing!"[2]

Pray to God to Forgive As in the Past (64:4-12)

[4]Since ancient times no one has heard, /no ear has perceived, /no eye has seen any God besides you, /who acts on behalf of those who wait for him. /[5]You come to the help of those who gladly do right, /who remember your ways. /But when we continued to sin against them, /you were angry. /How then can we be saved? /[6]All of us have become like one who is unclean, /and all our righteous acts are like filthy rags; /we all shrivel up like a leaf, /and like the

---

[1]Motyer, *Prophecy*, p. 518.
[2]Ibid., p. 519.

wind our sins sweep us away. / ⁷No one calls on your name / or strives to lay hold of you; / for you have hidden your face from us / and made us waste away because of our sins.

⁸Yet, O Lord, you are our Father. / We are the clay, you are the potter; / we are all the work of your hand. / ⁹Do not be angry beyond measure, O Lord; / do not remember our sins forever. / Oh, look upon us, we pray, / for we are all your people. / ¹⁰Your sacred cities have become a desert; / even Zion is a desert, Jerusalem a desolation. / ¹¹Our holy and glorious temple, where our fathers praised you, / has been burned with fire, / and all that we treasured lies in ruins. / ¹²After all this, O Lord, will you hold yourself back? / Will you keep silent and punish us beyond measure?

Isaiah's bold prayer begins with thankfulness for past mercies and concludes with a plea for fresh mercies. His frustrated longing for God to break into history on behalf of his people never loses sight of the root cause of the problem. It is sin, not the heavens that constitute a barrier between God and Israel (cf. 59:1-2). The prophet returns to the underlying issue, but here as well he realizes that God must take the initiative. When sin becomes deeply imbedded in a people, they lack both the perception and the will to overcome the problem without God's aid.

64:4-5 God is unparalleled in his willingness and capacity to work **on behalf of those who wait for him**. He makes himself available to **those who gladly do right, who remember [his] ways**. The problem, however, is that Israel at present neither waits for God nor gladly does right nor remembers his ways. They rightly receive God's anger, leading to Isaiah's critical question, **How then can we be saved?**

64:6 The purity laws of Leviticus warn Israel of the dangers of bringing that which is unclean into contact with the holy, yet Isaiah confesses that **all of us have become like one who is unclean**. Even their **righteous acts** are as unclean as a woman's menstrual cloths (cf. Lev 15:19 ff.; Ezek 36:17). This analogy may reflect Isaiah's opening chapter, in which Israel's religious deeds are contaminated by their sinful lives. Uncleanness that invalidates the cultic practices by which one maintains purity and fellowship with God yields disastrous results. Isaiah compares their state to a shriveled **leaf** that the **wind** blows away (cf. Ps 1).

64:7 Verses 4-5a describe a healthy relationship with God in which God readily comes to the aid of those who trust and seek him. Verse 7, on the other hand, presents the reality of Isaiah's day. **No**

one calls on your name or strives to lay hold of you may be hyperbole, but the purpose of the exaggeration is to demonstrate the radical extent of Israel's apostasy. The second half of verse 7 explains (כִּי, *kî*, **for**) the extremity of Israel's downward slide, not its origin. Isaiah says that it is **because of our sins** that God has **hidden [his] face** and **made us waste away**. The downward spiral appears to have reached its lowest possible point.

64:8 All Isaiah can do at this point is appeal again to God's compassion and the close connection between Israel's condition and his reputation and purpose. In verse 8 Isaiah describes Israel as God's children, **clay** that is **the work of [his] hand**, and his **people**. These designations acknowledge God's sovereign authority, but the relational nature of fatherhood implicitly appeals to his compassion as well. Hope remains that God, as a **Father**, will forgive. His children are "prodigals come home, daring to hope that father — simply because that is who he is — will not turn them from his door."[3] Hope remains that God, as the **potter**, will remold them (cf. Jer 18:1-10). Hope remains that the God who established a people from one man (cf. 51:2) and rescued that people from Egypt will redeem a remnant from Babylon and continue his work.

64:9-12 Israel has no hope if God remains **angry beyond measure** (= **remember our sins forever**) or if he determines to **punish [them] beyond measure** (= **hold yourself back**[4]). In addition to the appeals just mentioned, Isaiah adds the **desolation** of **Jerusalem** and its **holy and glorious temple**.[5] God had established Jerusalem as the place where he would be praised and as the focal point of drawing all nations to him (cf. 2:1-4). Israel's sins lead to Jerusalem's desolation, as God has already revealed to Isaiah. The prophet's penitence[6] in anticipation of that day models the proper response both for his contemporaries and for those who will experience destruction and exile. If sin is the fundamental problem, penitence is the key to the resolution of the problem.

Isaiah realizes the need for God's patience and intervention if Israel's repentance is to occur. He introduces his final questions in

---

[3] Webb, *Message*, p. 243.
[4] Cf. 63:15 and the comments there.
[5] Literally, "the house of our holiness and beauty" (בֵּית קָדְשֵׁנוּ וְתִפְאַרְתֵּנוּ, *bêth qodšēnû wᵉthiph'artēnû*).
[6] Note the first person plural pronouns as Isaiah again identifies himself with the sinful nation.

verse 12 with "Concerning these things . . . ."[7] In other words, in light of all that is at stake in the case Isaiah has made, can God possibly restrain himself and **keep silent**? The anticipated answer, of course, is "No." Isaiah may have deep questions about God's delays, but the elements of lament in his intercessory prayer should not obscure his underlying faith in the character of God. As the opening of the classic lament in Psalm 22 alternates between questions and reasons for confidence (cf. vv. 1-10), so Isaiah and all sensitive believers struggle to reconcile faith with God's apparent inactivity in the face of evil. The last two chapters of Isaiah contain a response from God to these questions about his commitment to the covenant people or the covenant promises.

---

[7]This translation is better than the NIV's "After all this," which implies a chronological relationship with the preceding verses.

ISAIAH 65

D. GOD'S COMMITMENT TO RENEW THE CREATION FOR HIS PEOPLE (65:1–66:24)

1. God's Response to Isaiah's Prayer (65:1-25)

God's silence in the midst of Israel's troubles has been a significant theme in Isaiah 40–66 (cf. 42:14; 57:11; 62:1), including the closing note of Isaiah's prayer (64:12) that precedes this final section of the book. God responds with a promise that he will not remain silent (65:6), but his answer probably exceeds anything the prophet expected. The necessity of judgment against the hardened rebels within Israel would not surprise, but the world that results so transcends the one Isaiah knows that it can only be described as a new creation.

God Will Repay Those Who Defy Him (65:1-7)

¹"I revealed myself to those who did not ask for me; / I was found by those who did not seek me. / To a nation that did not call on my name, / I said, 'Here am I, here am I.' / ²All day long I have held out my hands / to an obstinate people, / who walk in ways not good, / pursuing their own imaginations— / ³a people who continually provoke me / to my very face, / offering sacrifices in gardens / and burning incense on altars of brick; / ⁴who sit among the graves / and spend their nights keeping secret vigil; / who eat the flesh of pigs, / and whose pots hold broth of unclean meat; / ⁵who say, 'Keep away; don't come near me, / for I am too sacred for you!' / Such people are smoke in my nostrils, / a fire that keeps burning all day.

⁶"See, it stands written before me: / I will not keep silent but will pay back in full; / I will pay it back into their laps— / ⁷both your sins and the sins of your fathers," / says the LORD. / "Because they burned sacrifices on the mountains / and defied me on the hills, / I will measure into their laps / the full payment for their former deeds."

Disagreement exists over the identity of those about whom God speaks in verse 1. In Romans 10:20-21, Paul attributes verse 1 to the Gentiles and verse 2 to Israel. Motyer insists that the language of verse 1 is "too sweeping" to refer to Israel.[1] This case would seem to be strengthened by a more literal translation of the Hebrew text of the third line of verse 1: "To a nation (גוֹי, *gôy*) not called by my name.

In spite of these objections, the context of verses 1-7 indicates clearly that rebellious Israel is the subject of the whole passage. This identification also coheres with the apparent purpose of Isaiah 65 to convey God's response to Isaiah's prayer. Verses 8-10 point out the existence of a remnant in Israel, but the sinfulness of the people is so extensive that hyperbole such as in 64:6-7 fits this context. In 63:19 Israel confesses that "We . . . have not been called by your name."

65:1-2 As in 59:1-2, therefore, God insists that the problem is Israel's sin, not God's detachment. God has not been removed from the scene. Instead he has attempted to make himself known (cf. the NASB, "I permitted Myself to be sought/found") to a people not interested in receiving him. God even presents himself as one who pleads with his people, extending his **hands** and crying out, **Here am I, here am I**. His pleading has been met with indifference, however, from an **obstinate people** determined to **walk in ways not good** and to follow **their own imaginations**.[2] The real problem is that "we want God on our terms; when he does not respond, we blame him for being unresponsive. The result is, as 30:18 puts it, that God must simply wait until someone is ready to accept his terms — his ways and his thoughts — so that he can deliver them."[3]

65:3-5 Verses 3-5 characterize the evil ways of the unfaithful in Israel. The passage is bracketed by statements indicating the impact of their actions on God. He says that they **continually provoke me to my very face**, indicating that the regularity of their idolatrous practices reflects a callous disregard for God.[4] In verse 5 God says that the wicked **are smoke in my nostrils, a fire that keeps burning all day**. In contrast to the fire of the burnt offering that is to go up

---

[1]Motyer, *Prophecy*, p. 523.

[2]Cf. 55:8-9, which uses the same words for "ways" and "imaginations" ("thoughts").

[3]Oswalt, *Isaiah* 2, p. 637.

[4]Cf. Ezekiel 8, in which the prophet is transported to the temple to see the "utterly detestable things" Israel is doing that will drive God far from his sanctuary (v. 6).

continuously (Lev 6:8-13) as "an aroma pleasing to the LORD" (Lev 1:9), the actions of these individuals produce noxious fumes that anger God. Ironically, these individuals say to others, **Keep away; don't come near me, for I am too sacred for you!** They have become like those in 5:20, whose values have deteriorated so badly that they "call evil good and good evil."

65:6-7 God continually extends his hands to a people who persist in provoking his anger. Consequently, God **will pay back in full** their account, which he says **stands written before me**. Ezekiel 18 denies that children inherently bear the guilt of their parents or vice versa, but when children perpetuate the sinful ways of their parents or when parents adopt the sinful ways of their children,[5] the debt compounds. God might appear to be **silent** when in his mercy he allows people time for repentance, but in fact he calls out to sinners. His silence in terms of judgment, however, will not last if the wicked reject his appeals.

God Will Preserve Those Who Seek Him (65:8-12)

⁸**This is what the LORD says:**
"As when juice is still found in a cluster of grapes / and men say, 'Don't destroy it, / there is yet some good in it,' / so will I do in behalf of my servants; / I will not destroy them all. / ⁹I will bring forth descendants from Jacob, / and from Judah those who will possess my mountains; / my chosen people will inherit them, / and there will my servants live. / ¹⁰Sharon will become a pasture for flocks, / and the Valley of Achor a resting place for herds, / for my people who seek me.

¹¹**"But as for you who forsake the LORD / and forget my holy mountain, / who spread a table for Fortune / and fill bowls of mixed wine for Destiny, / ¹²I will destine you for the sword, / and you will all bend down for the slaughter; / for I called but you did not answer, / I spoke but you did not listen. / You did evil in my sight / and chose what displeases me."**

65:8-10 One of the most striking portrayals of Israel's failure to respond to God properly is the parable of the vineyard in Isaiah 5. The end of the parable holds forth little hope for the vineyard that bears only bad grapes. The apparent lack of hope in 65:1-7, on the

---

[5]Cf. Eli and the influence of Hophni and Phinehas in 1 Samuel 2–4.

other hand, is countered by the discovery of **juice** that exists in a **cluster of grapes**. This discovery leads those in charge to say, **Don't destroy it**. The **good** they have discovered in the cluster is literally a "blessing" (בְּרָכָה, *bᵊrākāh*). The analogy here points to the faithful remnant, described in these verses as **my chosen people, my servants**, and **my people who seek me**. God ultimately desires to bless all humanity through his people (Gen 12:3), so the existence of this remnant ensures that he **will not destroy them all**.

God multiplied the original descendants of Abraham, and he can do the same on behalf of the true descendants of Abraham in any age, those who trust God. They will be blessed by God (**possess, inherit**) and be a blessing to others. **Sharon** and the **Valley of Achor** represent the extent of God's blessings in several ways. Geographically, Sharon is a region on the Mediterranean coast in the west of Palestine, whereas Achor is in the far eastern part. They thus stand for the entire land (cf. "from Dan to Beersheba" for a north-south orientation). Sharon is a fertile plain that is associated with the fruitfulness of the land, whereas Achor is a barren wadi that is most famous as the location of the stoning of Achan (Josh 7:24-26). Isaiah has envisioned a devastated Sharon as a result of God's judgment (33:9), followed by its renewal (35:2). Hosea, on the other hand, has already used Achor to symbolize God's transformation of a bad memory to a place of hope (Hos 2:15). In addition to the geographical perspective, therefore, these two sites symbolize God's power to overcome the past and its judgment to bring about new possibilities.[6]

65:11-12 The preservative power of the remnant does not, however, secure the future of those who **forsake** and **forget** God.[7] Rather than respond obediently to God's call, they have preferred that which is **evil** in God's eyes. They will not possess God's mountains (v. 9) because they have forgotten God's **holy mountain** and the proper worship centered there. They are not among God's "chosen people" (בְּחִירִים, *bᵊḥîrîm*) because they have decided to **choose** (בחר, *bḥr*) that which **displeases** him.

The particular manifestation of forsaking God in this instance is the worship of **Fortune** and **Destiny**. The former was worshiped in

---

[6]Cf. Motyer, *Prophecy,* p. 527, Oswalt, *Isaiah* 2, p. 647.

[7]Verse 11 opens with an indication of strong contrast (וְאַתֶּם, *wᵊ'attem*, "But as for you").

the region of Syria,[8] but less is known about the worship of the latter. Both deities reflect the futile attempt of pagan religion either to know or to control the future. The tragic irony is that those who pursue such a course must answer to the God who alone knows and controls the future. This irony is reflected in the word play, apparent even in translation, between "Destiny" and "destine." Similarly, those who **bend down** (כרע, *krʻ*) to worship these Gods (cf. 1 Kgs 19:18) rather than bow down before God (cf. 45:22) actually assume the posture of execution as they must answer to God.

God Will Distinguish between His Servants and the Unresponsive (65:13-16)

¹³**Therefore this is what the Sovereign LORD says:**
"My servants will eat, / but you will go hungry; / my servants will drink, / but you will go thirsty; / my servants will rejoice, / but you will be put to shame. / ¹⁴My servants will sing / out of the joy of their hearts, / but you will cry out / from anguish of heart / and wail in brokenness of spirit. / ¹⁵You will leave your name / to my chosen ones as a curse; / the Sovereign LORD will put you to death, / but to his servants he will give another name. / ¹⁶Whoever invokes a blessing in the land / will do so by the God of truth; / he who takes an oath in the land / will swear by the God of truth. / For the past troubles will be forgotten / and hidden from my eyes.

65:13 The **Sovereign LORD** makes more explicit the contrast drawn between the faithful remnant in verses 8-10 and those who reject God in verses 11-12. He repeatedly refers to his **servants** and also calls them "my chosen ones" in verse 15. The contrast with the servants is expressed the same way (ואתם, *wəʼattem*, **but you**) as in the opening of verse 11. The reversal of circumstances between the two groups recalls the corresponding blessings and curses in Leviticus 26 and Deuteronomy 28. Just as God made a distinction between the Israelites and the Egyptians in some of the plagues, so here he promises to make a distinction between the true and the false among his own people.

65:15-16 Verses 15-16 place great emphasis upon a **name**. In the beginning of Scripture, the line of Cain is contrasted with the line of

---

[8]Cf. the use of the word for "Fortune" (גד, *gad*) in biblical place names (Josh 11:17; 12:7; 13:5; 15:37).

Seth, in whose days people "began to call on the name of the LORD" (Gen 4:26). The great sin at the tower of Babel occurs when people decide to "make a name" for themselves rather than call on God (Gen 11:4). Abraham, on the other hand, receives a promise that God will make his name great (Gen 12:2). The law classifies misusing the name of God as a serious offense (Exod 20:7; cf. Lev 19:12; 22:32; 24:16). Oaths should be taken only in God's name. In light of this background, human beings who seek to make a name for themselves without honoring the name of God, calling on him alone and seeking his glory, are bound to fail.

Those who have forsaken God leave the legacy of a name that signifies a **curse**. Like Abram, Sarai, and Jacob, however, God's servants will receive **another name** that signifies a new level of relationship with God (cf. 62:4,12). The resulting situation in the land is that God alone will be honored as the one in whose name blessings are invoked and oaths are taken. He alone is the **God of truth** (אֱלֹהֵי אָמֵן, *'ĕlōhê 'āmēn*), i.e., the true God. Since the rejection of God has caused Israel's problems, the recognition of God will introduce a new situation in which **the past troubles will be forgotten**. God reveals in the last portion of the chapter just how radically new the future will be.

God Will Create New Heavens and a New Earth (65:17-25)

¹⁷"Behold, I will create / new heavens and a new earth. / The former things will not be remembered, / nor will they come to mind. / ¹⁸But be glad and rejoice forever / in what I will create, / for I will create Jerusalem to be a delight / and its people a joy. / ¹⁹I will rejoice over Jerusalem / and take delight in my people; / the sound of weeping and of crying / will be heard in it no more.

²⁰"Never again will there be in it / an infant who lives but a few days, / or an old man who does not live out his years; / he who dies at a hundred / will be thought a mere youth; / he who fails to reach[a] a hundred / will be considered accursed. / ²¹They will build houses and dwell in them; / they will plant vineyards and eat their fruit. / ²²No longer will they build houses and others live in them, / or plant and others eat. / For as the days of a tree, / so will be the days of my people; / my chosen ones will long enjoy / the works of their hands. / ²³They will not toil in vain / or bear children doomed to misfortune; / for they will be a people blessed by the LORD, / they and their descendants with them. / ²⁴Before they call I will answer; / while they are still speaking I will hear. / ²⁵The wolf and the lamb

will feed together, / and the lion will eat straw like the ox, / but dust will be the serpent's food. / They will neither harm nor destroy / on all my holy mountain," / says the LORD.

ᵃ20 Or / *the sinner who reaches*

65:17 One message that rings throughout the Old Testament as a whole, and in Isaiah in particular, is that human beings are incapable of overcoming the problem of sin. Even with God's active involvement in the life of his covenant community, sin continues to cause havoc. As the prophets look to the future, they anticipate a better world. Jeremiah envisions it on the basis of a new covenant (31:31ff.). To that picture Ezekiel adds God's renewal of human hearts and the bestowal of his Spirit (36:24ff.). Isaiah's contribution to the prophetic vision of the future is the creation of **new heavens and a new earth**.[9] Not only humanity, but the physical creation also has been marred by sin.

Christians from the beginning have been influenced by certain strands of Greek thought (rather than the Hebrew roots of biblical theology) and favored a nonmaterial view of the future state. This mind-set has manifested numerous destructive influences over the centuries, including a rejection of the Old Testament God (who made the "mistake" of creating a material world and even calling it "good"), the incarnation of Christ, and a bodily resurrection. Paul addresses the latter extensively in 1 Corinthians 15. While the precise nature of the resurrection body and the new heavens and new earth remain something of a mystery, it is important to acknowledge the Bible's teachings in this regard.[10] The fact that John picks up and expands Isaiah's vision of the eternal state[11] in Revelation 21:1–22:5 highlights the significance of that vision.

65:17-19 The first verse of this section points back to the forgotten troubles of verse 16.[12] The God who demonstrated his power in the original creation will demonstrate his might again as he not only

---

[9]The combination of "the heavens and the earth" encompasses all of God's creation (cf. Gen 1:1).

[10]For an excellent treatment of the renewed creation, cf. Anthony A. Hoekema, *The Bible and the Future* (Grand Rapids: Eerdmans, 1979), pp. 274-287.

[11]The situation described by Isaiah and John does not refer to the notion of an earthly millennial kingdom as espoused by dispensational premillennialism. Hoekema includes a critique of a future 1000-year earthly reign of Christ.

[12]Verse 17 begins with "For" (כִּי, *kî*), which the NIV omits.

causes the **former things** to be forgotten, but also creates **Jerusalem to be a delight and its people a joy**. As in Revelation, the new creation is encapsulated in a single city, the city that most embodies God's presence with his people. Because of God's intimate presence, the creation will return to its original capacity to bring joy and delight to its inhabitants. Seeing the fulfillment of his purpose, God **will rejoice over Jerusalem and take delight in [his] people**. "This verse expresses one of the loveliest thoughts in the book. Zion will be a joy not only to itself but also to God."[13] He does not find his joy in **weeping**, but in the new state that exists when he removes the root cause of all sorrow.

65:20-24 Verses 20-25 give a figurative description of some of the details of life in the new creation. This future state is so far removed from the present order that flawed analogies must bridge the gap. Death, the ultimate consequence of the present creation's fallenness, will be overcome. Isaiah is aware of this fact (cf. 25:7-8), but here he remains closer to the normal sphere of human experience and emphasizes longevity. No one will suffer the curse of a life cut short (cf. 38:10; Ps 102:24). Similarly, the citizens of the new creation will not face the heartbreak of building and planting, only to see another reap the fruits of their labors (cf. Deut 28:30).

65:25 Positively, the blessings of the new creation will include intimacy with God (cf. 30:19) and harmony with the creation (cf. 11:6-9). The reference to **dust** as **the serpent's food** alludes to the judgment and ultimate destruction experienced by the instigator of the first sin (cf. Gen 3:14-15). Once again, judgment appears as an essential corollary to the completion of God's redemptive purpose. If the curse is to be removed, so must its cause and all those who have allied and identified themselves with it.

---

[13]Oswalt, *Isaiah* 2, p. 657.

ISAIAH 66

2. Two Approaches to God (66:1-24)

The biblical prophets use two basic types of communication: messages of judgment and messages of hope. The relationship between these two is particularly striking in Isaiah.[1] His messages of judgment are among the most devastating in the prophetic writings and frequently leave the reader with a sense of hopelessness. His messages of hope, however, are among the most sublime in all of Scripture. Isaiah's intended effect is to isolate God's gracious, powerful, creative work as humanity's only hope. God steps in to defeat his people's enemies when no other possibility exists. God succeeds through his servant when his people fail to respond. God turns the hearts of his people back to him when the downward spiral of sin has apparently hardened them beyond repair. One of the key words in Isaiah is "create" (ברא, *br'*), climaxing in 65:17-25. God's redemptive work provides such a dramatic change that it can only be compared to the original creation of heaven and earth.

The creative work of God does not leave mankind's freedom of choice out of the equation. Isaiah, like all the prophets, calls the covenant community to respond to what God has said and done in proving his commitment to the covenant. More than perhaps any of the other prophets, Isaiah points beyond God's relationship with Israel as he also calls them to fulfill their part in God's worldwide redemptive purpose. God recognizes only two responses to him: the way of faith and obedience that leads to life, and the way of self-determination and rebellion that leads to death (cf. Deut 30:15-20). These two responses correspond to the two types of prophetic messages. They come together in the final chapter of Isaiah as God sum-

---

[1] "When one observes the book as a whole, the interchange between judgment and hope is unmistakable" (Oswalt, *Isaiah* 2, p. 683).

marizes the two possibilities that lie before his people, presenting them with one final challenge to make the correct choice.

The Futility of Hypocritical Religion (66:1-6)

¹This is what the LORD says:
"Heaven is my throne, /and the earth is my footstool. / Where is the house you will build for me? / Where will my resting place be? / ²Has not my hand made all these things, /and so they came into being?" /declares the LORD.

"This is the one I esteem: /he who is humble and contrite in spirit, /and trembles at my word. / ³But whoever sacrifices a bull /is like one who kills a man, /and whoever offers a lamb, /like one who breaks a dog's neck; /whoever makes a grain offering /is like one who presents pig's blood, / and whoever burns memorial incense, /like one who worships an idol. / They have chosen their own ways, /and their souls delight in their abominations; /⁴so I also will choose harsh treatment for them /and will bring upon them what they dread. / For when I called, no one answered, / when I spoke, no one listened. / They did evil in my sight /and chose what displeases me."

⁵Hear the word of the LORD, /you who tremble at his word: / "Your brothers who hate you, /and exclude you because of my name, have said, / 'Let the LORD be glorified, / that we may see your joy!' /Yet they will be put to shame. /⁶Hear that uproar from the city, /hear that noise from the temple! / It is the sound of the LORD /repaying his enemies all they deserve.

The people of Isaiah's day would invariably be religious; the only issue is the form their religion would take. On the surface it might appear that the religion of Yahweh differs little from that of the surrounding paganism, apart from the belief in one God only. Beneath the surface similarities such as priesthood, sacrifice, and purity laws, however, the foundation of Israel's religion reveals radically different views of the nature of God and of the covenant relationship he desires to have with them. The notion that the pagan gods are dependent upon their human devotees permits the worshiper's manipulation of the gods. The importation of pagan elements into the lives of the covenant people compromises not only the exclusive allegiance God demands, therefore, but also the nature of God. The belief that God can be manipulated for one's own ends leads to disrespect for God and allows one to pursue the path of self-determination that falls under God's judgment.

66:1-2 The quality of a people's religion is reflected in their worship, which is why worship has been an important subject for Isaiah (cf. especially 1:10ff.; 58:1-14). Not surprisingly, therefore, the theme arises again at the outset of the final chapter. Typically the sanctuary represents God's **footstool** (1 Chr 28:2; Ps 99:5; 132:7), but here it is the **earth**, conveying a sense of God's greatness and transcendence (cf. 40:22). This observation leads to the same question Solomon raises in his dedicatory prayer for the temple (1 Kgs 8:27): Can anyone build a **house** that is capable of containing God? God might identify his presence with a building like the temple, but to see such a structure as containing or controlling God represents the dangerous importation of pagan notions. The rebuilding of the temple after exile serves as an important reminder of God's continuing commitment to dwell with his people, but its prior destruction should shatter superstitious views that it guarantees God's presence and protection (cf. Jer 7:1-15).

What God "esteems"[2] is not an elaborate structure, however, but a particular kind of person. In 57:15 God juxtaposes his residence "in a high and holy place" and the fact that he is at home "with him who is contrite and lowly in spirit." Similarly, in 66:2 the one who says **Heaven is my throne** gives his attention to the one **who is humble and contrite in spirit, and trembles at my word**. The complacent women in Jerusalem are exhorted to tremble at the message of impending judgment. The humble, penitent person feels the effect of God's word and responds to it. God desires to develop a relationship with and nurture the faith of such a person.

66:3 The picture in verses 1-2 contrasts with the group portrayed in the following verses. These are the ones who, as in 1:10ff., give the appearance of piety as they frequent the temple. Their conduct away from the temple, however, reveals hearts that are not committed to God. The language of comparison in verse 3 (**is like/like**) is added by the NIV and obscures the point. The text more literally reads, for example, "The one who sacrifices a bull kills a man." In other words, the same person who performs a religious act at the temple also commits murder. The other examples refer to acts of

---

[2] נבט (*nbṭ*) means to "look upon, regard" (cf. 22:11, where the verb is paralleled with ראה, *r'h*).

pagan worship which, though antithetical to the worship of Yahweh, are seen by these worshipers as legitimate rituals. The end of verse 3 summarizes the direction of their lives even as they appear to be godly. Choosing one's **own ways** inevitably means pleasing self rather than God. The dangerous result of such a course is that the person finds **delight** not in God (cf. 58:13-14), but in that which God labels **abominations**.[3]

66:4-6 God sees through hypocritical religion and promises to bring it under judgment. Those who choose this path do not tremble at God's word because they refuse to listen when he speaks, but they will be filled with **dread** when the **harsh treatment** that they cannot ignore comes upon them. They may seek to appease God by the external formality of worship, but because of their hypocrisy they only reinforce their status as his **enemies**. Their enmity with God manifests itself in part by their hatred and exclusion of those who sincerely seek God. The message at the end of verse 5 drips with sarcasm[4] as they derisively call for God to **be glorified** and for the **joy** of those who tremble at his word to be manifested.[5] It is not clear in what sense this group acts **because of [God's] name**.[6] Do they sincerely invoke God's name, having convinced themselves that they know and represent the true will of God? Or do they exclude the faithful because they are determined to do as they please and those who call on God's name are an inconvenience? The derision that follows supports the latter understanding.

The Power of Relational Religion (66:7-13)

[7]"Before she goes into labor, / she gives birth; / before the pains come upon her, / she delivers a son. / [8]Who has ever heard of such a thing? / Who has ever seen such things? / Can a country be born in a day / or a nation be brought forth in a moment? / Yet no sooner is Zion in labor / than she gives birth to her children. / [9]Do I bring to the moment of birth / and not give delivery?" says the LORD.

---

[3]Cf. the things labeled as "detestable" in 1 Kgs 11:5; 2 Kgs 23:24.

[4]Cf. the words of the arrogant in 5:19; 28:9-10; Ps 22:8.

[5]Interestingly, individuals are usually called to "tremble" at the judgment to come because they have not responded to God's word; here the faithful are warned of attacks against them by the hypocrites *because* they tremble at God's word.

[6]Cf. Motyer, *Prophecy*, p. 534.

/ "Do I close up the womb / when I bring to delivery?" says your God. / ¹⁰"Rejoice with Jerusalem and be glad for her, / all you who love her; / rejoice greatly with her, / all you who mourn over her. / ¹¹For you will nurse and be satisfied / at her comforting breasts; / you will drink deeply / and delight in her overflowing abundance."

¹²For this is what the LORD says:

"I will extend peace to her like a river, / and the wealth of nations like a flooding stream; / you will nurse and be carried on her arm / and dandled on her knees. / ¹³As a mother comforts her child, / so will I comfort you; / and you will be comforted over Jerusalem."

66:7-10 The focus in these verses shifts from the arrogant apostates to the humble believers. Religion is not a means to a selfish end for this group, but rather a means of knowing God and fulfilling his purpose. They **love** Jerusalem and **mourn over her** when appropriate, but they look forward to the day when they can **rejoice greatly with her**. Those who pursue this type of relationship with God, even if they suffer from the hatred of others for a time, will ultimately enjoy God's richest blessings.

In 26:17-18 Isaiah describes Israel as a pregnant woman who struggles but can only give birth to wind (cf. 37:3). Isaiah summarizes the significance of that image with the words, "We have not brought salvation to the earth; we have not given birth to people of the world." The prophet has also presented Israel as a formerly barren woman who will one day look around in wonder at the multitude of her children (49:19-21; 54:1). The frustration and barrenness stem from extreme sinfulness that cuts the people off from divine blessing. God, who is both powerful and faithful, makes possible the miraculous turnaround in 66:7-9. Israel may feel insufficient strength to complete the delivery, but no such limitation applies to God. He does not **bring to the moment of birth** without finishing the task. This work is only possible because God overcomes the barrier of sin and a faithful remnant responds to him. The significance of the problem of sin appears in a subtle way in the notion of a painless childbirth that represents "a symbol of Eden restored and the curse removed."[7]

66:11-13 Jerusalem stands as the geographical center of God's redemptive work. The condition of Jerusalem thus serves as something of a spiritual barometer for Israel's relationship with God. For

---

[7]Motyer, *Prophecy,* p. 536.

this reason Israel is to "mourn" Jerusalem's barrenness and "rejoice" when she gives birth and serves as a source of sustenance for her children.[8] The origin of Israel's blessings, however, is God himself. He **will extend peace to [Jerusalem] like a river**, a peace so long forfeited through unbelief (48:18-19). He will console **as a mother comforts her child**. The peace and comfort that God alone can provide come to those who are esteemed by God, to those who are humble and contrite in spirit and tremble at his word.

The End of the Two Approaches (66:14-24)

[14]When you see this, your heart will rejoice / and you will flourish like grass; / the hand of the LORD will be made known to his servants, / but his fury will be shown to his foes. / [15]See, the LORD is coming with fire, / and his chariots are like a whirlwind; / he will bring down his anger with fury, / and his rebuke with flames of fire. / [16]For with fire and with his sword / the LORD will execute judgment upon all men, / and many will be those slain by the LORD.

[17]"Those who consecrate and purify themselves to go into the gardens, following the one in the midst of[a] those who eat the flesh of pigs and rats and other abominable things—they will meet their end together," declares the LORD.

[18]"And I, because of their actions and their imaginations, am about to come[b] and gather all nations and tongues, and they will come and see my glory.

[19]"I will set a sign among them, and I will send some of those who survive to the nations—to Tarshish, to the Libyans[c] and Lydians (famous as archers), to Tubal and Greece, and to the distant islands that have not heard of my fame or seen my glory. They will proclaim my glory among the nations. [20]And they will bring all your brothers, from all the nations, to my holy mountain in Jerusalem as an offering to the LORD—on horses, in chariots and wagons, and on mules and camels," says the LORD. "They will bring them, as the Israelites bring their grain offerings, to the temple of the LORD in ceremonially clean vessels. [21]And I will select some of them also to be priests and Levites," says the LORD.

[22]"As the new heavens and the new earth that I make will endure before me," declares the LORD, "so will your name and descendants endure. [23]From one New Moon to another and from

---

[8]Cf. 60:16, in which Zion "will drink the milk of nations."

one Sabbath to another, all mankind will come and bow down before me," says the LORD. ²⁴"And they will go out and look upon the dead bodies of those who rebelled against me; their worm will not die, nor will their fire be quenched, and they will be loathsome to all mankind."

ᵃ*17* Or *gardens behind one of your temples, and*   ᵇ*18* The meaning of the Hebrew for this clause is uncertain.   ᶜ*19* Some Septuagint manuscripts *Put* (libyans); Hebrew *Pul*

66:14-17 Verse 14 begins the final stage of contrasts between the way of God's **servants** and the way of his **foes**. God's servants will **see** the accomplishment of his work and **rejoice**. Although **grass** can portray the fragile and temporary (cf. 40:6-8), here it represents life springing up in a formerly barren land by the power of God's Spirit as in 44:3-4. God will appear to his enemies, on the other hand, as an army on **chariots**, consuming like **fire**. The unfaithful within Israel have been the focus of God's anger in this context, but the reference to God's **judgment upon all men** (literally, "all flesh") in verse 16 indicates that ultimately God's judgment will take on a universal scope. Verse 17, however (cf. 65:2-5), maintains a connection at this point between the judgment of apostate Israel and God's larger redemptive purpose.

66:18-19 The opening of verse 18 (וְאָנֹכִי, *wᵊ'ānōkî*, "But I") presents a strong contrast between what the hypocrites in Israel do in their perversion of purity (v. 17) and what God does to allow **all nations and tongues** to see his **glory**. Where Israel as a whole has failed in revealing God's glory, God himself will succeed. The place names in verse 19 represent areas **that have not heard of [God's] fame or seen [his] glory**. The exact nature of the **sign** that precedes the spreading of God's glory to these distant lands is unclear. The connection of this sign to **those who survive** (cf. 4:2), however, indicates that it has to do with God's judgment of Israel. The survivors of that judgment **will proclaim [God's] glory among the nations**.

66:20-21 Those among the nations who acknowledge God's glory will bring back to Jerusalem the scattered remnant of Israel and present them **as an offering to the LORD** (cf. 49:22-23; 60:4,9). To demonstrate the full acceptance of these converts from the nations, they will even be allowed to serve as **priests and Levites**. Although the figurative nature of the language should promote caution in pressing the details, Isaiah presents a marvelous picture of God's work of redemption. Through the judgment of Israel, God forges a remnant that will carry the message of God's glory to the nations, who in turn aid in the restoration of Israel (cf. Rom 9–11).

66:22-24 The final contrast returns to **the new heavens and the new earth** that provide an enduring dwelling place wherein **all mankind will come and bow down before [God]**. The picture maintains elements relevant to Isaiah's original audience: a **name** and **descendants** associated with the covenant with Abraham and observances such as **New Moon** and **Sabbath**. Those who have **rebelled** against God, on the other hand, exist among the **dead bodies** in a place where **their worm will not die, nor will their fire be quenched** (cf. Jer 7:32).

> Thus Isaiah's great book comes to its end in ways not unlike those in which it began, with a reaffirmation of the great choice that lies before the human race: judgment or hope. But there is one great difference. The hope that the final chapters affirm is on the other side of judgment. Indeed, what they tell us is that since the Holy One of Israel is the Creator and the only God, even judgment can be turned to hope if we will let him do it for us. No tragedy, no disaster, no fate that has befallen us because of our stubborn self-worship need be the final word for us while we yet breathe. This is the great good news of Isa. 52:13–53:12: God has entered into our judgment and taken it on himself, and because of that he can declare that finally nothing can keep us from his love — except our own determination to persist in rebellion.[9]

---

[9]Oswalt, *Isaiah* 2, p. 693.